Wide-Eyed Wanderers

A Befuddling Journey From the Rat-Race To the Roads of Latin America & Africa.

By Richard Ligato
&
Amanda Bejarano-Ligato

Pop-Top Publishing   San Diego, California

Wide-Eyed Wanderers
A Befuddling Journey from the Rat-Race to the Roads
of Latin America and Africa
By Richard Ligato & Amanda Bejarano-Ligato

Published by:
Pop-Top Publishing
5694 Mission Center Road #360
San Diego, CA 92108 U.S.A.

http://www.VWVagabonds.com

ISBN 0-9761756-0-6
Library of Congress Control Number 2005901188

Acknowledgments

We owe a special thanks to my brother Maury, who was always there for us when we were half way around the world. He never complained, even when stuck with the tedious chores of sorting though our piles of mail, dealing with the DMV, the IRS, and getting us out of jury duty. Isabel Rodgers, a true inspiration and the person I most want to be like when I grow up. Your unconditional friendship and your caring guidance kept me centered, focused and in good spirits. You are always in my heart. Patrick and Marion Coyne, the dynamic duo. Your encouraging editorial notes and painstaking proofreading efforts maintained us on our path. The librarians at the Windemere branch of the Durban, Public Library, in Durban, South Africa, helped us to track down obscure facts about far-flung places. The Bell clan, owners of the San Diego KOA campground who always make us feel at home and have treated us as part of their family for many years. They have shown us how to balance a thriving modern business with good old-fashioned decency. David Greenway of Durban, South Africa offered us a quiet, well-lighted place with a tiny view of the Indian Ocean where we adapted our email into this book. And to my wonderful, husband Rich. Two pieces of such an unlikely puzzle that fit just right. It was meant to be – You and I.

Amanda Bejarano-Ligato

Typical! She takes up three-quarters of the page, leaving me this sliver at the bottom. To M&D for L,S&GMAS. To ATWHUATW TY. To R, ILY.

Richard Ligato

Disclaimer

This book describes the authors' drive through Latin America and Africa, and the subsequent changes they experienced. Some names and identifying details of individuals mentioned in the book have been changed to protect their privacy.

"All you need in this life is ignorance and confidence, and then success is sure."
Mark Twain

Preface

There are a few things I know for sure. The rest, well, any man who's been with a woman for more than a few years may be able to understand my problem.

I know, beyond any shadow of a doubt that each and every one of the stories in this book is true. I know it for a fact because I was the one who wrote them down, in most cases just a few hours after they happened. I would sit in the back of the van at night and scribble them out. No matter if we were free camping in a truck stop in Chile or bedding down in the parking lot of a sleazy motel in Mozambique, we would follow the same routine. Of course, my wife Amanda was there. She would sit in the swiveling passenger's seat, fixing something with Krazy Glue or reorganizing my toiletry bag, and she would say things like, "You forget about when I ......", or "Cross that out and write it like this....". And yes, I must admit that on more than a few occasions I would look up from writing and realize that I was taking dictation of her version of the story, word for word.

That's where the problem comes in. It took me a while to understand it, but living together in a Volkswagen van for more than three years in a space no larger than most people's closet gave me clarity I would not have had otherwise. Living in such close quarters Amanda and I really got to know each other well. I mean really, really well. All those little details that couples hide from one another in a big house with many rooms, were out in the open within the confines of our little rolling home. There was nowhere to hide.

At first this closeness was difficult to get used to. We had absolutely no personal space and we spent nearly every waking hour together. It wasn't long after we crossed the first border that I made an important discovery. In truth it wasn't really a discovery, it was more like a gut feeling I got. I suspected that Amanda had this ability, one I think many Mexican women have, of twisting the details of a story so tightly up in knots that the truth can no longer be distinguished. But that wasn't the discovery. If that was the only problem, a twisted up memory, I could happily go on without even mentioning it. But she's got another more subtle talent that makes me cross-eyed with fury because I know it exists, or at least I think it does, but I never seem to realize when she's using it. She can take those knots, the ones she's tied up so tightly, and she can untwist them in such a way that she reveals a whole new set of facts. By first confusing me, then saying things so many times, over and over, she can make me believe that her version of a story is actually my own. It's infuriating and I have no way of knowing when it's happened.

Nonetheless, I am starting off right now in the beginning with a disclaimer that the stories you are about to read are all absolutely true and are written from my point of view. Trouble is, after being squashed together in our rolling campervan for so long, my point of view, along with my toothbrush and my personal space, are no longer mine alone.

Introduction

150 Quetzals

Melchor de Mencos, Guatemala
8,459 miles

The soldier looked like a bulldog. He rested his arm on the dented, scratched automatic weapon strapped across his chest and drummed his chubby fingers on the barrel. He barked abruptly in Spanish, "You have crossed the bridge and must pay the toll," as he reached back for a tattered receipt book from the waist of his jungle-green camouflage pants.

Amanda rolled her eyes upward and gave the faintest hint of a sinister smile, a sign obvious to me, but the soldier had no idea.

"Why should we pay?" she yapped back in Spanish.

He tilted his black beret away from his hepatitis-yellow eyes as he impatiently thumbed the receipt book. "This is a toll bridge. You must pay or go back to Belize."

Amanda reached across in front of me and pointed through my window to the fast-moving traffic crossing the bridge. "Why must we pay when these cars can just pass by?"

I sat dumbly silent and he gave me a disdainful look that insinuated, "I see who wears the pants here."

He pointed with his thumb and offered halfheartedly, "I know all of these drivers, they are... uh, taxis. They have already paid the toll."

I decided to speak up for the first time in my limited Spanish. *"¿Cuanto cuesta, el ...?"*

Amanda interrupted, "No, Rich, no."

The soldier grasped on to my question. "It is 150 quetzels."

I calculated the price in my head and said to Amanda out of the side of my mouth, "A little more than twenty dollars."

She exploded from the passenger seat, *"¡Veinte dolares!* We're not paying that!"

The soldier opened his eyes wide and jerked his head back in surprise. "You must pay or you will go back."

Amanda leaned across from the passenger seat and pointed forward, telling him, "No, we will not pay and we will go ahead." The soldier moved in closer. "You will pay or you will go back."

Amanda moved even closer, purposely taunting him like a Chihuahua behind a fence. "We will NOT pay, and we WILL go forward."

She turned to me and said in English, "Roll up your window and let's get out of here."

I looked at her in disbelief. This was a soldier with a machine gun, and we were entering Guatemala, a country in civil war. Surely he would have plenty of practice shooting that gun, and not just target practice. This was all foreign to me. Was I missing something?

I hesitantly began to roll up my window and the soldier put his broad hand on the edge to stop it. "PAY!"

Amanda yelled, "¡NO!"

This was absurd. I felt trapped between two four-year-olds in a sand box, fighting over a toy.

He made a last attempt in his drill sergeant voice, "Turn back!"

Amanda pointed forward and yelled triumphantly, "Richard, move it!"

I was terrified. "Are you sure?"

"Go now!"

My heart was pounding. I smashed the pedal to the floor and nearly crashed into the traffic as I looked in the mirror to see if the soldier had raised his gun. Amanda let out a strange little laugh of exhilaration and fear. I watched in panic as he raised his hands in the air then moaned with relief when he rested them on his beret.

Numb with adrenalin, I drove into the chaos of the town of Melchor de Mencos, with no idea where we were heading. My mind was racing. "What am I doing here? Why would any sensible person subject himself to this? And who is this person next to me?

What have I gotten myself into?"

CHAPTER 1

Welcome to Tijuana

Tijuana, Mexico
0 miles

The California lottery billboard jolted me back to reality. I blinked a few times and looked around in confusion then banged the steering wheel and yelled, "Aaaarrrrrgggghhhh!" It was 5:30 in the morning. The sunrise had not yet peeked over the inland mountains and the red taillights combined with the misty coastal low clouds to create a glare on the dirty windshield of my old Volkswagen campervan. I had to squint to block out the bright yellow-white glow advertising that night's lottery jackpot. The number 14,000,000 magically imprinted itself on the back of my eyeballs and floated in my vision as I looked around, trying to figure out how I had gotten here.

This was happening more frequently and it was beginning to get frustrating. My memory of the morning was a complete blank. Without realizing what I was doing I had somehow managed to wake up, shut off the alarm, shower, get dressed, make coffee, drink it, warm up the van and drive off. It was as if I remained in a state of semi-consciousness until I was jerked back to reality and discovered that I was on a different freeway, not heading to work at all, but toward the border with Mexico.

I knew I had a tough day ahead. Before leaving work the previous night, I had left a to-do list on my desk containing a few unpleasant items, and the moment I snapped back to consciousness my mind instantly went to them. But then I blinked again to clear the lingering glow from my eyes and the number 14,000,000 stuck in my head. Fourteen million dollars is lot of money. As I veered on to Highway 54, turning away from Mexico, I thought about how Amanda and I would spend fourteen million dollars. What would we do differently? How would it change our lives?

Instantly settling into another blissful dream I imagined us sputtering along a narrow dirt road in the mountains of Southern Mexico, but then I pulled into the parking lot at work and suddenly flashed back to reality.

I had a good idea what Amanda would want to do with the money. She had grown up in Tijuana, just south of the border, and I knew that she wanted to introduce me to her home country. She was proud of her Mexican heritage and we often fantasized about how we would one day take an extended trip through the country. But no matter how often we thought about it we never seemed to get any closer to making the dream a reality.

On the weekends we would cross the border to visit Amanda's family, but we rarely made it further than a few miles into the country, and we knew that Tijuana, squashed between Mexico and the United States, was just the tip of the iceberg.

From a very early age Amanda had commuted across the border each morning to attend Catholic school, then University in San Diego. During the day she led a Southern Californian existence, shopping at the mall and eating at Bob's Big Boy, then crossed back each evening to her Mexican roots, where she spoke Spanish at home and her younger brothers chaperoned her on dates.

When we first met we had almost nothing in common other than the fact that we both worked for the City of Coronado, a small island community out in the middle of San Diego Bay. I was a carefree east coast transplant who spoke absolutely no Spanish and lived on a sailboat. Amanda was fresh from graduate school, setting out on a bright career with a Day-Timer full of commitments. I had strong reservations about the Catholic Church. Amanda was Catholic to the core.

After a few months of working alongside each other we discovered that we could both be ridiculously silly. She would make fun of my bumbling forgetfulness and I would laugh at her belief that she could take on the world despite her petite, almost childlike size. We began to take lunch together and I learned that she, in her own way, could be far more adventurous than me.

Before I knew what was happening I was dressed in a tux, standing next to a priest in the Chapel of Our Lady of Peace, waiting for the bride, who was on Mexican time.

It was a few years after we were married that I began to enter trances on my way to work and would find myself on a different freeway. Not long after they happened these moments would almost completely vanish from my memory. But that particular morning, when the lottery sign brought me back to reality, and the 14,000,000 imprinted itself on the back of my eyeballs, I didn't forget.

That night, just like a thousand other nights, Amanda and I watched television, lounging in our own personal dulled comas. It was the one moment of the day where our thoughts could wander into a mindless, sit-com induced stupor of time-killing numbness. Then the pithy lottery theme song came on and penetrated my stupefaction. I hit the mute button and Amanda blinked back to reality.

"That reminds me, I had this strange thing happen to me this morning." I said.

She looked around in confusion then turned to me, mildly perturbed that she had been disturbed.

"The lottery," I said nodding toward the television. "I was driving to work this morning and I guess I wasn't paying attention. I ended up on I-5 and I passed that giant lottery billboard. Anyway, that's not important."

Her eyes we drawn toward the television as the camera zoomed in on the balls bobbling around in the plexiglass bubble.

I could see I was losing her so I blurted out, "What if we won the lottery?"

"Did you buy a ticket? What are our numbers?" she asked, grabbing the remote to turn up the sound and looking at me with excited eyes.

"No, I didn't buy a ticket," I said as I reached for the remote, turning down the volume. "This morning I was just daydreaming or something like it, I guess...when I saw the sign...and I imagined that we won."

She curled up her cheek in a smirk and squinted her large brown eyes in suspicion.

"No, listen," I said. "What if we won? What would you want to do differently?"

She shrugged. I could see I was loosing her so I blurted out, "Why are we doing this?" Looking around the room I asked, "What are we doing here?"

Her eyes followed mine, wondering what had brought all this on.

Then I asked the question that changed everything. "Why don't we just live as if we won the lottery? I mean, you only live once, right?"

Slowly her eyes lit up. She leaned forward from her slouched position on the couch, thinking, but she didn't say anything. I could tell I had struck a nerve. But I'm not much of a salesman and I couldn't put into words everything I was feeling. I wanted to tell her about that Christmas morning feeling of my youth. That's what I wanted back from life, that feeling of uncontrollable excitement, my heart beating faster, my eyes wide open, ready for anything, ready to take on the world. I wanted to feel the same way I did when I moved into my first apartment. I wanted to face fear, to take a chance, to let go. I wanted the excitement. I wanted the unpredictability.

But all of these thoughts were new to me and I couldn't get them together into more than a few incoherent babbles. Then the sit-com theme music began. Our attention was drawn to the television and we settled back into our comfortable numbness.

That night I lay in bed, staring up at the ceiling and thought about how my life had taken a detour from the route I thought I would follow. The adventures I had expected and looked forward to when I got out of school had been sliced up, packaged and shrink-wrapped. Real world risk was cut away, piece by piece, as I passed through the system. Tangled up in the social safety net and anchored by a houseful of possessions, my life lacked something that I couldn't put my finger on.

Then I thought, "Who am I to complain?" We had it pretty good. I had a college degree, a nice home, a good job, and a great wife. As long as I went to work for forty-odd years and did whatever was asked of me with a smile, I was granted a good living, health insurance, and shelter from most of the uglier side of life. Was I just plain crazy to question the status quo? Was I overly selfish or did I lack something that those around me had in abundance? Why couldn't I just accept things the way they were? After all, it could have been worse. Much worse.

But underneath it all I had a gut feeling that we were missing out on the calluses of life. My fingernails were not getting dirty and my wits were becoming dulled. I had a very narrow base of experience and I was watching it becoming narrower each year. The routine of our lives was so predictable, so structured, that even a brief hiccup, like having to take one of the cars to the mechanic, caused turmoil. My calendar was ordered and set, with the same things happening at the same time, so much so that I could predict with unnerving accuracy where I would be, years in advance. Slowly but surely the routine became a rut, and the longer we stayed in the rut the harder it was to look outside of it.

To my surprise, Amanda was feeling much the same way. The day after the lottery drawing she came home from work and plunked down a pile of printed web pages on the dining room table. She was slightly out of breath with excitement, as if she had a thousand things to tell me at once, and she started, "Now if we really want to do this right we're gonna have to quit our jobs and go for six months."

"Go where?" I asked.

She stopped and took a breath as she banged the edge of the pile of papers on the table to straighten them. "To Mexico," she said as if it was obvious. "We've got to see something other than this," she said waiving the papers around the room. "But we'll have to get a new van. I started a list of things we need to do. Here." She handed me a printed, stapled list that ran for more than three pages. She had spent the entire workday researching the web sites of people who had driven through Mexico. My heart raced. It was Christmas morning again. That was the beginning.

It would take years of planning and careful saving to accumulate enough money to do it right, but it was a small price to pay. Suddenly, once we made the decision to go, the drudgery of work became easier to endure. A great weight had been lifted and we began moving toward a goal, toward something beyond the rut.

Before we knew what was happening we had crated up all of our belongings, the artwork and furniture, the books and diplomas, the computer and television, the light bulbs, linen, paper clips, photo albums, CD collection, and Christmas decorations. With supreme care we crammed it all, neatly boxed and labeled, into a large storage garage.

We left Amanda's parents' house early that first morning. As the Tijuana rush hour swept us around the massive traffic circle I looked up at the statue of Cuauhtémoc, the Aztec leader who had refused to reveal to the Spanish conquistadors the location of a cachet of gold and had his feet burned for his trouble. Turning to Amanda I asked, "Which way do we go?"

She shrugged. "*Yo no se.* Beyond here the city has changed so much."

It was the first day of a journey that would take years longer than imagined and cause fundamental changes in our lives. In our tiny Volkswagen van we would experience inconceivable difficulties. Our relationship would be tested, our ingenuity sharpened, and our forgotten sense of humor revived. Scouring markets, we would sample the cuisines of different cultures and learn to make much from little when among the desperately poor. Crossing borders alone and vulnerable, we would take chances, rely on help from strangers and make lifelong friends. Gripping the wheel, we would cross four continents, exploring the map and discovering the routes leading to what's important in life.

Driving in circles around Tijuana that morning, we were already lost, but we were moving in the right direction. In time we would learn that some of the best things in life happen at such a moment.

CHAPTER 2

The Third Member

Near Mazatlan, Mexico
1,394 miles

The Pemex gas station was teeming with cars waiting to fill and the attendants were taking their time, chatting with one another, otherwise ignoring the customers. When they saw us pull up, two of them jumped to attention and enthusiastically waved me to the end of an aisle.

The van rested off the edge of the cement pavement next to the pump and sat at an angle leaning toward the driver's side. The attendants fidgeted with the locking gas cap as I got out of the van. One guy held the nozzle and the other conveniently blocked my view of the counter on the pump. I unlocked the gas cap and insisted on seeing the zeros before they began to fill. The blocker grudgingly moved aside then shrugged and moved off in disappointment.

The attendant topped up the tank and took my money, then pointed confusedly at a puddle under the engine. I thought it was just another attempt at a scam until I realized that it was gasoline dripping from inside the engine compartment. In the time it took me to open the door the puddle had doubled in size and the attendant had signaled for the others to come over and look.

Suddenly, I realized that raw fuel was dripping, pouring actually, directly on the spare battery. Like a bunch of stray dogs the attendants scattered out into the street. Too stupid to run, I reached up and wrapped my fist around the tube that was leaking then yelled for Amanda.

"What's wrong? Is that our gasoline all over the ground?" She asked as she came running.

"Yeah, the fuel line is broken and it's pouring on to the battery. It might catch fire. Get me a rag, quick."

The fuel was running in a stream down my arm and soaking my shirt, but it no longer dripped on the battery.

"Never mind the rag. In my tool kit there's a piece of black rubber tubing. Get that for me."

I heard her frantically throwing around the spare parts and bags that were packed on top of the tool kit. "I can't find it. Where else do you think it is?" She yelled.

The gasoline seeped further down my shirt and into my shorts. "Look under my seat. Just pull everything out."

I heard banging. Jumper cables and a tow-strap landed on the ground. "It's not here. Where else could it be?"

Gas was trickling down my leg, soaking my sock and filling my shoe. In frustration I yelled, "We live in this tiny box and we can't find anything!"

Well over a year before leaving on the trip I began tormenting the staff of every Volkswagen supply shop in town while stocking up on cork gaskets, rubber seals, wires, plugs, lubricants, sealants, oils, and fluids. I purchased brake cylinders, generator brushes, fan belts, plug leads, and wheel-bearing grease. My pile grew and grew. I hadn't the slightest idea what I was buying. When I dropped off the van at the mechanic I would hang around the garage and repeat things I had read in the repair manual, in the form of a question. "What do you think of those sodium-filled valves?" "How do you like the solenoid bypasses?" Sunday mornings I roamed the swap-meet with a list of tools and bargained with second-hand vendors for ratchet hex keys, feeler gauges and cir-clip removers. In my ignorance I slowly collected a storehouse of used parts from junkyards: a spare cylinder head, a clutch cable, and a boxful of widgets for the carburetor. Every available space in the van was stuffed with the accumulated spare parts, tools, and supplies. They were crammed in cabinets, shoved in the glove box, strapped in the engine compartment, and squashed under the seats. I bolted old shocks to the chassis and heaped nuts, bolts, screws, and worm gear clamps into my tool kit, not knowing what they were for or if I would ever need them.

"Where else could it be? Think!" Amanda yelled from the van.

The whole left side of my body was soaked with gasoline but it appeared that the leaking had stopped. "Forget the tubing. Just get me a rag."

She came running with a grocery bag full of old clothing. "What happened?"

"I think it stopped. Hand me a sock and I'll tie it around the tube."

With the sock in place we slowly pushed the van to a parking spot and I went into the filthy toilet to change my fuel soaked clothing. When I returned Amanda was crouched in front of the engine compartment wearing her yellow kitchen gloves, sopping up the spilled gasoline. She poked her head out and said, "The only place I didn't check was the cabinet above the seat. Why don't you look there?"

I flipped open the cabinet door and pulled out a few boxes of mosquito coils, the sewing kit, an umbrella, the snorkeling gear, and there, way in the back, wrapped around the solar shower, was the spare fuel line. I kneeled down next to Amanda and asked, "Has it spilled any more?"

"No, it's actually drying," she said as she moved aside and I unwrapped the soaked sock. The tube had become brittle with age and a crack had developed. I cut a piece from the spare line and fit it in place.

That night, parked at a campsite, I admitted to Amanda, "I thought that was it, the end of the trip, and we've only just begun."

"Worse than that," she said as she threw her arms up in the air, "I thought our little home was going to blow up."

Even with all it's limitations we couldn't have imagined traveling in any other vehicle. The van was an old 1978 Volkswagen camper with no fancy gadgets. It wasn't four-wheel drive, it didn't have air-conditioning, and the radio and tape player barely worked. But from the moment we saw it we knew it was the one. It was love at first sight.

We found it parked in front of an antique shop on Fairmount Avenue in Ocean Beach, a funky little neighborhood in San Diego that typifies the California existence. It's the kind of place where professional long board surfers live next door to the vegan commune. On the beach, unleashed dogs dart through the surf as their rabid owners fight the encroaching tentacles of chain stores. Deadheads, tattoo artists, violin teachers, and feral cats all live together in a perplexing, dazed, laidback harmony. After drooling over the van for half an hour I jotted down the number on the for-sale sign as Amanda peeked through the windows.

Later we met the owner sitting on his front porch. He seemed a bit offbeat, but his white man's afro was downright Republican considering the neighborhood. As we walked up to the house he didn't stand. "So, you're interested in my kombi?" He said it like a man being offered money for his daughter.

Flattery was the only route to success. "It's in beautiful shape, almost perfect. What do you want for it?" I asked.

"Well, that's just it, I don't have an *asking* price," he said without hesitation. "Last week I had a guy from Del Mar make a low-ball offer, $200 below my price. I turned him down flat. He keeps calling me back but I know he's not the right person."

At first Amanda didn't recognize the signs of unnatural attachment between man and machine and she asked, "OK, so what is the price?"

He looked away, scratched his hair and said mysteriously, "See, I'm a Jehovah's Witness Minister, and I don't like to negotiate."

I thought we'd better tread carefully. "Fair enough. Mind if we take a look?"

We poked around the van, letting him get to the point in his own time. He showed off the cabinet doors he had tracked down at a junkyard in Escondido and the nearly-new seats he had bought at a swap-meet in Pasadena. The two-burner stove was spotless and the small icebox, exactly what we wanted. As we took it for a test drive along the beachfront road he relaxed his white-knuckled fists from the dashboard and said, "I see you know how to drive an old VW. Nice and easy."

I nodded. "I've owned three cars in my life, and they've all been 70's VeeDubs. This is by far the nicest I've ever seen." I didn't mention that I was completely ignorant about their inner workings, nor that I'd learned to drive a VW properly only through a series of mishaps that made several mechanics wealthy.

Back at his house we lifted the pop-top roof to check out the sleeping arrangements. There was a bed up top and another that folded out from the seat below.

As I was about to climb up and see if the mattress was comfortable Amanda spotted the owner's wife coming from the back yard and went for the jugular. "So, what is your price for the van?" she asked.

The woman answered without hesitation.

Amanda raised her eyebrows and looked at me with a smile. I accepted right there on the spot. The wife was thrilled. Her husband was stunned.

In desperation he sputtered, "Of course, I can only accept cash."

Amanda nodded, "What time can we bring it by tomorrow?"

To a longtime VW owner their bus is much more than simply a means of transportation. Volkswagens, especially the older ones, have such individual personalities that they seem to take on human characteristics. They are not mere cars or practical machines designed to move people, but are treated like a member of the family.

Stuffed full of spare parts and tools, having barely dodged a bus-b-que, our van was rapidly becoming the third member of our journey.

CHAPTER 3

Real de Catorce

Real de Catorce, Mexico
2,225 miles

The longhaired hawker leaned against a tree among piles of bootleg music at the flea market and peeked out from under a tattered leather hat as he said, "What has brought you to beautiful Matehuala?"

"We're going up into the mountains, to Real de Catorce," I said.

His posed indifference was penetrated. "Catorce...ah yes. A spiritual place...full of much power. It gives a lot of positive energy."

Amanda picked up one of his dust-covered cassettes and said, "We're going up for the pilgrimage. It begins tomorrow."

"Yes. I was there for the pilgrimage when I was small. My grandmother took me. She believed the statue was miraculous. But there is another pilgrimage, much, much older than this Catholic one. Have you heard about it?"

We shook our heads.

"No?" He said with surprise. "Each year the Huichol Indians walk from Nayarit to the desert up there..."

Amanda interrupted, "From Nayarit? It must take them weeks."

"A month, or more," he said. "They come to collect the pieces of the peyote cactus." He held his fingers apart to show the size and said, "They look like tiny carrots."

"What do they do with them?" Amanda asked.

"The Huichols believe dreams are a way for the gods to reveal secrets. They use the peyote to enhance their dreams."

"To hallucinate," I said to Amanda.

"You call it hallucinate," he said. "They believe it helps them to see things clearer. Like...like everything around us is not

reality. It is only *percepción*, perception. Peyote lets them see life
from a different perspective."

The arduous cobblestone road to the mountain village of Real
de Catorce was butt-numbing but the van relished it like a long-
lost friend. Enterprising locals parked ancient cattle trucks near
the pull-outs along the steep, winding road where two
overstuffed, mustachioed *policias* blocked the way. For five pesos
a raggedy-looking kid watched the van and his uncle hauled us in
the back of his truck the rest of the way up the mountain.

At the top we were dropped off at the entrance to a tunnel.
We followed the crowd into *El Ogarrio*, the access shaft built to
protect the old silver-mining town of Catorce from bandits.

After a few minutes of walking in near total darkness, hearing
nothing but the echoing of our footsteps, we turned a corner in
the damp cavern and were blinded by bright sunlight. Blaring
music foretold the chaos just outside the tunnel. We were swept
with the crowd down the main street, Lanza Gorto. The
megaphones of snake oil salesmen, blanket sellers and hypnotists
drowned each other out. Plastic clocks depicting the Last Supper
and six-foot wooden rosaries were leaned against stalls selling
dulce de leche and *gorditas*. Galvanized washtubs full of bloody
organ meats simmered over bonfires, giving off a noxious,
appetite-killing stench. A young woman reached into a bucket
full of *maza*, patting balls of dough flat with her tiny brown
hands, then fried them on a greased drum lid. With no
refrigeration, meat hung from hooks in the back of the food
stalls, on the verge of becoming jerky from the desert heat.

With just one telephone and a population of eight hundred
the town somehow accommodated over a hundred thousand
swelling souls as they inflicted unfettered adoration on the patron
saint, San Francisco de Assisi, affectionately known as Panchito.

Pilgrims wrapped in vibrant wool blankets used one another
as pillows and slept on the sidewalk under the shade of split
plastic rice bags. Vendors lounged under tables at noon while
their children covered chocolate crucifixes and Virgin of
Guadalupe *cocadas* with mosquito netting to protect against the

swarms of insatiable bees. No self-respecting pilgrim indulged in
the luxury of a hotel room and the *Hay Cuartos* sign rested in the
window of the town's dusty-floored inn. Waiting under the
balconies of a narrow alley, the devout piously queued for use of
the seatless, waterless public toilets.

Cloth tents lined the outskirts of town with brightly colored
banners advertising parish affiliation. Pilgrims organized into
massive groups as they departed the trail and entered the village,
with the young men struggling under the weight of car batteries
to power the megaphones that blended with one another into one
loud, unintelligible fit of sacred song. The tired pilgrims halfheartedly hummed a tune through the streets while the most
religious women walked up and down the line, prodding them to
sing louder.

We followed the groups into the church, where most of the
pews had been removed and steel barriers installed to herd the
anxious pilgrims toward the statue of St. Francis. Some crawled
on their knees across the hardwood floor as nuns stationed along
the edges kept order and quickly swooped on anyone with a
candle in the fire-trap church.

Amanda joined the long line and waited patiently to approach
the statue. The black clad woman in front of her shook with
emotion when she finally reached the saint and kissed the purple
robe hanging from Panchito. With tears streaming down her face
the woman prayed for a miracle, then reluctantly moved aside. I
watched as Amanda pinned a small silver charm among hundreds
attached to the robe.

In a side chamber the church walls were covered from floor
to ceiling with *retablos*, home-made tributes on tin plates with
glued pieces of hair and painted pictures. We squatted and
stretched to read some of the thousands of comic book like
tablets telling the stories of miracles performed by Panchito.

At the church courtyard we were herded along by the crowd
into a busy alley and we passed a small, informal eating place set
up by a local family in their home. Struggling against the throng
we made our way through their door. The mother sat us down at
her kitchen table as her husband grilled meat on a small barbeque

and piled *tacos de asada* on foam plates. The grandmother kept count of the number of tacos we ate and quickly served Coca-Colas, cleaning up before we were finished. Their young son wore a werewolf mask and went around the tables scaring patrons as an Indian family sat down with us and ate their tacos in the complete silence of total exhaustion.

The beer sellers and 'shroom-munchers, unwilling to relinquish the entire town, congregated near the Capilla de Guadalupe, an eerie chapel built using the gravestones and caskets of dead silver miners. A young guy sat cross-legged on a tattered blanket, dirty feet turned upward, twisting pieces of bailing wire into ornate shapes with miniature needle-nose pliers as a girl dressed in a flowing cotton skirt and skimpy Ché t-shirt braided another's hair. They set out handmade jewelry and piles of colorful rocks on a faded sarong next to a decrepit Volkswagen van.

A young Argentinean girl with dreadlocks and a tie-dyed dress that barely contained her large, hanging breasts sat with a baby in her lap, smoking a hand-rolled cigarette. Amanda stopped to look at the jewelry and I asked her in Spanish about the van.

She stretched a bangled hand to keep the smoke from reaching the baby. "A guy from Texas left it here a few months ago. We sleep in it when we're not trekking in the hills."

We sat down next to the girl in the shade of the van and Amanda asked, "What do you do in the hills?"

"Every few weeks we go out on a pilgrimage. We collect buttons. You know, the kind the Huichols have collected for thousands of years. Then we come back here and chill."

Amanda reached over and the baby grabbed her pinky finger. "The mushrooms, what do they do for you?"

The girl smiled and said, "For everyone it is different. Some smell strange odors. Others hear noises or see wild colors and shapes." She stood and opened the rickety back door of the van, carefully resting her baby on the back seat then she turned to look over the valley below. "A few weeks ago we got some fresh buttons, mashed them up and made a drink. I swear to God I flew." She swept her matted hair from her eyes and pointed to a boulder below. "I swooped down and landed on that rock, then I shot up into the clouds. It was unreal." Then she turned with a start and looked toward her baby with a dazed, surprised expression.

Just after sunset an old pick-up truck dropped us off near the side of the road where we had parked the van. The boy sat on the ground leaning against our back bumper and jumped to his feet when we approached. I handed him a few pesos for guarding the van while Amanda unlocked the door. As he looked inside he asked, "Did you see Panchito?"

"Um hum," Amanda said. "I did."

"Last year my aunt asked Panchito to make my cousin's eye better, and he did."

"Ah, that's good," Amanda said as she sat in the passenger's seat and I started the engine.

The boy said something we were unable to hear over the sputtering purr of the van so Amanda opened her door and asked, "*¿Perdon?*"

The boy moved closet and said a little louder, "I hope you get what you asked for too."

CHAPTER 4

Don & Sancho's Walk

Guanajuato, Mexico
2,929 miles

As we were pulling out of the campsite in Guadalajara Amanda said, "OK, we follow Avenida Vallarta all the way out of town. Remember, this is the second biggest city in Mexico so we're going to have to be a little patient, ok...OK?"

I grumbled, "OK. Avenida Vallarta all the way across town to the highway."

It took teamwork and an amazing amount of patience to find our way through the twisting confusion of one-way streets and kamikaze drivers of a Mexican city. I did much of the driving since I was familiar with the van's sticky third gear and the lack of visibility through the back window. Amanda was the navigator. She was more organized and would normally plan our route the night before by marking the maps with a highlighter and sticky-notes.

As we approached the center of Guadalajara cars buzzed by at amazing speed, passing on the right and the left. "It looks like we're coming to a fork. Should I take Avenida Vallarta or Avenida Cárdenas?" I asked.

No answer.

"Vallarta or Cárdenas?" I asked more forcefully.

Amanda looked down at her map and answered with a bit of frustration in her voice, "I told you, Avenida Vallarta all the way across town. Just like when we came in."

The job of navigator was, in many ways, more difficult than driving because Amanda had to look at the map, watch for street signs, and make split-second decisions all at once. Highway signs in Mexico did not specify north, south, east, or west, but indicated the city the road headed toward. To confuse matters, right at the exit, when chaotic drivers frantically changed lanes, the sign indicated a small town not listed on the map. In the heart of downtown Guadalajara Amanda was studying the route with great intent and said, "OK, at some point Avenida Vallarta becomes Avenida Cárdenas. We want Avenida Cárdenas."

I took a deep breath, trying to remain calm. Then I exploded, "I just asked you that five minutes ago when we passed it! The split was way back there and there is no way we can turn around here!"

Amanda searched the map for a way back to Cárdenas. Our map gave a general overview of the city, but showed only a few large avenues, and we were about to plunge into a neighborhood with small, winding, one-way streets. Not the best way to start off a long day of driving.

After forty-five minutes of asking directions, doubling back, spinning around traffic circles, and quietly fuming, the argument began. Amanda yelled, "This isn't going to be the last time we get lost. Driving through cities is hard and we've got to be patient!"

I yelled louder, "But it was right there on the map. You just had to look at it!"

Amanda yelled a little louder, "This isn't easy, and it's why most people don't even try to make a trip like this!"

The rest of the drive was pure silence.

Hours later we reached the city of Guanajuato. The highway abruptly threw us onto Calle Hidalgo and we found ourselves once again hopelessly lost. Shot through one tunnel, then another, we ended up in the city center. Getting lost in Guanajuato was not like getting lost anywhere else in the world. The center resembled the bottom of a bowl, with the pastel-colored colonial homes clinging to the inside slopes.

It was hard to believe that a town this compact would have a campground, but we had fuzzy directions to a place that involved weaving through a labyrinth of cobblestone streets and climbing a steep hill, while going the wrong way in a one-way alley. We were bound to get lost.

Pulling over several times to ask directions we eventually found the proper alley. It gradually narrowed to the point where the van could just barely fit and became so steep that with the pedal to the floor the van was on the verge of stalling. As we ascended I was yelling and honking to keep stray dogs, pregnant women and donkey carts out of the way. If for any reason we were stopped, we would never get the van moving again.

The alley eventually flattened and we rolled into the driveway of a house perched on the hillside overlooking the city. The campground was a large tiered yard behind the house that was also used as the neighborhood parking lot. We were so relieved to be on flat ground that we completely forgot the argument.

An old inebriated American waddled over to greet us as Amanda got out of the van to look for the owner. "Hello there. You look like you've had a helluva drive." He rested his thick forearm on the front door and wheezed to regain his breath from the strain of the ten steps he had taken. "You must be here for the Cervantino Festival like everyone else." He swung his arm in a gesture to indicate the four other campers.

"Yeah, the first few days at least. We're not sure if we'll stay for the entire event." I said.

He reached through the window and took my hand to shake it as his other hand went to a large scab on the top of his bald, discolored head. "I'm John. If you have any questions I live over there." He pointed to an ancient, rusted trailer in the corner of the campsite among the overgrown weeds and piles of junk. "I'll let you get settled. We can talk more later tonight." He let go of my hand and started back.

That evening we walked through the Plaza San Roque in the midst of a Cervantes frenzy. The celebration honoring Miguel de Cervantes, the Spanish author of the novel about the crusading, overly noble Don Quixote de la Mancha, had taken over the city. The plaza was filled with the sound of blaring trumpets from mariachis ambushing unsuspecting diners. Student minstrels warmed up on the steps of the market, competing for space with a group of young Mexican students who pounded bongos as they passed a knitted ski cap for donations. A brush-headed kid poked at the fire under his washtub full of corn, and I bought a cupful for seven pesos, with mayonnaise, ground cheese and chili sauce. A stilted Don Quixote, Sancho Panza and Dulce danced through the streets pausing briefly for photos. Amanda made her way to an ice cream stand that scooped unusual flavors like *elote* (corn), *tequila*, *zanahoria* (carrot), and *nopal* (cactus). She returned with her hands full and found me sitting on the fountain watching the mimes, jugglers, unicyclists, and clowns as they playfully insulted the crowd.

While the Cervantes festival made Guanajuato renowned throughout the world, in Mexico the town is famous for a far more gruesome attraction. By some freak of nature the highly acidic soil in the area has a tremendous preserving effect on corpses. Years ago the owners of the local cemetery began digging up the bodies of the deceased whose families could no longer pay the plot fee. An entrepreneurial genius put them on display and began charging admission to a museum that includes, among other rarities, the smallest mummy in the world.

Early the next morning we lined up with a horde of Mexican tourists to visit the Mummy Museum. The leathery bodies of over a hundred mummified adults and children in antiquated funeral attire lined the walls behind glass cases. We walked through the museum with a family from Mexico City who stopped and stared in amazement at one particular case. The father squatted down between his young sons and said in Spanish, "Look at this one."

One of the boys said, "Eeeewww", as the mother covered the eyes of her daughter and moved on. Huddled together the boys stared into the case while we zipped by the other displays. As we came up behind them they broke into a giggle and their mother embarrassedly called out to them.

The display contained a young man who had been buried without clothing and was revealing his mummified private parts.

Back at the campsite, old man John sat on a pile of stones in the dark, waiting for us to return. He held a bottle of cheap tequila and looked out over the lights of the town as he caressed the scab on his head. We talked for a while about life as an expat' in Mexico. He said CNN and the movie channels made him feel at home and he enjoyed the Saturday morning American Club meeting at a small greasy spoon. After a few swigs he asked if I would walk with him to an all-night grocery shop just down the hill.

I doubted he would make it all the way down and asked, "What do you need? I'll go and get it for you."

He struggled to stand and mumbled, "No, let's walk."

The cobblestone hill was steep, and John stopped every ten or fifteen steps to gulp in the cool, thin mountain air. The grocery shop resembled a small stall, but the tightly confined space did not limit the selection. A young woman peeked from behind the bars of the night window and greeted us with a sugary voice, *"Buenas noches."*

John just nodded and pointed with his eyes.

Without turning her head the young woman pulled a condom from a long roll behind her and passed it through the bars. John dug in his pocket and slipped her a five-peso coin.

As he started away from the window she leaned forward and said, *"Buena suerte, caballero."*

He smiled over his shoulder and said with a thick American accent, *"Gracias,"* then turned to me and said, "Okay, I'll take it from here. See you tomorrow."

He hobbled away, disappearing down the narrow lane.

A few weeks later word passed through the travelers' grapevine that John had succumbed to the cancer that had started as a small dot on his head and relentlessly spread throughout his body.

CHAPTER 5

Natual Selection

El Rosario, Mexico
3,274 miles

The new pavement abruptly ended, dropping us on a dirt track that became extremely steep and rocky. The steeper it got, the slower we chugged along and the van barely made it past a few rutted, sandy sections. Less than half a mile from the entrance to the El Rosario Monarch Butterfly Sanctuary the road became even steeper and sandier.

A group of indigenous women squatting over baskets of clean laundry watched as I disrupted the tranquility of the mountains by revving the engine to five thousand rpms, then popped the clutch. The van spewed a cloud of sand and dust behind. Even with the pedal to the floor it felt as if we were moving in slow motion, and nearing the ridge the power finally gave out. We came to a complete stop.

The women giggled and called for the others to watch as we backed down the hill to a relatively flat spot and tried a different route, not as steep, but a bit more rutted. As we hit the first set of bumps the van slowed but continued inching its way forward. Then we hit an unavoidable rock in the road. It stopped us dead in our tracks. The engine stalled. Turning tail we headed back down the mountain.

Before leaving home we changed the van's engine from a complicated fuel-injected motor to a low power, easy to repair Beetle motor. The compact Volkswagen Beetle has infested virtually every corner of the globe, making it easier to find spare parts in even the most remote locale. I figured it was a reasonable trade-off, giving up raw power for versatility.

At the time it didn't occur to me that the engine and transmission work together as a team. The engine provides the power and the transmission delivers it to the wheels. When we changed the amount of power and mixed in some environmental variables like high altitude, the whole system became confused. At the coast or on flat ground the van surfed along happily but at elevation, with diminished oxygen, it barely sputtered along. I figured this out the hard way.

As we passed the village of El Rosario on the way down the mountain, an old *indigena* wearing the traditional wool skirt and shawl of the mountain women frantically waved at us and asked for a ride down to the village of Ocampo. Amanda opened the sliding door and helped her in. The elfin woman placed a bony, arthritic hand on Amanda's shoulder and propped herself up, barely hunching to get in the van. She settled on the back seat and positioned a colorful pouch on the floor beneath dangling feet. Her thick dark braid and small stature gave her a childlike quality, out of place with her worn, sun-damaged face. She explained with disgust in basic Spanish, "They took all of the local buses for the tourists. Now we have no way to get down to town and my grandson needs medicine." She glanced around the van and asked, "And where are your children?"

Amanda paused for a moment and answered tactfully, "God hasn't sent them to us yet."

The woman persisted, "I've heard that some women do not want children. Is this true?"

"Yes, there are women, even some here in Mexico, who don't want children. But we do. We'll welcome them when they come."

Now she was even more perplexed. "Here, we don't think about it. They just come."

We drove on silently for a while, pondering the conversation, and passed a young girl struggling up the hill with a child strapped to her back, another in her arms, and a third, no more than four years old, carrying firewood in a bundle slung around his forehead.

The old woman directed us to the pharmacy where we dropped her off. Then we headed to the mining town of Angangueo to figure out another way into the sanctuary. With no campgrounds in sight we stopped at several hotels to ask if we could camp in their parking area. They all refused. Eventually one man gave us directions to a hotel with a grassy area where camping was sometimes permitted. We turned off the main street and found ourselves on an extremely narrow cobblestone path that tailed up into the mountain. I sped up to gain momentum, but after a short stretch the van sputtered and stalled. The mountain had defeated us. A truck followed closely behind and blocked our only downward escape route.

I cursed myself for being such a fool, failing to think through the consequences of changing the motor and not the transmission. The truck driver understood our dilemma and reversed all the way down the hill, allowing us to back into a driveway. Without realizing it, we had passed the hotel we were looking for and backed right into their grassy parking area. It was an old miners lodge and the owner graciously allowed us to pop up the roof and set up camp.

Early the next morning, after a bumpy ride in the back of a cattle truck and a steep hour-long hike, we arrived at the sanctuary. Our guide, Ramon, led us through the fog along the narrow paths of the dense forest as he explained that each year hundreds of millions of Monarch butterflies leave their summer homes in North America and migrate for six weeks to this tiny dot of mountaintop in central Mexico to spend the winter. It is a mystery of nature how they find their way more than three thousand miles to this remote place.

As we walked, we saw only a few butterflies fluttering between the trees. Amanda whispered, "I expected to see millions." Looking closer, she noticed that the pine trees appeared unusually dark and realized that the velvety, clinging coats were actually thousands of butterflies draping the branches.

Then the sun came out. The trees burst to a bright orange life. The swarms looked like orange snowflakes against the blue sky and butterflies clumsily fell to earth without warning. Each step on the mountainside had to be taken with extreme caution to avoid crushing them underfoot but children ran with wild abandon, collecting as many as possible.

And then the sun went behind a cloud. The bright spectacle was shut off like a light bulb, only to return again and again with the appearance of the sun. We found an isolated spot in the sun, carefully spread out a blanket, and sat in awe, eating our sack lunch of refried beans and goat cheese wrapped in flour tortillas.

A year later while camping on the edge of the Kalahari Desert we were listening to the BBC on our shortwave radio as we got ready to go to sleep. Amanda had already climbed up into the pop-top bed and I was about to shut off the radio when a report began about the butterflies of the El Rosario Reserve.

A freak storm had passed through the area, dumping a large amount of rain during the dry season. This rain was followed within hours by a freezing coldfront. A record number of butterflies arrived in the mountains of Mexico that year and millions of them froze, dropping into massive piles on the ground.

Researchers estimated the dead at more than twenty-two million per hectare. When digging to the bottom of the piles they found that a small percentage of the butterflies were still alive, insulated by the warmth of the dead. The report ended with a researcher explaining how he felt profoundly saddened by the large-scale death of the beautiful insects while at the same time being fascinated by the clear and unambiguous glimpse the tragedy had given him into the evolutionary process.

As I switched off the radio I realized we had been instantly transported from the center of Africa to that small mountain community in Mexico. We laid in the pop-top bed talking.

"Remember that little old *indigena* we picked up on our way down the hill?" Amanda asked in a drowsy voice. "She had those long braids and her feet didn't even touch the floor when she sat on the seat. I wonder if her grandson got better."

"We were so worried about the van," I said. "Can you believe we actually considered turning back toward home?" Amanda laughed. "It's gotten us through so much since then. Imagine everything we would have missed."

She was quiet for a long while and I had almost drifted off to sleep when she whispered, almost to herself, "Strange…It's strange…Such a terrible thing but they will be so much stronger for it."

CHAPTER 6

Tail of the Devil

Pátzcuaro, Mexico
3,366 miles

As we sat in the waiting room of the Mexican government health clinic in Pátzcuaro Amanda teased, "I remember hearing stories about the IMSS clinic in Tijuana. People would go in with a cut finger and come out with an amputated leg." She added with a chuckle, "But I'm sure it's gotten much better since then."

A vile sickness had spread through my body. A simple headache bulged into a throbbing pain and my stomach churned. Throughout the night a fever rose, then plunged, alternating between shivering chills and overwhelming heat. The cycle of high fever and cold sweats continued for another day and night, and I no longer cared if I died. Amanda threatened to dress me in a mustard-colored suit for my funeral. I hate mustard.

Coincidentally, we were in the right place at the right time. On the shores of Lake Pátzcuaro the indigenous and Christian beliefs are meshed together to create a unique holiday at the beginning of November. The Tarascan Indians added a pinch of chili to the bland Catholic tradition of All Souls Day and created the unique *Dia de Los Muertos* or Day of the Dead.

In Diego Rivera's famous painting, Dream of a Sunday Afternoon in the Alameda, he includes *La Catrina,* an elegantly clad skeleton woman, who represents the gleefully macabre black humor of Mexico's unique relationship with death. Mexicans enjoy yanking the tail of the devil, almost ridiculing mortality. Using laughter to conceal their fear of death, they have a unique view of the spirit world.

On *Dia de Los Muertos* homes in Pátzcuaro and many throughout Mexico create an *ofrenda,* an offering with their deceased relatives' favorite food and drink. On the days leading up to the holiday street vendors sell joyous, dancing skeletons and festive chocolate skulls to be added to the offering. Life was difficult for the Tarascans, with mortality a constant companion, snatching nearly half the children. Few lived to reach the age of forty and death was seen as a relief; almost a reward to be rejoiced upon.

I flipped though our medical emergency book, *Where There is No Doctor,* and discovered a handful of ailments that matched my symptoms, but none better than malaria. Skeptical that malaria even existed in Mexico, I scanned a pamphlet we brought with us published by The World Health Organization. There, under the light blue wave that indicated the malarial zone, was the region we were in. It was definite. I had malaria. Of that there was no doubt. I thought, "What in the world do I do now?"

I showed the evidence to Amanda and she looked at me with true concern in her eyes. "You might be right, but you know it could also be," she flipped through the book, "that you have ringworm," she kept turning the pages, "or maybe you were bitten by tsetse flies and you have sleeping sickness," she flipped to the back of the book, "Ah, here it is. I got it. You're pregnant!"

The IMSS doctor was starting the holiday a day early. A dark little man practically hidden behind the huge desk, he was hunched over the newspaper, tapping a chewed pencil on the metal surface as he completed a puzzle. His thick black hair appeared almost blue and covered his head like a military helmet. His nurse ushered us in and he lazily looked up. I described my symptoms in detail and Amanda translated the high fever, the freezing chills, and the upset stomach. He patiently listened and cracked a very slight smile when I told him I was convinced I had malaria. He shook his head doubtfully and gave a questioning glance toward Amanda, "*Ahhhh sí*, with my experience those symptoms would indicate a viral infection."

"A viral infection?" I could not accept this explanation. I knew for sure what it was and persisted by asking, "Are you sure it is not malaria?"

He thought for a moment and answered with a hint of mirth, "Malaria is highly unlikely here in Mexico. Perhaps twenty years ago, yes, but not now." He dismissed us with a wave of the hand.

There was no bill.

I was feeling horrible but Amanda insisted, "We can't miss the most famous celebration for the Day of the Dead. We've got to go."

Popping a handful of aspirin, I relented.

Each year several thousand Tarascan Indians descend on the tiny island of Janitzio in the center of the lake. They believe that the lake is the doorway to heaven through which the gods come down to earth.

Leaving the dock in Pátzcuaro, we could clearly see the island with its white houses and red-tiled roofs, topped by an enormous statue, giving it the appearance of a steep floating muffin crowned by a wedding-cake figurine. The long, narrow boat slowly putted forward as a bank of fog rolled in and the sun disappeared. I looked back to the tiller and found the captain of our vessel was no more than fifteen years old. Rain began to pour down in large heavy drops that made the water seem alive. Hazy figures took shape through the thick fog. The sound of a distant bell reverberated a continuous, gentle chime, calling the wandering souls to the celebration. In what seemed to be the center of the lake, the boy cut the engine and we coasted through the obscurity to a gentle stop along a pier.

We hopped onto the dock with Stefan and Vivien, German friends from the campground, and together we strolled the steep, slick, cobbled streets, stopping to enjoy *pescado blanco* in a makeshift restaurant overlooking the lake. Glassfuls of tequila sold for ten pesos and Stefan indulged himself each time he passed the stall of a pretty Tarascan girl. After the third drink I asked her a question we would all regret in the morning, the cost of the entire bottle. Stefan's eyes nearly popped out of his head when she replied, *"Solo treinta pesos."* (Only thirty pesos.)

Young children roamed with candle-lit *calabazas* (jack-o-lanterns) and asked for a *donativo* as a form of trick-or-treat. Vendors sold earthen jars of *pulpa de tamarindo* and we sat on the wall overlooking the lake, spitting tamarind seeds into the trees below. The sweet smell of the bubbling hot fruit ciders enticed us to try the different flavors. The narrow walkways were lined by stalls piled high with *buñuelos*, a sweet hard tortilla with hot syrup and *pan de muerto*, bread adorned with strips of dough to resemble bones. Tiny restaurants served miniature fried fish and bubbling vats of *sopa tarasca*, a spicy tomato soup.

Dancing began on a stage at sea level but only a few paid to sit in the official seats with most propped up on the rooftops overlooking the stage. At 6'2" Vivien scanned the roofs and found one unoccupied. She jumped above and scooped Amanda up with one arm. The view was perfect. We clapped and laughed along with the *Danza de Los Viejitos* (Dance of the Old Men) and were awed by the fishermen as they rowed their canoes onto the pitch black lake and fanned their butterfly nets, eerily illuminated by torchlight.

At the stroke of midnight, a disjointed procession began to move toward the cemetery. Families came prepared to spend the entire night in the graveyard, carrying fruit baskets, flowers, and clay plates of food covered with intricately embroidered napkins. They set out their *ofrendas* at the graves, surrounding them with candles and incense, to guide the souls of their loved ones on their journey back. Millions of orange marigolds covered the burial chambers and candles illuminated the night. The chapel was filled with an offering of gourds, bananas, corn, and colorful flowers for those who no longer had anyone to remember them. Women and children spread out blankets, leaning against their relatives' gravestones, praying and chanting. The mood in the air swung toward festive.

Vivien and Stefan created a miniature shrine in the cramped graveyard on a tiny cement ledge to honor the memory of a friend who had recently passed away. They placed a few marigolds in a circle around a handful of the fast-burning thin candles and held one another as they silently wept. Children who were hopping from grave to grave, playing games and enjoying the moment, stopped to stare at them in confusion. As I looked around I realized that no one else seemed sad.

Just before dawn we boarded the boat to return to town. The mountain air was cold and we bundled to keep warm as I counted the firepot buoys on the lake that lined the way back to Pátzcuaro. I was able to see a few ahead and a few behind, but those further away were obscured by the fog. They passed slowly. As my mind wandered, I silently counted. "Are they the years ticking off toward death?" I thought.

Life for many of us is no longer the endless toil it once was, and consequently, death is not a release from hell on earth. For us, remembrance of the dead has gradually become a sad event. As my mind was dulled by the hum of the old outboard motor, the tequila, the passing firepots and the mysterious fever, I wondered, "If I were to die now would I go without regret? Have I really lived? Unlike many of those who created these ancient traditions, I've been given the free will to choose my path. Have I?"

The bitter cold and the mesmerizing firepots lulled me unknowingly into a groggy half-sleep as we glided by. Suddenly, I was jolted wide-awake when the boat bumped the pier, all the fire-pots past, the journey complete.

CHAPTER 7

Something Old, Something New

Mexico City, Mexico
5,162 miles

"You must like pain or be insane." That's the advice a guidebook offered to anyone considering driving through Mexico City. Other travelers warned us to leave the van with Don Pepe at his campground and take a bus. But the temptation was far too great, and we left Cuernavaca on a Sunday morning determined to drive into Mexico City, the labyrinth above.

Climbing on Highway 95, Amanda nervously planned our route through the city as I read a billboard announcing the government's anti-pollution plan. It prohibited cars from being driven in the downtown area on certain days of the week depending on the last number of the license plate. Thursdays were off-limits for us since the van's plates ended in two, but the weekends were a free-for-all.

While highlighting the street map Amanda said, "I can't believe it. It looks like there are more than a hundred streets in the city named Hidalgo."

I glanced over and asked, "Which street will we be taking?"

She answered worriedly, "Hmmm, Hidalgo."

With more than one quarter of the country's population, Mexico City is one of the world's largest cities. Over twenty-five million people live in this sediment bowl of a valley ringed by mountains, preventing smog and sewage from leaving, and fresh water from entering. The summer rainy season often brings relief by washing the pollution down to earth, but during the dry winter, the smog collects for days. We were arriving in the heart of winter, after weeks with no rain, when breathing in a daily dose of city air was the equivalent to smoking a pack of cigarettes.

With no ring road, the only way to attack this beast was to plunge in. While the historic center was laid out in a fairly even grid, the rest of the massive tangle was haphazard and dizzying. Amanda had three maps spread on the dashboard and I chanted a mantra, "patience... patience... patience". The highway narrowed to a two-lane street and then a detour shot us into a neighborhood before we knew what happened. We followed another car the wrong way down a long one-way street and made a quick illegal U-turn to work around the detour. The term "to merge" was meaningless so I fought with two buses and a taxi to get back on to the same main street toward *el centro*.

After doubling back twice we found a hotel in the historical center advertising that it had parking. Only blocks from *La Plaza de la Constitución*, the Hotel Monte Carlo, a former Augustinian monastery, won us over with its faded elegance and over-the-top grandeur. At the front desk Amanda insisted to the rotund deskman, "We must have a secure parking place."

"Yes, we have parking. Right here," he said, pointing toward the back of the brightly tiled lobby.

I said to Amanda, "Let's go take a look to make sure it's safe before we commit ourselves."

Standing in the cramped indoor parking garage, I noticed that most of the spaces were occupied, then it occurred to me that something was missing.

"How do you think that cars get in here?" I asked.

She looked around at the three solid block walls then back toward the doorway we had used to enter from the lobby, and answered, "I have no idea."

Back at the desk she began interrogating the round man, "How do we get the van into the garage?"

He smiled and said, "Don't worry," in true Mexican fashion. "There is room for your vehicle. No problem."

She said a bit abruptly, "We don't want to register until we know we can park the van safely."

He relented and said, "Go, bring your car around. Guillermo will wait in front of the hotel and take you to the garage." He motioned toward a hunched little man wearing a maintenance uniform who lazily mopped the tiled floor.

Walking back to the van neither of us could imagine how we would drive into the parking garage.

Pulling around the corner, Amanda spotted Guillermo waving at us from the foyer of the hotel. He bent down and unlatched a series of bolts from the vestibule doors, folding them against the wall. With the expertise of an airport ground crew, he guided us directly into the lobby. The opening was just wide enough for the van to squeeze through, and we drove past several guests sitting in the plush lounge conducting business. Guillermo was well practiced and steered us far to the right to avoid the front desk. Under the arch of the rounded staircase he signaled us to stop while he folded back another set of accordion-like doors, clearing the way into the garage.

Once settled in our room we opened the French doors to our tiny balcony and stood overlooking the bustling *Avenida Uruguay*. No matter how nice the hotel, we really disliked having to be away from the van. We were far more comfortable in our own pop-top bed, with familiar sheets and pillows, close to our tiny kitchen to make coffee in the morning and prepare dinner in the evenings. It was a hassle to have to pull out our clothing from the microwave-sized closet and lug our books, shortwave radio, toiletries, food, campstove, and utensils into the room. At night in the van the porta-potty was just a hop away, while in a hotel getting to the toilet often involved a dark, stumbling journey. Our simple routine of life in the van was disrupted each time we spent the night away.

That evening we walked to the plaza and watched the military guard perform the elaborate flag-lowering ceremony. Amanda smiled with pride as the soldiers folded the enormous banner, then she turned to me and asked, "Do you know the meaning of the symbol in the center of the flag?"

"No," I answered. "I always wondered."

"It's an Aztec legend," she said. "They believed the gods would show them a sign of an eagle on a cactus eating a snake, at the place they were to settle. They saw it right here." She looked around in quiet awe.

Walking around the plaza, we passed the elaborate government buildings and stopped in front of the cathedral.

"Look how crooked it is," I said.

"It's sinking." Amanda said. "This area was once a small island in the center of a lake. They filled it in to build the city."

As we stood next to the cathedral she rubbed her hand on the stone wall and said, "These stones were once part of a pyramid. Cortéz and the *conquistadores* destroyed the Aztec structures that were here and used the stones to build the city."

We entered the cathedral and admired the ornate altar and the statues of the different saints. From a distance I noticed that one statue was illuminated with more candles than any other. Stepping between the pews, we walked closer and I heard Amanda whisper, *"La Virgen."*

The Virgin of Guadalupe is Mexico's patron saint and is the one icon prominently displayed in every car, bus, taxi, government office, and home. The appearance of this dark-complexioned Virgin with Indian features was the single most dramatic event in the conversion of the indigenous population to Christianity. Her image, once simply a religious symbol, has come to represent for many the Mexican identity.

An old woman knelt in front of the statue, sliding the beads of her rosary between her fingers, as Amanda whispered to me the five-hundred-year-old story of the Virgin.

Juan Diego, a recently converted Indian, was crossing the barren hill of Tepeyac. The Virgin appeared to him and told him she wanted a church built on the spot where Indians previously worshipped a mother figure that pre-dated the Aztecs. She instructed Juan to pick the roses that had miraculously grown on the top of the hill in December and take them to Bishop Zumarraga. Juan carried the flowers in his cloak, but when he arrived with the Bishop, the roses had disappeared and were replaced by an image of the dark-complexioned Virgin, modestly adorned in Indian garb.

Amanda said, "Every year on the day of the apparition millions of people gather at the hill." Looking at me hopefully she said, "It's the day after tomorrow. Do you want to go?"

That year nine million people came to celebrate. Nine million.

We paid the one-and-a-half-peso (sixteen-cent) fare and squashed on to the subway line toward the Basilica/Tepeyac stop. The subway was spotless, fast and remarkably efficient for the super-low price. At every stop a loud, barking vendor with a monotonous, nasal voice would enter our subway car and begin a long speech about some ridiculous product pulled from an overstuffed bag. One guy pitched a cookbook with over a hundred traditional Mexican recipes for only ten pesos. We were not the only ones to buy it as we got off and followed the crushing crowd to Tepeyac.

The Basilica was inside a gated compound that included several chapels bordering an enormous open courtyard the size of several dozen football fields. Once inside we felt as if we were in a massive concert. Groups of Indian performers formed circles and lost themselves in the beat of the dance, with headdresses of feathers flowing like waves. *Campesinos*, having walked for days over the mountains, were rolled up in their blankets, asleep in the shade as their children wandered freely and danced with the competing drumbeats.

An overzealous young priest doused everyone in the vicinity by dipping a palm branch in a bucket filled with holy water and showered it over the crowd with almost violent efficiency. At the top of the hill there was a chapel, and Amanda got in a long line behind a family that carried an immense framed picture of the Virgin, to receive a blessing from a fine, patient old priest who radiated a pious calm amidst the overwhelming chaos.

Searching for tranquility we traveled to the quaint colonial suburb of Tepotzotlán. In front of the elaborate chapel an elegant *charro* (Mexican cowboy) held the reins of a beautiful horse-drawn carriage, waiting for a newly-married couple to depart. Two little boys decked out in full *charro* costume entered the courtyard on ponies and were followed by the exquisitely dressed *novios*.

The groom wore a traditional burnt-orange leather suit with a matching sombrero and a revolver on his hip. The bride's elegant gown was equally traditional. The skirt was delicately embroidered and her flowing lace veil embraced her body like a shawl. Posing for photographs, the groom held the reins as the bride sat sidesaddle on a white stallion.

We both watched for a while, then Amanda continued translating a brochure about the chapel, "This is one of the churches that was founded by the Jesuits."

As the groom helped the bride descend from the horse her gown was caught.

"...They finished it in 1762..."

The groom held her hips and lowered her to her feet slowly, but the skirt of the gown was caught in the reins.

"...it was first a seminary..."

When I saw her bare calves I was surprised, then the garter belt came into view. It was like watching a car crash.

"...They say it's one of the finest..."

The bride slowly dropped to her feet but the flowing gown did not. There she was for the world to see.

"....examples of churrigueresque architecture..."

I could not believe my eyes.

"...in the country, It's really beautiful, isn't it? Rich, are you listening?"

This exquisitely dressed bridal couple were celebrating their wedding in one of the most traditional towns in Mexico, but under her antique gown, perhaps the same one worn by her grandmother, the modern bride did not wear underwear.

48

CHAPTER 8

Moctezuma's Revenge

Cholula, Mexico
5,270 miles

Amanda filled a small bucket with puke. Not regular puke, but puke full of the hairy legs and hard-shelled bodies of grasshoppers. I had an altogether different problem. I kept the grasshoppers down but could not stop them from coming out the other end. Moctezuma had enacted his revenge.

A few days before, as we drove into the city of Cholula, the volcano Popocatépetl spewed ash, and filled the sky with powdery gray flakes. People in the streets wore masks to keep from inhaling the particles. The government tried to encourage the *campesinos* who lived on the slopes of the erupting volcano to leave their homes and descend to shelters below, but they refused. The village shaman insisted that there was nothing to fear. The *campesinos* believed that they were protected because they had lived in harmony with the mountain for ages and had no intention of leaving. Frustrated officials threatened to use the military to forcibly evacuate the mountain.

Nearly five hundred years earlier Cortéz and the conquistadors had marched into Cholula, describing it as "the most beautiful city outside of Spain". Unknowingly they also marched into an Aztec trap. Initially the Spanish soldiers were ceremoniously welcomed, but Cortéz soon discovered that they were to be captured, their breasts split and their still-beating hearts cut out. He pre-empted the attack and slaughtered his hosts, convincing the already fearful leader Moctezuma of his suspicion.

Aztec oral tradition predicted the vengeful return of the god Quetzalcoatl (The Plumed Serpent), described as having light skin, hair on the face and emerald eyes. Cortéz's unique appearance, his red hair and bearded face, proved to Moctezuma that the unusual visitors were indeed the return of Quetzalcoatl, back to seek unavoidable retribution.

It is said that Moctezuma takes revenge for the conquest of his people through the guts of travelers, but our case of Moctezuma's revenge was caused by my naïve curiosity. Just outside the pyramid of Quetzalcoatl, in Cholula, the dilapidated market stalls sold marinated *hormigas* (ants), roasted *gusanos* (caterpillars), and fried *chapulines* (grasshoppers).

We joined a group of Mexicans huddled around a wrinkled, indigenous woman who sat on a colorful blanket with a basket of fried red grasshoppers. She held her polished brass scoop up to me and said in Spanish, "Try one."

I crunched the grasshopper between my teeth and said to Amanda, "Tastes like popcorn. I think I'll get a bag."

"You tried it," Amanda said. "We don't need any more."

But it was too late. I had already taken the five-peso coin from my pocket and we watched as the woman filled the tiny bag, using her miniature, dirty fingers to squeeze fresh lime on the creatures. With a flourish she sprinkled powdered chili on top and handed them to me.

We ate the entire bag.

Our first-aid kit was stocked full of a strange assortment of emergency supplies, but the ingenious Moctezuma attacked in a way we had foolishly neglected. We were equipped to perform surgery using our stainless steel scalpel and ready to give each other injections or temporary fillings. We even had a fully stocked homeopathic kit. But we failed to include the most basic useful items, Pepto Bismol and Milk of Magnesia.

I spent a day on the filthy seat-less toilet of our campsite with non-stop diarrhea as Amanda lay in the upstairs bed of the van, laundry bucket close at hand, puking her guts out. Neither of us felt well enough to risk a trip to the *farmacia* so we suffered in silence, punctuated by fits of laughter at our own stupidity. After two days the torture abated and we ventured out to the corner market.

As I bought supplies for our first-aid kit Amanda read the front page of the newspaper. It showed a photograph of a confused truckload of *campesinos* being returned to their mountainside homes. The army had forcibly removed them to shelters but the shaman had been correct. As predicted, Popocatépetl calmed. All was well.

That afternoon as we strolled around town a little brown woman followed close behind and did the bidding of Moctezuma by yelling in a nasally, sing-song voice, *"CHAPULINES...CHAPULINES."* (Grasshoppers...Grasshoppers.)

As she came up behind we stopped to let her pass. She brought the wicker basket down from her head and rested it just under my nose as she said, *"Pruebe uno güero."* (Try one, whitey.)

CHAPTER 9

The Mechanical Mocho

Zipolite, Mexico
5,914 miles

Wearing little more than jewelry and a somewhat dazed smile, backpackers from all over the world unite at Zipolite, a small strip of beach on the Southwestern coast of Mexico, in the state of Oaxaca. In Zipolite minimalism is the key. It is virtually gratis to hang a hammock beneath a *palapa* on the beach and relax without a care in the world.

A few open-minded, free thinkers moved to Zipolite in the 1960s. They built retreats for reinvigoration of the soul amidst the palm trees and warm sand.   Shambhala, one of the first retreats, at the far end of the beach, is just above the cove where everyone sunbathes in the buff.

We arrived in Zipolite almost by chance just at sundown, and found a familiar Volkswagen van parked in a grassy lot a few yards from the beach. It belonged to Commie Bob, a remarkable fellow we had met at another beach weeks before. He inhabited a bare, thatched roof cabaña and I weaved through a throng of occupied hammocks to find him with his feet up and his nose in a Vonnegut book.

He introduced us to Angelina, the manageress of *Palapas Tiburon,* who charged $2 a night to park the van in a mosquito-filled bog. Angelina ran her place with a slow and steady efficiency. A few tables offered a spectacular view of the two-kilometer beach and she was willing to serve up whatever happened to be in the pot. Throughout the day, unwashed, bleary-eyed travelers arrived with their lives on their backs and Angelina hung them a hammock. After lunch they took a nap swinging between tables.

Locals in Zipolite took well to the naked invasion of their peaceful community and a few enjoyed the freedom of strolling unclothed themselves. Unlike other areas in the world where nudity is permitted, in Zipolite the proportion of attractive nudists was actually quite high. Young people came to counter the effects of seasonal light-deprivation disorder and to lose tan lines. They arrived a pasty pink-white and left a toasty Kahlúa brown.

Of course, there were some really unusual-looking people too. At first I thought these misfits shouldn't even be allowed on the beach fully clothed and definitely not stark naked, but after a while I began to appreciate the interesting bodies with their hanging parts and pieces much more than the sculpted bodies of the perfectly proportioned.

Commie Bob and I would lie in our hammocks along the water and watch the bobblers jiggle up and down the beach, admiring some of the more extraordinary forms the human body could assume, the same way others marveled at the variety of seashells. One morning we watched an obese man strolled naked while his companion built a drizzle castle in the sand, one breast drooping far below the other.

Bob led an interesting life. He spent his first thirty years doing little more than drinking and drugs. Becoming a communist is easy when one does nothing useful, but somehow he managed to adhere to his beliefs through twenty years of sobriety and relative productivity. Not long after his first AA meeting Bob joined the union and became a stagehand, periodically working as a member of a road crew for rock bands. Mostly he enjoyed the freedom of his job and would call into the union hall when he felt like working.

One afternoon he set down his book and perched his reading glasses on his gray head as he said, "Right now I could be at home freezing to death. I never understood why people stay in Minnesota for the winter."

"How many years have you been coming down here?" I asked.

"To Zipolite? Just a few years," he said. "Before that I would go to Nicaragua for the winter and volunteer to work with the Sandinistas."

"You did what?" I asked. "Why would you want to go to Nicaragua?"

"It's a beautiful place," he answered defensively. "One year I built a few homes. Another year I helped set up a sustainable logging operation."

"Why don't you go any more?" I asked.

"The government found out what I was doing and refused to give me a visa." He answered with a shrug.

Surprisingly for a communist with an aversion to work, Bob managed to save enough money to take early retirement.

I asked him, "How did you do it when you only worked half the year?"

He took his glasses off and rubbed his eyes as he said, "No matter what I earned I always put some away. It's simple. Just don't buy things you don't need."

Parked next to us in the mosquito-filled bog was Mario, a speed propelled middle-aged Quebequer who enjoyed chatting with Amanda in a free-flowing babble of French and English mixed with Spanish. He came to Zipolite each year in a homemade camper that was stuffed with a remarkable array of unusual items. One morning we watched as he worked like a

Tasmanian devil to unpack a small moped. He fought for twenty minutes to get it started, but failed to produce even a sputter.

A few hours later he and a fellow Quebequer were hunched over the disassembled pieces spitting out rapid-fire French. His mechanical friend was remarkable because he was what the Mexicans call a *mocho*, slang for a one-armed man. In a short time the *mocho* mechanic had the moped spinning like a top.

With the newly-repaired moped Super Mario and his friend became highly mobile. The *mocho* held on tight as the pair sped away.

In the evening Mario returned and circled around the grassy bog with his feet in the air as he said to Amanda, "Even zo he solo one arm, he'z gud mecanico."

Amanda called out and he stopped the moped next to the van. "How'd he lose his arm?"

"Es interessante, oui. He crash avec un machina for snow, snowmobile, et'vas caught en ze belt of ze machina, horror. But he get beaucoup money from gobernmento de Canada."

"So he lives here year round?" Amanda asked.

"Oui, he will never go back."

The next morning Bob and I were in our familiar pose, with our feet up in our hammocks, when the *mocho* mechanic strolled nude down the beach with two young Nordic girls. He turned and waved to us with a blissful smile across his face.

Bob stretched his neck around clumsily in the hammock and said, "You may get further in life on the middle road, but the extremes are so much more interesting. So it goes." (Shrug)

CHAPTER 10

¡Viva Zapata!

San Cristóbal de las Casas, Mexico
6,281 miles

Just before leaving on the trip we visited my father-in-law at his home in Tijuana. He sat content and cross-legged at the head of the table one Saturday afternoon, looking me dead in the eyes. With a voice full of gravel that comes from somewhere deep down inside he said, "There are two places I don't want you to go." He paused, gulped down tequila from a shot-glass, then wiped his mouth in an almost violent gesture using the napkin on his lap. "Central America is *la ruta de drogas*, the drug route. Smugglers use the route on their way to the U.S. Drugs are the only reason anyone passes through those countries." He refilled the glass, then shook his head and chopped his hand in the air for emphasis. "*La ruta de drogas.* The authorities, politicians, and all the *pendejos* around them are contaminated, involved one way or another. Drugs make decent people turn bad, like that." He silently snapped his fingers. "I've seen it here a million times. Listen to me, you're going to be an easy target taking that route." He screwed the glass down into the table for emphasis. "The money, the power, it twists normal people to do things..." He paused, left it hanging.

Pointing at the floor he continued, "Here in Mexico you have to watch those little *cabroncitos* in Chiapas." He held the shot-glass by the tips of his fingers and laughed coarsely. "Those Indians in the south are different from the ones here or from anywhere in *todo México.* They fight. They don't take no-thing. Remember in '94 they took over the whole place with machetes and the world watching them? They're still out there living in the jungle. Listen to me, don't go to Chiapas. Especially in the kombi."

We turned off the two-lane tarmac road and followed a hand-painted sign pointing us to a muddy path worn by rutted tire tracks. The smell of rain was in the air. Milky orange puddles lined the track as it breasted a rolling, tree-covered hill and slithered down around a field with cattle grazing behind barbed wire.

An adolescent girl walked alone in the direction we were headed. She stepped aside to let us by and bent to pick up something from the ground. As we were passing she swung her arm back and threw a rock with all her might, pelting the side of the van with a large thud.

She didn't run. She stood there facing us with those Asiatic eyes that look as if they've been crying.

Amanda yelled, "*¡Ay!* What...what...what are you doing?"

The girl went on staring, unmoving, looking through us, almost but not quite frowning, blinking but unconcerned, unaffected. When we pulled away she stepped back on to the path, continuing on her way as if nothing had happened.

Cresting the last steep, rolling hill we passed through the entrance gate to Rancho Esmeralda, stopping in front of a small thatched-roofed patio surrounded with a thick bed of tropical plants and flowers. A row of bungalows lined the edge of a grassy field and a grove of neatly planted young trees stood along the rolling manicured hills.

The screen door squeaked and pulled shut behind us with a slam loud enough to draw a young local man from one of the bungalows. He entered, wiping his hands on a towel, and greeted us warmly in English. When I mentioned the girl on the path he nodded and continued with his explanation. "When you take a beer or pop, write it in the book. If you want dinner, mark it here before ten a.m. so we know to prepare enough. Don't worry about paying until you leave." He added proudly, "We work on the honor system."

I pressed for an answer about the girl and he asked us to wait for a moment as he left the room.

A few moments later the screen door slammed behind Glen, a good-natured lanky American, perhaps in his early fifties, wearing jeans and a western shirt. The only thing out of place was the felt, Indiana Jones-style hat on a head made for a Stetson.

We shook hands and he reached for a beer, offering one to each of us.

He took a gulp, then leaned against the cooler and crossed his legs. "I hear you had some trouble on the road."

"Yeah, it was the strangest thing," I said. "A girl threw a rock at the van and then she just stood there, staring at us."

He nodded, took a deep breath, and explained, "Ellen and I bought the place from a rancher in '93 after we finished up with the Peace Corps. When we moved in there was nothing out here, nothing but empty ranch land. We graded it out and planted the macadamias," he pointed to the grove with the pride of a father. "We went back to Idaho for the holidays and the Zapatista thing happened."

Amanda had mentioned to me earlier that the town of Ocosingo, just a few miles down the dirt road, was one of the towns taken over by the rebels.

Glen said, "We treat our employees well so we didn't have major problems and the government built that military base over there." On the way into the ranch we had passed a massive, heavily guarded military base with American-made Humvees neatly lined up.

"Then, 'few years ago those people you passed along my access road moved in. They call 'em *paracaidistas*, parachutists, 'cause they sneak in and set up a shack. They're just squatters really, but the land along the road isn't mine so I couldn't stop 'em. We get along well with most of 'em. I take 'em into town or pick up their supplies. My wife reads their letters for 'em and helps out with their medical problems. But a few of 'em do stupid things like throw rocks at the cars coming our way." He was more irritated than angry.

Amanda asked, "Why do they do it?"

He shrugged, "Don't want gringos here I guess." Then he turned, looked out the window, and smiled, "The trees take a few years to start producin' but the gardens are doing great. Next year should be our first harvest. 'Few years back we put in two cabins, then some more. Now there are ten and the place is nearly always full. We came here to grow plants and macadamia nuts. The cabins are holding us over until everything matures."

It was hard to believe him. He was too outgoing and talkative to live so far from others. I knew he had built the cabins to lure visitors to the remote jungle hills.

Glen walked with us part way down the hill and said, "You can set up your camper anywhere down there. There's electric on the fence if you need to hook up. We have a group staying up here in the cabins tonight, so you're more than welcome to join us at the bar and the bonfire."

The place was paradise, within walking distance of the Mayan ruins of Toniná, peaceful, green and lush. The gardens overflowed with rare tropical plants and the massive green lawn invited us to spread out and relax.

For most of the night a violent storm pelted the outside of the van with loud, banging drops, but we slept peacefully in our little home. The next morning as we were leaving Glen followed us in his pick-up until we reached the main junction. He turned to town and we headed up into the mountains.

A few hours later we drove toward the pink baroque Church of Santo Domingo in the town of San Cristóbal de las Casas. The tiny streets narrowed and became crowded with market stalls. Vendors sold small piles of tomatoes and live hens by the crate full. A man in a coarse wool poncho weaved cactus-fiber sacks and another strung together custom-made leather sandals with tire-tread soles. A woman with red patches on dark brown cheeks carried a docile infant tied to her back with a colorful shawl. Her doe-eyed, sullen daughters wore coarse woolen, potato sack-like skirts, and had bright blue blouses with intricate embroidery. Their long braids were linked across their backs with purple-red strings of yarn that swayed as they walked. At the corner a woman folded a cloth inside a wicker basket as she sang out, "Tor-tee-assss."

We were slowly moving through the traffic when suddenly the van burst forward in frenzied acceleration. I instinctively jammed in the clutch and slammed down on the brake pedal, stopping a hair short of smashing into a frightened young woman with a bag of onions balanced on her back. The leather strap across her forehead held the bundle and pulled her face into a distorted, fearful look. With the clutch depressed, the engine roared at full throttle as the accelerator pedal defied normality and stuck to the floor. I reached down and pulled it up and the engine quieted. "What was that all about?" Amanda asked.

"I don't know. It got stuck."

"Is the pedal OK? Do you think we can move?"

I pressed on the pedal several times and it popped right up. "Seems OK."

Moving again, the van drove fine, but once I relaxed my grip on the wheel and eased back into calmness, the pedal stuck again. The van continued moving forward long after I released my foot from the accelerator, propelling us through a stop sign and halfway through the intersection. I slammed in the clutch and slammed down the brake. Amanda frantically reached down and grabbed the pedal to pull it up. Cars honked, people yelled, and the engine roared as we coasted to the side of the street, up on to the stone curb, blocking the sidewalk.

I jumped out and opened the engine compartment while Amanda worked the pedal. The cable connecting the pedal with the motor looked just fine. It swept back and forth, accelerating and releasing exactly as it should. I slammed down the compartment lid, the pressure of a hundred eyes watching my every move, frustrated that I couldn't figure out what was wrong.

Amanda asked a flurry of questions. "Is it catching on something?"

"I don't know."

"Well, what's under the pedal down there?"

"I don't know!"

"Is it caught on something underneath or is it broken?"

"I DON'T KNOW!"

"Could duct tape or maybe Krazy Glue keep it in place?"

"Eeeerrrrgggggggg!" I exploded.

The van was not the only thing out of control in San Cristóbal. My father-in-law had warned us about this place. A few years earlier on December 31st the town was a powder keg with a burning fuse. Mexico had signed a free trade agreement with the U.S. and Canada. As part of the agreement Mexico revoked sections of the constitution dealing with collective ownership of land, reopening battles that Emiliano Zapata had won nearly ninety years earlier.

On New Year's Day, just as the deal took effect, the Zapatistas struck. Emerging from the jungle with machetes and machine guns, they took control of San Cristóbal and five other towns.

In the small village of San Juan Chamula, a few kilometers from San Cristóbal, we visited the church packed with pilgrims for the annual Festival of San Juan. A cloud of incense filled the pewless colonial church as an old shaman sat on the dusty floor, surrounded by the light of a thousand thin, colored candles. The troubled look on his grooved face contrasted with the placid expressions of the life-sized statues, with their exaggerated European features. His black, wire-like hair was indented by the large-brimmed hat that lay at his side, its colorful tassels indicating his standing as village doctor, priest, psychologist, and politician.

The woman sitting across from him, skirt bunched up under her, with a baby strapped on her back, had come with a complaint that she whispered in his ear. The shaman quietly contemplated for a moment, then diagnosed the problem and devised a solution that required the rubbing of a whole egg over the woman's shoulder and head to draw the evil spirits from within.

Another shaman sat with a man at his side, chanting and lighting candles as the man gulped from a Coca-Cola bottle. The soft drink, used as a replacement for their traditional fermented orange drink, was believed to purge evil spirits from the body by causing belching.

As we left the church we met a young woman who slowly walked along with us through the village and asked Amanda questions about life in the United States. At the edge of the small community she pointed out a group of corrugated shacks and said, "These are the *expulsados*. They have been expelled from the village by the elders and have lost their home and land. Most of those you see in San Cristóbal selling crafts are *expulsados*."

Amanda asked, "Why were they expelled from the village?"

The woman said, "They have been converted by the missionaries and adopted the modern ways. The shaman says the *expulsados* contaminate our ways."

Almost two years later we came upon a newspaper article about Glen and Ellen's macadamia-nut ranch in Ocosingo. The *Lonely Planet* guidebook had listed it as one of the ten best places to stay in Mexico. But their good fortune soon changed. The entry gate to the ranch was blocked by the squatters, who intimidated the guests and cut off the electricity. Calling themselves Zapatistas, the squatters sent a message to Glen and Ellen, threatening to take over the ranch on New Year's Day. A spokesperson for the group said, "The gringos must leave but cannot take anything with them."

The couple closed the ranch, vowing to stay behind to defend their property, and New Year's Day came and went without trouble. But the harassment continued. Appealing to the authorities, they were told, "They are Zapatistas. They are untouchable."

Finally, in February, the inevitable happened. A hundred machete-wielding squatters, invaded the property. In anticipation, Glen and Ellen had fled a few days earlier.

One can only imagine the fate of the once-immaculate bungalows and the tended beds of tropical plants. Will the jungle vines strangle the neat lines of macadamia trees, or will they thrive? How long will it take for the jungle canopy to reclaim the man-made world? Or will it survive like the immortal call to arms of Emiliano Zapata, "It is better to die on your feet than live on your knees."

Container ship from Colon Panama to South America

CHAPTER 11

Betta No Litta

Bermudian Landing, Belize
7,878 miles

A crazy-looking black guy with a five-inch afro, a scraggly beard, and filthy Swiss cheese clothing flapped his arms in the air and tried to wave us down as we negotiated the narrow bridge across the Belize River. We had driven miles down a rough dirt road to get to the rural village of Bermudian Landing to visit the Community Baboon Sanctuary that was just up ahead. I sped up to get away from the madman as he frantically ran after us.

Earlier in the week we endured almost five hours of hide-and-go-seek with border officials, processing our paperwork, purchasing the obligatory car insurance, and fumigating the van, before being allowed to approach the final entry post of the other English speaking country connected to Mexico. Unlike the behemoth to the north the tiny country of Belize is roughly the size of Massachusetts with only two paved roads and three traffic lights. As we parked at the final checkpoint the sky opened up with an afternoon downpour and the officials waved us through, showing no interest in the documents we had spent the entire morning collecting.

Having barely escaped the crazy guy back at the bridge, we parked in front of a small wooden house that had been converted into the Visitors' Center, under a sign that read "Betta no litta." I kept half an eye on the van as we entered the reception area.

An older black lady with a kind face wiped her hands on her bright green smock and adjusted her white turban as she came to greet us. She explained in Creole-accented English that we were welcome to camp in the field behind the Visitors' Center for a small fee. She led us on a tour of the compound, showing us the pit toilets and shower stalls out in the yard, and mentioned that a guide would be along shortly to take us to visit the "baboons", as the endangered black howler monkeys are known locally.

We were signing our names in the registry as the crazy-looking guy we had seen earlier entered, out of breath from the long jog. He wagged his finger at us. "You not stoppin' for me when I callin'. I know you was hearin' my yellin'."

The turbaned lady looked at him quizzically, then turned her palm upward in a gracious, sweeping gesture, "This is Mr. Johnson. He is one of the founders of the sanctuary and an expert in medicinal plants."

He shook our hand and raised his eyebrows, offering a half-knowing smile that insinuated, "This world is not the same as the one you come from."

I stammered, "Oh...I thought...I didn't know you...were...coming in this direction."

In Caribbean fashion he allowed the uncomfortable moment to dissipate and graciously said, "So, you here to see b-boons," in a matter of fact way. "You betta' be puttin' on some bug cream and long clothes if you wanna getta good look 'round."

After pulling the van behind the Visitors' Center I hurried with a roll of paper to the basic wooden structure surrounding the pit toilet. When I opened the door I found that it was just a box with a round hole cut into a piece of plywood. Squatting over the hole was impossible, as the covering was built so high up that my feet could not reach the ground while seated. The opening was so far back on the wooden structure that the edge dug into the back of my calves and I had to hold my legs out straight in front of me to assume the proper position. To remain balanced I had to use stomach muscles to keep my legs horizontal. I quickly realized that these same muscles were involved in the procedure at hand. An interesting vicious circle developed and I discovered that the only way to success was to assume the lotus position.

Toilet paper was another problem. Most of the toilets we encountered did not provide paper and I often wondered how my fellow users, those who did not carry a roll, attacked this problem. Sometimes there was a pile of old newspapers shoved in a corner but often there was nothing. In Mexico and Belize we began a routine that we would follow for the next three years, advertising our intentions by carrying the roll, as discreetly as possible, when we visited the *baños*.

For Amanda the thought of having to sit on an unfamiliar toilet was agonizing and the pit toilet at the baboon sanctuary would have sent even the heartiest lavatory adventurer running for cover.

When I returned to the van I told Amanda about my experience and she said, "See, I told you that yoga class would come in handy one day. Thank goodness we have Porta."

Amanda was so dependent on our little porta-potty that she christened it with a name. A square portable toilet with a seat on top and a tank connected to the bottom, Porta was her lifesaver. When we discovered that Porta was too big to fit into any of the cabinets, Amanda creatively sewed together a few pieces of upholstery material and insisted we keep the potty undercover. She did such a good job at concealment that most people who looked into the van's living space assumed the covered porta-potty was an unusual footstool.

When we divided up the daily chores for our life on the road, somehow I got stuck with the job of cleaning out the porta-potty's tank. Since we never used it for "number two", it was not as horribly unpleasant as it might have seemed, but it was not my favorite part of the day. Each morning I would disconnect the seat from the tank and carry it to the nearest toilet stall where I would wait my turn to complete the errand. While I knew it was a dirty job that someone had to do, I never got used to the strange looks from my fellow campers.

Mr. Johnson waited at the Visitors' Center and together we set out on our trek to find the howler monkeys. He swung his machete with expertise and hacked through a patch of dense jungle until we came upon a large clearing at a family farm. He said, "For years they been a-cuttin' down the jungle to farm an' the b-boons was losin' habitat. The farmers for almose twenny miles promise to keep from cuttin' the trees and from killin' the b-boons. They're sharen' the proceeds from the sanctuary."

Suddenly the trees above us sprung to life. Two troops of howler monkeys were within calling range and Mr. Johnson said, "You gonna' hear some yellin'." The treetops erupted in a howl that sounded like the combination of a growling grizzly bear and a lion's roar. I thought that the remarkably loud and ferocious noise could only emanate from an animal at least the size of a human being.

No bigger than a poodle, the howler monkeys were yelling and jumping from treetop to treetop and it seemed clear that we were unwelcome. Mr. Johnson stood back against the trunk of a tree and pointed, "Go ahead, you can get closer."

As we moved in the howlers began to throw things. At first Amanda thought they were branches but then I got a whiff of a piece that whizzed by my head.

Fleeing to the trunk of the tree we both looked at Mr. Johnson, surprised. He offered his half-knowing smile in return.

CHAPTER 12

Fatalistic Free Will

Poptún, Guatemala
8,658 miles

In the early seventies an idealistic young couple purchased a large piece of land in the Petén region of Guatemala, along the only paved road between the ruins of Tikal in the north and the population centers in the south. Mike and Carol Devine built a modest ranch in the tropical forest and named it Finca Ixobel. They opened a restaurant in town, adopted two Maya children, and fit in well among their neighbors in the remote region. The location guaranteed a steady stream of hearty travelers and their ranch became a popular stopping-point. Eventually they offered campsites for the impoverished, tree houses for the adventurous, and cabañas for the luxurious.

As we entered the finca house a young Maya man said from across the large room, "Hi guys, welcome. Go ahead and write your names down in this book. You can help yourself to anything you'd like from the bar and the bakery. Just mark it down here. At the end when you're ready to leave we'll tally everything up."

Amanda was distracted by the well-stocked kitchen and was drooling over the crates-full of fresh fruits and vegetables.

The young man noticed and said, "Oh, we grow our own organic produce. The farm is out that way."

The finca had the vibrant feeling of a commune. Everyone was busy with some project: baking in the kitchen, gathering tomatoes from the garden, or inflating the inner-tubes for the afternoon tubing trip on the Rio Machquila. A young Dutch couple wrote in their journals on the spacious patio. A chubby Guatemalan girl fed the pet monkeys from a basket of fruit. Blond, dreadlocked British guys rested their feet on their packs while leafing through the collection of National Geographic in the library.

In the evening a couple of girls sliced whole grain loaves and placed them on clay plates with churned butter in preparation for the candlelit buffet dinner. The room was full to overflowing with guests and cheerful volunteers, who worked in exchange for room and board. From the head of the table the perky American owner, Carol, made a short speech, offering everyone a warm welcome, and invited us to "dig in". We had entered a time warp where the idealism of the seventies was alive and well.

As I lay down to sleep that first night the gyrating, clicking call of a giant tropical beetle penetrated the thin tent sided walls of the pop top roof and entered my dreams.

Early the next morning I wolfed down a plate of homemade fruit yogurt while Amanda munched on handfuls of nutty granola. Eggs were fried up just moments after being laid and the smell of steaming banana bread filled the rooms of the guesthouse.

One afternoon while Amanda and I gorged on a pan of brownies still warm from the finca's oven, one of the volunteers, a short, stocky girl from New Orleans, came out to our campsite.

She introduced herself as Silvia and said, "I heard you were from the States. I wanted to come over to see if you have any books to trade." She carried a small plastic bag with a few tattered paperbacks.

Before leaving home we had accumulated a collection of used books, those that we had always wanted to read but never found the time. I said, "Sure, we've got a handful that we've both finished."

"Take your pick," Amanda said as she opened the wicker basket and placed them on our table.

"Wow, you've got a whole library in there. I've been waiting months for someone to trade with," Silvia said excitedly.

After she chose her books she asked, "Have you heard the story about this place?"

Amanda shook her head as I answered, "No, but it must be interesting."

Silvia plopped herself down on one of our chairs and reached over as she said, "It gives me an excuse to have a brownie. May I?"

"Help yourself," I said.

She grabbed a brownie, the biggest of the bunch, and told us how, years ago, the government had built a training base for the elite Guatemalan Special Forces not far down the road. The country was in the grips of a civil war, and the remote Petén region was the epicenter. One night in the mid-eighties a soldier from the nearby base had had a little too much to drink at the restaurant. He became enraged when Carol's husband Mike served a Maya Indian before serving him and banged his bottle on the table. Mike, a burly Vietnam veteran, promptly threw the soldier out and ignored his threats. Years later the soldier returned for revenge.

On one of his regular trips to town to buy supplies Mike was late returning. Neighbors had seen a white pick-up truck with armed men waiting outside the ranch. When Carol went to the nearby military base for help in locating her husband, the colonel in charge refused to see her. Mike was found the following day along the road near their ranch. He had been killed.

The soldier was tried and found guilty of the crime. He escaped from prison days after his conviction.

Leaving the finca, we drove south on the narrow two-lane road and felt a strange eeriness in being almost completely alone while traveling through the jungle. For a while we followed a Coca-Cola delivery truck with two guards perilously balanced on the front and rear bumpers, wearing full body armor and carrying automatic weapons. When they stopped at a small village to make a delivery we continued down the road on our own.

As we crossed southern Guatemala we came upon a massive traffic jam. A bridge on the only road across the country had collapsed, effectively cutting the country in two.

One of the truck drivers waiting in the long line of traffic told us that a short detour existed from a town we had passed about half an hour before. He said the road crossed a banana plantation along the border with Honduras and ended at the main road on the other side of the bridge.

As we approached the town a local radio announcer broadcast that the mayor had declared the collapsed bridge a state of emergency and ordered the plantation owner to open their road to traffic. After driving more than an hour on a network of dirt roads we found ourselves, with a handful of other vehicles, at the plantation's gate.

Amanda got out of the van and walked to the gate to see what was happening. A group of truck drivers were huddled around a security guard. She pushed her way to the front. The guard, a stocky man with a belly that drooped over his belt and dark little eyes that darted back and forth, was nervously cradling his shotgun, "…no, you cannot cross the plantation."

Amanda butted in, "But on the radio they announced that the mayor has declared a state of emergency and ordered the company to open the road." The group of truck drivers grumbled in agreement.

The guard stuck out his chest and belly. "The mayor has nothing to do with us. I have orders to not let anyone in." He slowly backed up a few steps to get behind the gate.

Amanda pointed to the guard shack. "You have a radio there. You must have heard the announcement. This road should be open."

The guard became bolder from behind the fence. "The road will remain closed. Now get in your trucks and go!"

"*¡Imposible!* The road is too narrow for me to turn around," one of the drivers pleaded.

"It's obvious they can't turn around. The only way for us to move is to drive through the plantation. So open the gate!" Amanda demanded.

"That is not my problem. Clear the area now or I will clear it," the guard yelled more forcefully, shaking his shotgun. Slowly the drivers drifted away from the gate mockingly repeating what the guard had said, and Amanda returned to the van.

We waited in the blazing sun, listening to the radio. The announcer broadcast an apology, saying that a misunderstanding had occurred and vehicles were not being permitted to drive through the plantation. As we were getting ready to leave the security guard slunk out from behind the gate carrying his shotgun, and peered into each of the vehicles as if he was searching for someone. Amanda tried to hide by ducking down in her seat but he saw her and came over to the van.

"*Señor, Señora,* there is a dirt path through the hills. It is a long way but it enters the main road after the bridge. Only small vehicles with high clearance can make it. I will give you directions." He stood for ten minutes and outlined the route on the back of an envelope.

The path was horrible, with rutted sections and steep grades. After two deep-water crossings the powdery sand and muddy water combined to coat the van like a piece of fried chicken.

Driving off-road for hours it seemed we were getting further and further from the road. Studying the scribbles on the envelope Amanda asked, "Do you think these directions are right?"

"He seemed to know what he was talking about. I just didn't expect it to take so long," I answered.

"This road is worse that what he described. It's really torturing the van," Amanda said. "Do you think we took a wrong turn?"

"I hope not," I said "We might have crossed into Honduras without even knowing it."

Several four-wheel drive vehicles came from the other direction, filling the air with clouds of dust, and we were forced to drive with the windows rolled up. With no air conditioning the van began to feel like a dirty sauna in the tropical heat.

At sundown we reached the chaotic main road, just beyond the collapsed bridge. We parked the van and walked toward the scene where a semi-truck transporting a Caterpillar crane had smashed into the overhead steel supports of the bridge. Simultaneously, a cargo truck coming in the opposite direction tried to cross. The weight of the two caused the entire bridge to collapse, dropping the trucks and their loads to the river below.

It was amazing to see how the locals reacted to the disaster. Kids climbed on the mangled girders and hung from the crumbling cement to get a better view of the wreckage. Hundreds of semi-trucks lined the road for miles. The drivers, faced with hours of idle delay, did not display any measure of distress. They gathered in groups, drinking Gallo beer, and playing cards. Quick-thinking vendors had set up shop within moments of the accident, selling every type of food and drink imaginable. Loads of bus passengers left by their drivers without hope of reaching their destination anytime soon had spread out blankets along the edge of the road.

I said to Amanda, "It's extraordinary how they just accept things."

She looked at me with surprise and said, "There are times when there is nothing you can do."

For some reason that struck me as ridiculous. It had not even occurred to me to just sit at the other side of the bridge and wait. I had to continue moving, no matter what.

Like most Americans, I was brought up worshipping doers, those who recognize what needs to be done, then roll up their sleeves and just do it. It is one of the defining traits of our culture and it was ingrained deep inside me. Fatalism is a dirty word. While we may give lip service to the prudence of accepting what lies beyond our control, we fight to keep from admitting that there is much outside our grasp. We admire the man who makes a superhuman effort and we cheer on the woman who fights tooth and nail against all odds.

But then I thought about Carol, the owner of Finca Ixobel. As I looked around at the wreckage I thought how she could have just packed up and gone back to America. She didn't have to stay and endure the chaos of this country, the place that took her husband. She could have gotten on the first plane out of there.

Yet she didn't. Perhaps she simply resigned herself to live with both the good and the bad of Guatemala. Obviously she accepted those things that couldn't be change and made the best of what remained. But she was not weak in accepting. She was not meek in remaining behind. She had the courage to be a fatalist. .

In wasn't until the following day while reading the newspaper article about the bridge collapse that we discovered the rest of the story. Just a short time after we left the bridge, the plantation owner had opened the gates, permitting traffic to pass freely on the paved road. Had we restrained our need to keep moving and relaxed for a short time we would have spared ourselves the hours of torturous driving. If only we had controlled our need to move for the sake of moving, the route would have been much easier.

CHAPTER 13

To Give and Take

Antigua, Guatemala
9,251 miles

I wore the same few pieces of clothing daily. Alternating shorts every so often, changing shirts every three days and socks a couple of times a week. I would wash them when I showered and hang them to flutter dry in the back of the van as we drove. Amanda was cleaner than me and could wear the same pants for over a week before they needed a soaking. Our opinions on cleanliness had not really changed much, but since we washed all our clothing by hand we would inspect every piece thoroughly for signs of dirt before deciding we needed to make the effort. I never felt smelly, tried to find a place to shower nearly every day, sometimes every other day, and considered myself fairly respectable-looking compared to the backpackers we met along the way.

It was my shoes that were taking a beating. I wore my one pair of mid-height hiking boots everywhere we went and we walked a lot, sometimes five or six hours straight. The heels were worn through and holes were sprouting through the toes. After seven months on the road it was time for new shoes but in Guatemala the choices were limited. A good durable pair of tire-soled boots was available from the local shoemaker for about $10 but they were thick, solid leather, with no vents for breathing. This was not an option considering my sock changing routine.

In Antigua we found a mountain-climbing shop, an outfitter and tour company that led trips up into the surrounding volcanoes. The Australian guy behind the counter shook his head. "No, mate. No place in town to get good shoes." As I turned to leave he added, "Well, unless you check the second hand stalls behind the market."

"Huh?" I turned back.

"Yeah, in the back of the market they sell all the second-hand clothes donated by American charities. Most of it is too big for the locals." My interest encouraged him to elaborate, "There's a row of shoe sellers. If you have big feet you can get some really good shoes for two or three U.S." He propped a foot on the counter to reveal an expensive hiking boot. "I bought these there."

The next morning we dug through piles of clothing with the locals and were surprised at the high quality stuff thrown out on the blankets. I found a nearly new pair of Lowa boots, unfortunately a half-size too small, for only $2.75. Amanda could barely contain herself when she uncovered two lightweight long-sleeve GAP shirts in a pile below a sign scribbled on cardboard indicating the price, equivalent to four U.S. cents. She approached the man to pay but he was deep in concentration, drawing in a sketchpad with colored pencils, and looked up in surprise. *"Disculpeme, señora."*

"Are you an artist?" Amanda asked.

He scratched his head sheepishly. "No, well, no, not really. I draw my customers sometimes."

"Your customers?"

With a shrug he said, "We all have to make money somehow."

Amanda assumed he was embarrassed to be selling clothing that was sent as charity but then he added, "I try to capture their appearance, the different patterns, and ask them what village they come from. I want to get it down before they disappear. Before they only wear this." He nodded toward the piles of clothing. Thumbing through the sketchbook he showed Amanda amateurish drawings of the traditional clothing of the local people. "Not many of the men wear their village clothing anymore." He turned to a few pages with men's shirts and pants, "So whenever I see one I draw his clothing. But many of the women and children still do. You know, each village uses a different pattern of embroidery. It breaks my heart when I sell them something... but it is inevitable."

As Amanda paid for her shirts the young man looked away, obviously embarrassed, then went back to his drawings.

CHAPTER 14

Banana Republic

Gracias, Honduras
9,502 miles

Eli Black flung his briefcase through the sealed window of his office on the 44th floor of the Pan American building in bustling downtown Manhattan, then followed it himself.

He should have been on top of the world as the Director of United Brands, the banana importer that would later become Chiquita. A few years earlier he had engineered the takeover of the company, installed himself as chairman and accepted the widely-held belief that the cost of doing business in Central America included certain under-handed methods. He negotiated a lowered taxation on his bananas with the help of an alleged bribe of more than a million dollars to the Honduran administration. Before he knew what was happening the press got wind of the payment, the Honduran government was toppled, and the U.S. Congress wanted to investigate. Rather than face the music, he jumped, and splattered himself, like the fruit that made his empire, on the sidewalk of New York City.

A few thousand miles south, Honduras held the dubious distinction of having coined the phrase "Banana Republic". Long before the safari-chic clothing store twisted the expression, Banana Republic was used to describe a country virtually ruled by a single powerful company. The tangled tentacles of *"El Pulpo"* or The Octopus, as the United Fruit Company became known, extended into virtually every facet of Honduran life. Remarkably, the simple, cheap, nutritious yellow fruit wields the power to topple presidents and squash executives.

Driving the van through the chaotic capital of Tegucigalpa was an unsettling experience. Street signs were non-existent, the few tall buildings were crumbling and one-way streets turned into dead-ends. We had heard that *"Tegus"* had one of the highest rates of murder in the world and that the police were accused of forming vigilante hit squads to exterminate the *maras* or swarming ants, as the street gangs were known. With a defeated demeanor people squatted on the sidewalks, were sprawled out on public benches and leaned against trees watching the day go by with glassy-eyed disenchantment.

True to Latin American character, the real ruler in this land of guerrilla wars and steaming jungles is not generally exported. While daily life is controlled by a small group of *ladrones*, the emotional existence of the nation revolves around the all-encompassing sport of *fútbol*.

In the late sixties Honduras and neighboring El Salvador faced each other in the qualifying match of soccer's World Cup. The relationship between the two countries had been simmering for years and a disputed call by a referee sparked a riot that exploded into an all-out war. It took more than ten years of cooling tempers and intensive negotiations for a peace agreement to be signed. This *Guerra Fútbol* ignited a perverse national pride in Honduras that has become intermeshed with the sport in such a way that the two appear inseparable.

On the way to the remote town of Gracias we noticed that nearly all of the trucks and cars on the road displayed their affiliation with a non-governmental aid organization. A line of Hummers full of American soldiers passed as we entered the town and we saw their large encampment that flew both the Honduran and American flags. Gracias gave us the feeling of a run-down, wild west, one-horse town as we arrived during siesta. With the entire town resting behind closed doors and shutters we reluctantly ate soggy pizza at the only small restaurant open for lunch. We were the only customers until a couple of young U.S. soldiers sat down at the table next to us.

"What is it that you do here?" I asked.

The fit young woman with an impeccable uniform answered warily, "Well, we're helping the Hondurans with humanitarian stuff." She looked at us curiously, "And you, what are you doing in the middle of nowhere?"

Amanda told them a little about our trip, then asked, "What sort of humanitarian work are you doing?"

The other soldier was a baby-faced young man who could have been away at summer camp. "We're medics. I drive a mobile hospital. 'Cause of the roads, you know? Hurricane Mitch really messed them up. Our trucks are made to go anywhere."

The young woman added, "Most times we're the only medical care these people ever see."

She went on to tell us about the devastation that Hurricane Mitch had caused. Five thousand people were killed, two hundred bridges collapsed and 82,000 homes were destroyed.

Both soldiers had a slight accent so I asked, "And where are you from?"

She answered, "We're all from Puerto Rico. They brought us in because we speak Spanish."

Through the window of the restaurant we saw a group of extra large, geriatric American church leaders struggling to get out of an old school bus. They stared at our camper as they walked into the restaurant. It didn't take them long to figure out that we were the owners of the van and they came to our table to bombard us with questions about our travels. After a few minutes we asked them what they were doing in Honduras and the head of the group, a husky Oklahoman, said, "We're all from different churches from around Oklahoma City and we've been raisin' funds to build an orphanage and a church down here. I guess you could say we're here to see how the work's comin' along."

His wife, an overly made-up platinum blonde with a giant dome of hair added, "Every year we take a pilgrimage to a different project our church has sponsored. This year it's Honduras. Last year it was Guatemala. The year before that..." She stopped, trying to remember.

"Nope," her husband said. "Year before that we went to see Elizabeth and the kids in Florida."

She ignored him and said, "You know, this is one of the poorest countries in the world. We loaded our luggage with school supplies, pencils, pens, and books. This afternoon we gave out two thousand pencils. I was glad to get them out of my bag. They weighed a ton."

This busload of well-intentioned, pasty white church elders looked so out of place to us. As she blabbed away I could not avoid the mental picture of how this inspection visit must appear to the rural Hondurans.

That evening the World Cup qualifying match between the U.S. and Honduras took place. The van was parked on the street near our hotel and a group of young men were sitting on their front steps, drinking Salva Vida beer, listening to the game on the radio. I went out to check on the van, and a half drunk young guy with a thin, fuzzy mustache pointed to our license plates disbelievingly and asked in Spanish, "You are from California?"

I nodded yes.

"That's a long drive. Which organization do you work for?"

"Oh no. No organization. We're just visiting."

"Are you missionaries?"

"No, we're traveling."

"Peace Corps?"

"No, *turistas*. Here to see your country."

"*¿Turistas?* Honduras does not have *turistas*. Maybe out on the islands or at the ruins, but not here. You must work or do something, no?"

"No, only *turistas*." I pointed to the radio in an effort to change the conversation. "And the game, what's the score?"

He waved his hand in disgust. "It was supposed to be on television," he pointed to a small black-and-white TV propped on the windowsill. "But the local station did not pay. Radio is not so good. It is half-time and the score is 1-1."

As I locked the van and reluctantly walked away he offered, "We will watch the car for you. Do not worry, *amigo*."

I wished him good luck and went back into the hotel, secretly rooting for Honduras to beat the U.S. team.

In our cramped little room we turned on our shortwave radio and listened to the game. The stadium erupted with rage when the referee called a foul against the Honduran defender with just four minutes to go. The score was still tied 1-1 and the defenders lined up in a five-man wall to block the free kick. The American striker positioned the ball and delivered it like a swooping right hook. The announcer described the shot as it passed just over the heads of the defending wall and bent in an unbelievable arc, dipping beyond the reach of the goalie. The U.S. won, but a vast majority of Americans were not even aware. Every Honduran was devastated.

The next morning I went out to check on the van not long after sunrise. The young man from the night before was sitting on the step smoking a cigarette.

"Buenos dias," he called as I walked toward the van. *"Felicidades.* Your team won."

As I unlocked the door I said in Spanish, "Good morning. Yes, I listened on the radio."

The van was exactly as I had left it and he said, "I told you I would watch your car. With me here you had nothing to worry about." He strolled over to the open door and peeked in. Our fruit bowl was on the seat with apples and pears piled high. He said, "You have a lot of fruit."

"Yes," I said.

"May I have one?" He asked, hesitating. "For watching the van."

"OK. Would you like an apple or a pear?"

He pointed upward to a bunch hanging from a hook and he asked, "May I have a banana?"

CHAPTER 15

Border Crossings

Honduras-Nicaragua Border
9,887 miles

Groups of filthy young men ran after the van like kids chasing an ice cream truck as we searched for a place to park close to the gate that separated the *zona de frontera* from the village of Las Manos.

Surviving off the scraps from the few trucks crossing daily between the two desperately poor countries, the herd of men elbowed one another, waving bundles of Honduran lempiras and Nicaraguan córdobas at us. The less fortunate, those without bills, simply pressed their calculator against the windshield to let us know they could change our remaining currency. These gold-toothed masters of deception have thousands of tricks, often rearranging the buttons on their calculators to multiply the level of confusion from which they profit. They carry outdated bills that are no longer in circulation and count out the money using well-practiced sleight of hand.

A cloud of thick red-brown dust swelled around the con artists as they followed the van to the gate where Amanda asked the guard permission to be admitted into the border zone.

Crossing Central American borders was not something we took lightly. The night before, we camped as close to the border as possible. We would pull out the laminated color copies of our driver's licenses and vehicle title, stashing away the originals in a safe I built under the closet. Our money belts were packed with our passports, immunization cards, travelers' checks, ATM cards, and just enough local currency to pay the inevitable exit fees. We set our watch alarm and planned to arrive just after the border opened, hoping to complete the tedious process long before the midday *siesta*.

Once inside the border zone the only place to park was in a large puddle of water in front of a shed made from several sheets of corrugated metal nailed to a tree with a sign above that read *Migración de Honduras*. Amanda locked the security bars over the windows and I padlocked the sliding door. As the *migración* line inched forward the dirt path became a mud bog.

At the counter stood a greasy-looking, disheveled man with a giant belly and a tattered uniform. The tassels hanging from his sleeves indicated that he was the supervisor of the shed and he took obvious pleasure in the fact that everyone had to stand in two inches of muddy water to answer his questions.

Sliding our passports back across the counter, he refused to stamp them without a payment of $7 per person, a fee that everyone in line had grudgingly paid.

Amanda couldn't hold back and blurted out, "But that sign behind you says that there is no fee to cross this border."

He looked up at her with contempt and said, "This is a legitimate requirement. I guarantee you that the new sign is due to arrive tomorrow."

When we entered the *Aduana* (Customs Office) we found it far more chaotic than Immigration and we were forced to use our most basic survival skills. Surrounded by burly truck drivers who spent their lives crossing borders, outnumbered and out-skilled, we resorted to pushing and shoving to hold our place in line. The lone customs officer processed the paperwork with the speed of a sloth, and after an hour of watching his slow, methodical movements, we arrived at the head of the line. He carefully wrote the van's information into a dusty old ledger book and took back the temporary import permit we had been given when we entered the country. Stamping our papers, he set us free to travel the road through no-man's-land to the other side.

We were driving into Nicaragua from the Northwest, the area where gun barrels and tempers remained scalding hot from years of guerrilla insurrection fueled by the Cold War. The border barrier was a metal post with a cinder block attached to the end. A young boy raised the post as moneychangers appeared from out of the dust, swarming around us like human flies, blocking our way. One tugged at my sleeve through the open window and another began counting his wad of córdobas while attempting to hand each bill to Amanda. They encircled the van and shouldered one another to get at us. Our insistence of *"no gracias"* was ignored with ingratiating smiles.

Another more prosperous group waited for us on the other side of the post, judiciously respecting the barrier. These unofficial customs agents were slightly more civil as they pressed laminated identification badges in our faces. Each insisted that he could assist us to zip through *los tramites* (the transactions). In essence, these guys were little more than conduits to funnel under-the-table payments to their friends in the offices.

After parking the van we skipped right by them, but one persistent guy followed us from window to window, offering unsolicited advice on what to do and where to go next. At the immigration window he peered over Amanda's shoulder and pointed to the form, suggesting what to write in each blank space.

I told him, *"No pagamos"*, in pidgin Spanish but he followed us to the next window as we paid a fee and got the entry stamp in our passports.

Here he yelled to a friend behind the window and Amanda told him, *"No te necesitamos."*

After following us for another ten minutes he got the message and left us alone.

By the time we arrived at Customs the office was closed for *siesta*.

With nothing to do but wait, we moved the van to the only shady spot under a massive Coca-Cola billboard to prepare lunch. As Amanda chopped up a quick salad a customs official approached.

The small lean man spoke in a whisper and introduced himself as Officer Dominguez. He said in Spanish, "We're in *siesta* but I've brought forms for you." He held two sheets of paper and said, "When they are complete I will stamp them for you." He added with a smile, "There is no reason to keep you waiting."

Suspicious of his intentions, Amanda said, "Oh, thank you. But we don't want to interrupt your lunch. We don't mind waiting."

Shoving the forms in my hand, he insisted, "It is not a problem. Please, take the forms and fill them out."

He leaned against the van chatting with Amanda through the sliding door as I completed the sheets. When I handed them back, he took them, along with the title to the van and our passports, into his office. A few minutes later he returned with the paperwork stamped and ready to go.

I wanted to thank him for his trouble so I carefully folded a few crisp new dollar bills, like I'd seen people do in the movies, and I slipped them into his hand when we shook.

He stared at the bills in his open palm and said, "*Rishard, Rishard, Rissshard....¿Que es esto?*" (What is this?)

"Well...ah...a tip."

"*¿Propina?*" Like a bad rash he shoved the bills back into my hand. "There are many eyes watching us."

Gruffly he said to both of us, "Close up the van and follow me."

As Officer Dominguez walked straight to the building marked *Policia* we followed behind. Amanda smacked me on the arm and hissed in English, "What were you thinking?"

"I thought...he was so nice...," I mumbled.

Pointing to a bench outside the office he said, "Sit right here and don't move."

He disappeared into the office and we sat on the hard bench for over an hour. My imagination ran wild with visions of third world jail cells. Frantically whispering, I said to Amanda, "I know what I can say. I'll say I thought there was a fee."

She looked at me as if I had lost my mind and spit out, "They'll never believe that." Then she put her hands over her face and mumbled, "Why? Why did you have to give him money? Can you tell me that? What got into your head?"

"I don't know. I thought that's what you do in Latin America," I said.

"Yeah, but you never offer a bribe. If they want one, you'll know," she said.

"Oh no. What happens now?" I asked.

She stared at me incredulously and said, "How should I know?"

Officer Dominguez poked his head out the door and led us into a minuscule, sky-blue chamber with folding chairs, a metal desk, and an ancient typewriter. Giant stacks of yellowing paper were piled everywhere and the walls were covered with old health department posters: "Mother's milk builds stronger children," and "Protect the water supply to fight typhoid."

The pint-sized police officer behind the desk ignored us as if we were two of the thousands of flies in the office while he meticulously pounded away at the typewriter with thundering blows. He removed an inkpad from the top drawer, clobbering each page of a multi-page document with ornately detailed stamps.

Without looking up, he slid several sheets across the desk and told us out of the side of his mouth, "You can go."

"We can go?" I asked.

He looked at us for the first time and said, *"¡Vayanse de aqui!"* (Get out of here!)

From the doorway Officer Dominguez said, "You were lucky to catch him on a good day."

CHAPTER 16

The Widow's Shawl

Estelí, Nicaragua
9,962 miles

Driving through the sleepy town of Estelí in Northern Nicaragua, we passed the central square and a building with colorful murals on the wall. A sign over the door read FSLN *Casa de Campaña.* Over the years the clubhouse had become the Sandinista museum of martyrs and heroes.

I had wanted to see the town that I had read so much about, run by the Sandinistas, a group that the U.S. played a part in defeating during the Cold War. But being there I felt uncomfortable. My effort to keep a low profile was fruitless as we inevitably had to drive up and down *Avenida Central,* the only main road in town, with our license plates screaming out, *"Americano, Americano."*

We took turns reading a brief history of Nicaragua while eating leftover cold pasta in the park across from the *Casa de Campaña.* After siesta we visited the museum, and signed our names in the reception book. The older woman at the desk flipped the book around. Her plump brown fingers scanned across the lines to the *nacionalidad* column. She smiled and said, *"Bienvenido."* (Welcome)

The walls were covered with large full-faced photos of bug-eyed young fighters who had been killed in the war. The museum was a memorial, perhaps even a cemetery, with images of saints stuffed neatly behind the picture frames.

The museum was empty except for one petite woman who wore a long black shawl over her head that wrapped around her shoulders. She stood with her back toward us facing a photograph mounted on the far wall. We slowly made our way around the room, looking at the hundreds of young faces staring back at us. As we got closer Amanda elbowed me and nodded toward the woman.

I looked over as she removed a wilted flower from behind the corner of a picture frame and placed it carefully between the pages of a book. She gently slid the stem of a fresh wildflower between the frame and wall. She kissed her fingers and pressed them against the glass, then turned and walked toward the door.

The older woman at the desk stood and hugged her, then tenderly readjusted the woman's shawl as they said goodbye. And she was gone.

Amanda walked over and looked at the photo closely. She said, "He looks so young, almost like a child."

The old woman from the desk came up behind us as we stared at the photo and said in Spanish, "That was Isabel. She has been coming every week for thirteen years. This was her husband." She nodded toward the photograph and gave a sad smile.

Amanda asked, "How long were they married before he…?"

"I am not sure," the woman said. "But she has two children. For many years she would bring them but they no longer remember their father. How sad, no?"

As we were leaving the museum the old woman said, "I hope you enjoy your visit."

The streets of Estelí were lined by low cinderblock homes with corrugated roofs and barred windows. Bright colors had been slapped over the pockmarks of bullet holes, and splattered paint littered the cement sidewalks. Young boys passed us in small groups, carrying oversized backpacks, wearing the white polyester shirts and uncomfortable blue pants of the typical school uniform. Motorcycles and bicycles buzzed around. Street sweepers lazily pushed their broomfuls into dustpans made from split tin cans. Telephone and electrical wires hung from rooftops to lampposts to poles and buildings, covering the town in a spider web of hanging wires. Despite their efforts to move forward, the people, even the kids, had the glum, resigned look of flies caught in a web.

On the Pan American highway between Estelí and Masaya we saw a disturbance on the horizon. From a distance it looked as if a small dust-devil had touched down to swirl up the brown, fertile earth. As we approached a gritty cowboy sat on a gaunt horse waving a red handkerchief, indicating us to stop while the cattle trod by. We were in the middle of a broad, empty rangeland, and the cattle extended in a long line for as far as we could see. A few scraggly men lay in the shade of a small bush next to the road. As I shut off the van one of the men tilted up his hat to watch the commotion of the cattle. He gave us an uninterested glance, then went back to his slumber.

Except for a moaning cow in the distance and the sound of the slight breeze rustling the bushes, there was almost complete silence. The afternoon sun beat down hard on the road and the sky was full of gray-bellied clouds that stood out against the deep, bright blue.

I closed one eye and watched in the side mirror as a cloud floated by.

Amanda broke the silence as she said, "Every week for thirteen years."

It had been more than two hours since we left Estelí but we were thinking the same thing. I took a deep breath, "Whenever I think of the Cold War, I picture the wall coming down in Berlin. All those happy faces on television crossing from East Germany. It was as if everyone had won."

"Um," Amanda said under her breath. "I don't think that's what the widow feels."

The cowboy kicked his skinny horse and blocked the long line of cattle, then waved his red handkerchief toward us in an overly grand gesture.

As we drove past I said, *"Muchas Gracias"*.

He graciously tilted his hat in return.

CHAPTER 17

Hopelessly Lost

Somewhere in Nicaragua
10,044 miles

I stopped at a fork in the road to ask a man, "How do you get to the capital?"

Rather than pointing to one of the two roads ahead, he motioned backward the way we had come. When he saw our confusion he continued in absolute seriousness, "First I walk back to the station, and then I get on the bus."

Unfamiliar territory can be disorienting. In a foreign land, with the basic elements of life different from those that we know, one takes great pleasure in the simplest of familiarities. Answers to basic questions like: "What is the name of this village?"; "Where is the main road?"; or "When will we get there?"; provide a sense, just a hint, of solid footing. To pinpoint a spot and say, "I am here," gives a comforting feeling. That tiny fact becomes something we can comprehend in an environment chock-full of the incomprehensible.

Mapmakers, the translators of unfamiliar territory, bridge the gap between the natural human desire to conquer the unknown, and our love of a neat and tidy package. The vast imagined nothingness of uncharted terrain can be interpreted with a map, and the apprehension caused by unfamiliarity is partially conquered. Once charted and placed in an understandable format, the mystery is somewhat revealed and our trepidation diminished.

The maps that we brought along with us cleared the obscurity by using dashed lines to designate dirt roads, blue curlicues to represent stream crossings, and wavy lines to indicate mountains. They gave us an idea as to where we were on earth in relation to other places: fifty kilometers from Córdoba, a thousand feet from an intersection, or a million miles from home. Our maps made us feel just a tad more in control.

Asking for directions was fraught with perilous misinterpretations. Six blocks means different things to different people. *"Seis cuadras"* to a rural villager whose everyday routes follow those of ancient goat tracks, is incomprehensible. The scale of perspective of any two people can vary remarkably. Asking a person the road to the next big town, perhaps a journey they have never made, can be both enlightening and infuriating.

Heading south through Nicaragua, we were using a horrible map we had picked up for free from the Auto Club. The scale was so small that one inch equaled a whopping 145 miles of land. Any useful features like mile markers, intersecting roads, small towns, rivers, lakes, mountains, bridges, anything that could help pinpoint our position, was not indicated.

Every so often I glanced over at Amanda, the navigator, and became irritated as I discovered our only tool, unreliable as it was, taped to her window as a sunshade, or spread out on her lap as a food tray. She would fold it into a fancy fan to get relief from the sweltering heat or roll it into a baton and use it as a fly swatter. It never failed to amaze me how the map could morph into some absurd gadget, rendering it temporarily off-limits at the precise moment I needed directions.

To bring her back to reality I would ask through gritted teeth, "Eh, how many more kilometers, do you think?"

She would shrug, tap on the bobbing compass on the dashboard and answer unconcernedly, "We're going south."

Amanda could go for hours not knowing where we were or if we were headed into some unknown corner of the globe. Perfectly content, it did not seem to bother her one whit.

Our compass was one of those little plastic dashboard jiggamabobbers sold at the 99 Cent store. The day before we left on the trip I saw it hanging on the hook by the plastic bubble wrap and felt it was something we should have. It just seemed like one of those things that someone setting out into the great reaches of the unknown on a big road trip might find useful.

The compass was paired together with another useful device, a thermometer that registered temperatures between -20° and 120°. In my mind's eye I pictured us being snowed in somewhere high up in the Andes, watching this thermometer as the temperature gradually dropped, then regaining hope as it slowly inched upward.

In the real world, the useless device rarely read a temperature below 100° except on bitterly cold mornings when it plunged immediately to -20°. It had no middle ground. A balmy 70° did not exist in the world it passed through.

But that didn't stop Amanda from using it to prove a convenient point. She would say things like, "Look, it's 110° in here. I'm turning on the fan," or "Brrrrr, it's freezing. The thermometer says it's twenty below. Put on the heater will ya?"

A tiny screwdriver was included in the plastic packaging. As I unfolded the directions to determine the use for this added tool I envisioned the person, somewhere deep in China, who used their baby-sized hands to fold the Bible-paper sheets into a thousand minute squares and stuff it into the package. The directions explained that the compass could be adversely affected by electrical devices mounted in the cockpit. A car stereo, for example, could cause disorienting variation and the screwdriver was provided to make the proper adjustments to compensate. It recommended we park the van facing directly north, then turn on the radio, or any other piece of equipment that may cause interference, and fiddle with the compass until it pointed north.

Problem was, I did not know which way north was, precisely. That was why I bought the thing in the first place. I knew the general direction but was in no way comfortable making such an important fine-tuning without being sure. So the compass was mounted on the dash, with all the variation-producing interference pulsing away.

Not that it mattered. The thing would swing back and forth with wild abandon, one moment reading south, the next northwest, then abruptly back to south. Radio on, radio off, it made no difference. It would jiggle away in its fishbowl environment and turn wherever it fancied.

In desperation I would glance quickly down and catch it pointing south at a moment when I knew for sure we were heading in that direction.

Instantly it would swing passionately past west, skim by north, before settling firmly on east.

Many times I was tempted to tear the thing from the dash and toss it out the window, but Amanda would intervene, placing a protective hand over it. She seemed to think it was helpful, found it reassuring, and somehow communicated with it just fine. They had a language all their own and only she could interpret its swinging moods. "Oh, it's pointing east, so we're definitely going south now. Good, we're on the right track."

Before leaving on the trip we shopped around for a GPS receiver. The Global Positioning System has revolutionized navigation, making it possible to know the exact position on the globe, down to a fraction of a foot. The tiny device displays a string of numbers, a numerical address, using the ancient artificial slices of the globe, parallels of latitude and meridians of longitude.

The basic model was downright reasonable in price, but spit out only the untranslated numerical address. The salesman stressed that the super-advanced, scrolling-screen, removable-chip device with separate map software was just the thing we needed. It cost a fortune. Rejecting modern technology, we took a chance and set out into the unknown the old-fashioned way.

As we continued through the journey and got further away from our uptight world, I learned to concentrate less on how we got to where we were, or the route we would take to leave. I began to enjoy the world, not in the way a map shows, but quite the opposite, by experiencing one place at a time. Rather than looking to what was next, or to what had been, I began to enjoy what was now.

Back in the U.S. more than three years later, we attacked the chore of sorting through the massive piles of mail that had accumulated in our absence. One piece from our credit card company tallied the amount of mystery points we had earned while circling the globe. Flipping through the thick, glossy catalog accompanying the letter we were mesmerized by the expensive and useless possibilities our points could get us.

Then we turned the page and there it was, displayed in full color, with its own prominent fold-out. Everything we had dreamed of before leaving home. It was the best brand, the perfect size, and included all the components. In our travels we had accumulated just enough points for the GPS receiver we no longer needed.

CHAPTER 18

Easter Karma

Sámara, Costa Rica
10,344 miles

The old lady shook her fist and yelled, *"¡Tiene que pagar por esto!"* (You are going to pay for this!)

I roared the engine and backed up over the tent before speeding away down the beach. The sun had barely risen on the Easter holiday but Costa Rican families were already arriving to stake out their sunbathing spots for the day. I drove as fast as I could on the dry sand, swerving to dodge beachgoers as Amanda kept a lookout for the police.

The week leading up to Easter Sunday was notorious as the worst time to travel in Latin America. Knowing this before we arrived in Costa Rica, we had hoped to find a comfortable, secluded hideaway to wait out the storm. On the Nicoya Peninsula, the tiny beach town of Sámara, at the end of a rough dirt track, seemed as obscure as any.

When we arrived nearly a week before the holiday the lazy town was virtually deserted. Some local surfers poked their boards in the sand waiting for the waves to pick up. A lone ice cream vendor rested his cooler in the shade and leaned against a palm tree with his straw hat pulled down over his eyes. Teenage boys rode wild-looking horses bareback along the beach, trailing along a string of sickly mounts, trying to drum up business from the few visitors.

The sandy campground was practically empty, with the boundaries between campsites well marked by mature palm trees. We pulled out our awning, set up our chairs and relaxed as the waves broke at our feet. It was a tranquil tropical paradise and we shared it with a handful of pleasant families. One balmy evening we watched as two Costa Rican girls taught a Japanese exchange student how to salsa and merengue as the sun set. Then came Wednesday.

The sounds of slamming trunks and banging doors woke us before dawn. Our neighbors were frantically stuffing their tents, barbecues, and beach gear into their cars. Abandoned within minutes, we were unaware that somewhere at the other end of the campsite a floodgate had opened. A torrent of locals inundated the place. Mobs raced to stake out every square inch of the campground in a beachfront version of the Oklahoma land rush.

Rubbing the sleep from our eyes, we watched the human deluge in a confused haze. Rusted jalopies were packed with every comfort of home. Mattresses were strapped to the roofs of the cars with clinging sheets and pillows. These ready-made accommodations were haphazardly thrown down on the sand. Dining tables were set up between mini refrigerators and cable spools were used as chairs. Each group brought their own boom box and Britany Spears competed with Ziggy Marley for our groggy attention.

Improvised tents were made by tying dirty curtains to the palm trees and cramming the edges beneath the mattresses. Several young guys set their tents up on the opposite side of the van, and another group tied theirs to the spare gas canisters on the rear. The village of tents blocked any path through the campsite. Before we knew it we were surrounded on all sides. One family set up a makeshift wood-burning kitchen made from old tire rims just upwind from the van. The insufferable smoke from the continual fire engulfed our space.

"I don't know if I'll be able to take four days of this." I yelled, over the roar of the music as we sat in a haze of smoke that evening.

Amanda spouted, "I thought the same thing. But no matter where we go it's going to be the same."

"It can't be this bad everywhere," I said.

"Maybe not, but we're trapped. How can we possibly get out of here?"

"The only way is by the beach," I said.

"The beach? There's no way. No vehicles are allowed on the beach. You've seen the police."

"I know. We'll just have to go really early. Hopefully the tide will be low."

"That means I'll have to wake up our neighbors to get them to move their tents and all their stuff."

"Well, I have to dig out that fence post." I walked over to the post and gave it a good shake to see how deep it was buried. It didn't budge.

The next morning, with the sun just cracking the horizon, we watched carefully as the tide reached the perfect level, leaving a thin sliver of hard-packed sand to drive on. Amanda woke the families around us as I frantically dug out the post. Our neighbors were excited to be getting our beachfront site but they were not enthusiastic about moving. Lazily they dropped the ties from the palm trees and insisted we drive over their homemade tents.

With a crowd of onlookers I began inching slowly back. Amanda was giving me directions and some overzealous young guys decided they also wanted to help. In the rear-view mirror I saw six people pointing in six different directions. I could not see the first few tents and was worried that the van might get bogged down in the sand, but I continued to reverse. Women struggled to corral their children to safety while the young guys blurted conflicting commands to me in Spanish. Engulfed by the crowd,

I completely lost sight of Amanda. In front of the van, women fought over the few inches of sand I had just relinquished and eagerly set down their beach chairs. I continued reversing and saw a big bump in one of the crude tents, but the guys waved me on.

Suddenly out of nowhere Amanda yelled, "STOP!"

I slammed on the brakes as a bleary-eyed, chubby teenage girl came crawling out of the tent. With her safely out of the way, I continued to back up over the last pile, of material.

Then a high-pitched shrieking caused everyone to go silent. I looked in the rear view mirror. The guys had faded away. The teenage girl held a piece of fabric in her hands as she cried, "I borrowed this."

The van rolled off the pile to reveal a large tear where the material had caught on the bumper. The greedy crowd in front of the van stopped fighting for our space and quickly became a part of the commotion, surrounding the van on all sides.

A mole-covered grandmother elbowed through the mob and poked her face into my window, "You must give her money to repair the damage."

Amanda jumped into the van and said, "I'm sorry but I asked you to move the tents."

The old woman shook her fist and began to yell at us.

Clearly outnumbered, I slammed the pedal to the floor, and the sea of people parted as we made our getaway.

Turning inland, we drove for hours and headed toward the high mountain area around Lake Arenal. Every campsite around the lake was occupied, so we continued on the road to a wilderness area surrounding a nearby volcano. Once paved, the road had disintegrated into a string of potholes separated by a few flat pieces of asphalt. The jungle canopy enveloped the bumpy road, blocking the sun and filling the air with the damp, sticky-sweet smell of summer after a hard rain.

Just before dark we found a place on a grassy lawn that an enterprising local had turned into a makeshift campsite. Reaching high into the atmosphere, the volcano created a strange funnel effect, driving clouds with precipitation directly over us. The rain fell hard and the massive drops pelted the roof of the van with a deafening drumming.

As I climbed up to bed after the tiring day I noticed water seeping through the canvas siding of the van's pop-top roof. Amanda quickly grabbed a rag and wiped the droplets from the inside. As she dabbed at the canvas it let out a loud, zipping "snap" and gave way, splitting into a two-foot long tear.

We both stared at the opening in disbelief as the rain poured in on our bed.

The pop-top had held up through far more furious storms. It had survived more than twenty years without so much as a pinhole. But that day, of all days, it gave way.

The van had taught us an important lesson.

CHAPTER 19

Four Worms and a Mouse

Monteverde, Costa Rica
10,631 miles

It sounded like the purr of a cat, deep like a growl, reverberating. I heard it first and stopped dead in my tracks. We had passed a sign an hour before saying that if we walked quietly there was a better chance of seeing wildlife. We were silent, hiking into the depths of the dense jungle.

Amanda was daydreaming behind me, and bumped right up my heels. "Oops, why did you...?" As the words were leaving her mouth she heard it too and her eyes grew wide. She stood frozen in a panic.

Miles from the ranger station, I had no desire to see this kind of wildlife outside of a really big cage. I whispered to her the thing every terrified fool says at such moments, "It's as afraid of us as we are of it."

Amanda looked at me unconvinced, and hissed back, "Oh, and how do you know that?"

"Well, I would guess."

"Guess?!"

Of all the ways I thought I could die on this trip, not in my wildest dreams had I considered feline attack as an option. Rebels in the jungle, riots in the streets, or a civil war were all possible, but I had put those thoughts out of my mind the moment we entered Costa Rica. I pictured the headline back home, "American Mauled Fleeing Jaguar. Mexican Wife Says He Guessed Wrong".

Known as the "Switzerland of Central America", Costa Rica is a peaceful country that did away with their military in the late 1940s. Traveling in the one Central American nation where coups are less frequent than flying saucers was somewhat predictable. It lacked the spontaneity that came from knowing the floor might fall out from underneath at any time.

Not only was it safe, Costa Rica was also revoltingly clean. The fluttering plastic grocery bags and tangerine peels that decorate the roadside throughout the continent were blatantly absent. There were recycling programs and public trashcans that people actually used. Toilets flushed and had paper. The currency was stable and the telephone system functioned. We could even drink the water right out of the tap. Where was the fun in that?

After traveling for a while we began to appreciate the advantages of this upside-down world. I never worried about turning a bend on some remote jungle road and being ambushed at a detour, or getting caught in the crossfire between two warring guerrilla factions. The expatriates we met did not share the typical stories of dream jungle lodges that ended in disaster. They just had dream jungle lodges. Chipper backpackers said things like, "Why buy a bus ticket when it's safe to hitchhike?"

Even the hazards seem contrived. The roads were crumbling and full of potholes, but only in the tourist areas. As a local explained, "Our roads are paved. It's the roads around the nature reserves that are a mess, to make it seem more adventurous."

We learned it was true as we bounced along a rocky dirt road to get to the Monteverde Cloudforest Biological Reserve. The massive chunk of land was donated by a group of peace-loving Quakers who moved to Costa Rica in the fifties in protest of the draft back in the U.S.

From the ranger station we obtained a permit to spend the night in a lone primitive hut deep in the dense jungle. Before starting our hike the Ranger warned us with a chuckle, "A big Australian girl stayed there last night. She told me she broke some floorboards when she stepped into the shelter. We have not been out to inspect yet, so be careful."

The main trail was tame, with tree stumps cut into stepping-stones, but when we branched off toward the hut on the less-traveled path it became more challenging. The long, muddy trail passed through several different life zones of varying humidity. When we started our hike it was a bright sunny day but under the jungle canopy it was dark, damp, misty, wet, and cold. We crossed several deep streams, completely submerging our boots. Sloshing through sticky orange mud, we ended up sliding on our butts and clinging to wet, rubbery vines. Through it all we kept completely quiet, stopping when we heard a tree shake or a scamper among the ferns. The ranger had told us that we were bound to see something interesting with over six hundred species of animals prowling the area, but after hours of hiking we had only spotted four colorful centipedes.

That was until we heard the growling purr. We stood still for what seemed an eternity. Thump, thump, thump my heart pounded. Listening, looking, silently wondering. I peered into the blackness just beyond the thick foliage, saw nothing and said, "Maybe we should head back."

"Back to where?" Amanda whispered.

"I don't know, the ranger station."

"No way," she insisted. In that brief moment she had acquired confidence and marched in the direction of the shelter.

"But the hole in the floor," I called after her, "with jaguars out here..."

"Let's go." She didn't even turn to see if I followed.

The shelter was elevated on stilts and the hole in the floor was massive, about the size of a hearty Australian girl. It punched straight through, leaving a wide-open gap down to the sticky black earth below. The hut had a vile, moldy smell and the floor was filthy from the leaves and debris that blew in.

Just after sunset we whipped up a quick meal, rolled out our sleeping bags and tried to fall asleep. When we turned off the flashlights a handful of fireflies came in through the hole and illuminated the pitch darkness. Crickets had taken refuge beneath the shelter and their chirping echoed through the opening, reverberating between the four walls. I lay there, unable to get the jaguar out of my head. "I think they hunt at night. Isn't that what the poster back at the ranger station said?"

Amanda was already snoring.

A plastic trash bag on the floor began to make a rustling sound so I jumped up, switching on my flashlight. Nothing there, must have been the wind. Off went the light, back into the sleeping bag and the rustling began again. On went the light and this time, inside the bag, I found a little mouse. As I swatted, it ran down on to the floor and out the hole before I could catch it. I tied the bag from a hook in the ceiling and imagined the mouse mocking, "You think that'll stop me."

Amanda went on sleeping, undisturbed.

The moment I turned out the light I heard him scurry through the hole, up the wall, across the ceiling and into the bag. I turned on the flashlight and he scurried out again. We played the game several times, flashlight off, into the bag, flashlight on, out the hole. Finally I tired of it and left the flashlight on, staring furiously at the black hole until I drifted off to sleep.

I was jolted wide-awake by the mouse's sharp claws and stringy tail scurrying right across my face. I jumped up and chased him to the edge of the hole, peering down into the darkness and said, "You think you've won, don't you."

Amanda slept with a peaceful smile.

I grabbed a piece of the floorboard and pointed my flashlight down into the darkness. I lay there quietly and listened as my heartbeat settled back to normal, never taking my eyes off the hole. Fifteen minutes passed, half an hour, then an hour. Nothing. The little bugger knew what was up. I began to get drowsy and closed my eyes for just a moment, peering through a droopy lid. Nothing. Then my eyes closed and I drifted off.

The rustling bag woke me.

Furious and defeated, I shut off my flashlight, zipped the sleeping bag up over my head and fell sound asleep.

CHAPTER 20

Pan American Highway

Panama City, Panama
11,580 miles

We camped at a miserable beachfront resort in Uvita, Costa Rica, where a bunch of derelict American expatriates wasted their disability checks swilling *guaro*, the local moonshine, and ingesting painkillers. Early the next morning we headed for the border. Our map showed a dirt road but surprisingly it turned out to be newly paved and we sped into Paso Canoas at half past ten.

The immigration officer refused to give us an exit stamp unless we purchased stickers from a young lady standing next to his window wearing a Red Cross uniform. The stickers cost 250 colones (76 cents) and she placed one in each of our passports, then handed them to the officer. Amanda inspected hers after it was stamped, "The sticker says 200 colones, but you charged us 250."

The young woman looked away without interest and said, "Service charge."

Crossing the border, we drove on the final section of the Pan American highway that runs unbroken from Mexico to the Panama canal. Several years earlier my imagination had been set ablaze by a newspaper article about the Pan American highway, the road designed to link the major trade routes of the Western Hemisphere. Before reading the article it never occurred to me that the roads I used every morning to commute to work were somehow linked to places like Mexico City and the Panama Canal. I always thought of my commute as a means to an end, a way to get where I needed to go. But the article sparked my imagination. As I drove to work I would picture the vast stretches of asphalt as an opportunity, a challenge.

We were soon to discover that there was one small stretch where the road was nonexistent. The break was at the remote strip of jungle where Central and South America are linked, a place called the Darién Gap.

It seemed absurd that nearly 18,000 miles of road and two geographically connected continents were kept apart by a tiny, almost insignificant morsel. The impenetrable fifty-four mile gap was between the towns of Yaviza Palo de Las Letras in Panama and Mutata in Colombia.

Environmental organizations argued that plowing a road into the region would expose it to logging and farming. The Panamanian government was half-hearted about the project since it could open the door for Colombian rebel groups. And the deep pockets of U.S. government were reluctant to fund and promote what would essentially become a pipeline for South American drugs.

With these overwhelming factors blocking the continuation of the road, it appeared the Pan American highway might never be complete. Clearly if we wanted to continue our journey, we would have to put the van on a ship sailing to South America.

Crossing the mile-long Bridge of the Americas over the Panama Canal, we headed towards the Manzanillo International Port in Colon. When we stopped to ask directions in Colon, the man who pointed the way looked at Amanda with great concern and said, "*Suerte*" (good luck). The shipping office of the Crawley Lines was just across the street from the women's prison.

Fernando Anderson, a jovial black Panamanian who spoke impeccable English, greeted us at the door and ushered us into his office. The cramped, cluttered space was divided into small cubicles with modular furniture shared by several employees including his boss. The walls were covered with shipping schedules and maps decorated with push pins. A schoolroom chalkboard listed arrivals and departures.

The next ship to South America was scheduled to depart in five days, and Fernando said, "You must hurry and collect the necessary documents. First you must take a copy of the Bill of Lading to the National Police office in Panama City. They will give you another document to take to the motor vehicle department…"

I interrupted him, "But I thought you took care of all the documentation."

He laughed loud enough for the others in the room to hear. "Oh no. We are a shipping company. We move cargo, not paperwork. You must take care of the documents yourself."

'But we've never done this before," Amanda said. "How will we know what to do?"

I heard a man in the next cubicle snort a laugh. Fernando looked in his direction and said with a smirk, "You will learn."

Five days seemed like plenty of time but we were dealing with government officials who took six hours to place one precious stamp on a piece of paper. They opened their offices late, took generous siestas then closed early. These maddening circumstances left us with plenty of time to explore the city.

We spent hours at the Miraflores Locks, awestruck as massive ships moved, as if in a giant liquid elevator, through the flooded gates of the Panama Canal. I bought a pamphlet on the history of the canal and read aloud to Amanda as we sat in the spectator gallery.

In 1848 a Frenchman, Ferdinand de Lesseps, famous for his success as the builder of the Suez Canal, began work on a canal across Central America. Disease and landslides caused the project to fail but another Frenchman revived it near the turn of the century. A second failure found the French begging the United States to purchase the half-finished project. At the time Panama was a province of Colombia, who objected to the transfer, so the U.S. stoked the flames of revolution and the nation of Panama came into existence. The new government granted the United States an eight-kilometer belt of land across the country along with the right to protect it from invasion. Paid for in lives sucked away by malarial mosquitoes, yellow fever and bubonic plague, the Panama Canal, considered one of the greatest engineering marvels of the world, was completed in 1914.

The U.S. government always claimed the canal was a break-even proposition but military expenses may have factored into the cost. By the seventies resentment among the Panamanian people towards the U.S. presence was so great that President Carter signed a treaty guaranteeing local jurisdiction over the canal by New Year's Day 2000.

On the day our ship was scheduled to depart we met Fernando at the Crawley office and followed him to the port. The stress of running around and getting the paperwork had blocked out the reality of the moment. Our little home for nearly a year was about to sail away.

The shipping container was placed on the cement dock, doors were opened, and ramps positioned for the van to be driven in. Port employees hovered around with ropes, ties and wooden blocks to secure the van. The container looked eerily like a car coffin, and the Panamanian dockworkers did not instill a feeling of confidence. As they closed the door, a lump formed in my throat. I looked at Amanda as she tried to hold back the tears. The dockworkers inserted a pin in one hasp and I placed an uncuttable lock on the other.

Turning our backs on the container, we walked away from the van with our hearts heavy and our minds whizzing. Departing the port, we felt as if we were deserting the third member of our trip.

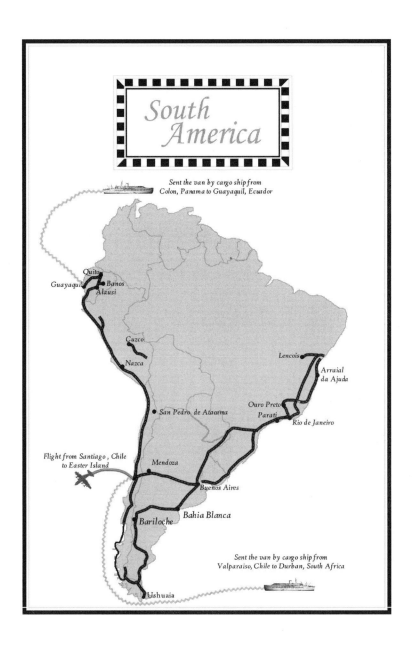

CHAPTER 21

The Fireplug

Guayaquil, Ecuador
11,646 miles

The port security officer in high heels, skin-tight blouse and remarkably short skirt blocked the entrance, "The only way you can get in is if you have a pass from your agent."

"But we don't have an agent," Amanda said.

She stopped picking her fingernails to look up at us, "You must have an agent. Everyone must have an agent to pass here. Except for agents."

We had no choice. We sat in the muggy hotel room, flipping through the Ecuadorian Yellow Pages trying to find an agent.

By that afternoon, Benito Muñoz, a squat little fireplug of a man, had acquired all of the documents we needed, including a long, peculiar explanation of our trip written into my passport, and stamped by an endless array of officials. With keys in hand, we were poised to remove the van from the container.

Two weeks later we were still holding the keys, waiting to receive the van. Guayaquil is one of those sweltering, dirty port cities where we felt as if everything, from the tops of our heads to the bottoms of our shoes, was covered in a sticky black paste of grime. The mosquito-infested Rio Guayas flows through the town like molasses, carrying piles of trash and clumps of vegetation on the sludge-black journey to the sea. Dengue fever, an incurable viral disease, flourishes among the mosquitoes in the stagnant water of the river. The main tourist attraction is the above- ground cemetery that protects the occupants from the frequent floods.

Each day we packed a bag lunch and flashed our expired one-day pass to get on to the port, trying to find the proper person with the powerful connection that could get our van out. We were sent round and round in several giant bureaucratic circles, each office blaming another, until finally we narrowed the delay down to one person on the third floor of the customs building shielded behind two levels of security.

Butting to the front of the line, we pushed past the first level of security while flashing our California driver's license. Not knowing what to make of us, the second guard hesitantly unlatched the door and we stuck close as he ushered us directly to the desk of Veronica Esquer, the director in charge of receiving for the port. Her astonishment at seeing us standing in front of her desk could not be disguised and she hung up the telephone in mid-sentence. Once we were there, she had to deal with us. While Latin America may have many faults, impoliteness is considered unacceptable, and she felt obligated to assist us.

Later in the day our fireplug agent hissed with mock anger, "This is why no one wants to come to my backward country."

We had spent several hours standing just outside the office, of the *Gerente de la Bodega*, the man in charge of the warehouse. He had ignored us all day and spoke only with our agent. We waited as Benito discussed our dilemma with him once again.

Stepping out of the office Benito said almost in a whisper, "*Gerente* Robles will not let the van out."

We were amazed at the audacity of the warehouse manager.

"What about the special letter we got from Ms. Esquer?" I insisted. "She told us this was all we needed."

"I think it is going to take more than official documents to get your vehicle out," Benito said.

"But it's Friday already. I can't spend another weekend staring at the walls in the hotel room," Amanda whined.

I asked in frustration, "What do we need to do? Is there anyone else we can talk to?"

"Let me see what I can do," Benito said as he walked back over to the *Gerente's* office.

Irritated, I turned to Amanda and said, "He's talking about a bribe."

"A bribe! Aaagh, that's just great. I am so sick and tired of this. All I want is to get the van out of here." Amanda whined a little louder.

Benito returned within minutes. "This is it. There is no one else," he said. "If you want the van out before they close tonight we need to do what he wants."

I got the feeling that under his perturbed demeanor Benito was actually enjoying our troubles.

"What will it take to get the van out?" I demanded.

He turned his head away embarrassedly, then turned back and mumbled, "Normally, it would be around $15."

We hated the idea of paying a bribe, no matter how small. If we did we were nurturing the disease of corruption, but if we refused, the van would be held hostage indefinitely.

I pulled three crisp five-dollar bills from my money belt and slapped them into Benito's outstretched hand. Within minutes we were driving the van from the container and out of the port. We never looked back.

CHAPTER 22

Idiots and Airheads

Quito, Ecuador
11,944 miles

As much as I had wanted to, I could no longer ignore the problem. We were about to enter the Andes, some of the highest, steepest mountains in the world. Like a student cramming for a final exam while the teacher handed out the test, I had to study the problem, understand it and find a solution.

On the Central Route, surrounded by banana plantations and palm trees, we stopped by the side of the road near Santo Domingo de Los Colorados at the foothills of the Andes to make adjustments to the van.

I had a basic understanding of the workings of the Volkswagen motor. I knew that the gas exploded inside somewhere and that the explosions were converted into motion. On the practical side of things, I could change the spark plugs and the oil, and follow the tedious directions to adjust the valves, because everyone said, "You gotta adjust the valves." I had no idea why the valves needed adjustment, no clue how they got out of adjustment, in fact I did not know what the valves did, but I routinely lay down under the rear end of the van every 1500 miles and adjusted them with a greasy discomfort.

It was at these times, looking up under the van from the rear end that I realized, when pushed into a corner with nowhere to turn, I was not a complete mechanical fool. It took me a long time to figure out a problem, especially if it was complicated by more than one variable, but once diagnosed, I could generally find a solution.

Our library in the van included the book *How to Keep Your Volkswagen Alive, A Manual of Step-by-Step Procedures for the Complete Idiot.* At first I was insulted by the title but later realized that the book and I were made for each other. Written in the sixties and seventies by a Santa Fe hippy couple who understood the value of learning from experience, *The Idiot's Guide,* as we affectionately called it, starts from scratch by assuming that the reader knows absolutely nothing. Front is front. The left side of the car is the driver's side and the engine is in the rear.

I propped open the engine compartment, squatted down to look at the spaghetti system of tangled wires and parts with their mysterious functions, and tossed down *The Idiot's Guide.* The book flopped open to a cartoon of a guy crouched in much the same position I was in, with an incredulous expression, scratching his head.

This was a complicated procedure, so Amanda stuck a sticky-note on the page that showed the various pieces of the engine with lines pointing out the name of each part. I paged through and found the details explaining how to make adjustments to improve power at altitude. I understood the theory behind the adjustment perfectly well. Fuel + Oxygen + Spark = Explosion.

With less oxygen it was difficult for the thousands of explosions to happen efficiently so I had to give them a little more time to do their thing. If I loosened the bolt and turned the distributor just a fraction of a hair it would send the spark out earlier giving the explosion more time to happen and the van more power. At least it seemed like I understood it.

I took out a wrench and looked at the place where I was to loosen the nut, and just then it struck me. Why did I wait so long to solve this problem? I switched on the engine, loosened the nut, spun around the distributor and, voila, it sounded really good. I listened for a while and wondered, does it really sound better or am I just hopeful. Lo and behold, I pulled out on to the road and we had more power. For that brief moment I felt elated and turned to Amanda with the look of smug satisfaction.

She replied, "Chalk one up for Inspector Gadget."

Up into the Andes we climbed, leaving the steamy, sticky banana plantations, the papaya trees with their strange upturned umbrella shapes, and the pineapple palms, low and spread-eagled in the afternoon sun. The air was cooler, drier, and significantly thinner. Abruptly the rich red soil was gone and the gray, sandy, death-filled earth appeared. From months of living in the dense tropical life at sea level to gulping for air in the wind-driven stillness of altitude.

The road bent and twisted round and round as we climbed. We were overlooking the lush green valley with cultivated blocks that appeared to be a giant jigsaw puzzle, each piece fitting snugly in place. Tiny huts clung to the cliff-sides and villagers plodded along the road carrying their bundles as young boys prodded miserable donkeys loaded with wood.

As we entered the historic area of Quito I felt the first twinges of pain. It was as if a metal band was slowly tightening around the front of my head. The headache was combined with a strange shortness of breath. Sitting in a hole-in-the-wall restaurant near the *Iglesia de la Merced*, I began to suck in air and could not get enough. I consciously sped up my breathing almost as if I was hyperventilating, but it didn't help.

Oxygen was one of those things I had always taken for granted. Then suddenly it was gone. With less oxygen in my blood I had less energy and felt lethargic, sluggish, exhausted, but by a strange trick of metabolic fate, I could not sleep. Interestingly, there is no way to know who will suffer from altitude sickness. Amanda showed absolutely no effects and was up and perky the next morning, ready to go for our daily run.

For thousands of years the Andean Indians have chewed the coca leaves to deal with the effects of altitude. These are the same leaves used to make cocaine. Chewing them produces only a mildly intoxicating effect, reducing fatigue and relieving pain. We bought a small bag in the market and I shoveled a handful into my mouth. Chewing them into a messy green ball of mush deadened the feeling in my lips and took away my hunger, but otherwise had little effect.

Just outside Quito the Ecuadorian government had built a monument to mark the line where the equator passes, but they mistakenly chose a spot two hundred meters too far south. A resourceful Ecuadorian built an alternative museum on the exact equator line. This mad scientist created a few cheesy exhibits from things he pulled out of the trash and manipulated them to show visitors the freaky effects of being at the center of the earth.

We waited along with a handful of other curious spectators for the afternoon show. The owner appeared in a dingy light-blue lab coat with his assistant, a stick-thin teenage boy who wore thick glasses and struggled under the weight of several props.

"Welcome to my museum," he greeted us in Spanish. "Today we will learn about the equator. This line you see running through my property cuts the globe in half." He stood with one foot on each side of a stone pathway that marked the equator. "Anywhere else on earth it is impossible to balance an egg on the head of a nail, but here…" He turned to his assistant who was struggling to make a brown egg stand on the head of a rusty nail poking from a pillar. When he realized the assistant would not succeed he asked, "Would anyone like to try?"

One by one the entire group tried, without success.

As he walked away he said, "Please, believe me when I tell you that it can be done."

Amanda stayed behind, struggling to get the egg to balance as the scientist turned the group to face his assistant, who was standing on an old bathroom scale, and said, "Can I have a volunteer, please."

A group of five Israeli students were traveling with a chaperone, a woman of about thirty, and together they pushed her forward. Reluctantly she followed the direction of the assistant and stepped on the scale.

The assistant knelt down to look at her weight and announced, "Eighty-two kilos."

The Israeli students laughed in unison.

The scientist asked, "What is your weight at home in Israel?"

"About the same, I guess," the woman answered with bright red cheeks.

The scientist looked confused and said, "But here you should weigh less. You must have gained some weight recently. Can I have another volunteer?"

No one volunteered.

He continued by explaining, "When you are standing on the equator you are on the outside edge of a ball spinning round and round at thousands of miles per hour. The centrifugal force counteracts the effects of gravity and pulls you away from the earth. So, the closer you are to the equator, the less you weigh."

Taking away the scale his assistant brought out a portable stainless steel kitchen sink with four wooden legs. As the scientist positioned the sink a few feet to the north of the equator the assistant filled a paint bucket with water from a nearby tap. We all stood around the basin as the assistant poured the water into the sink. The scientist said, "Notice how the water flows down counterclockwise in the northern hemisphere." Then he moved the basin to the south of the line while his helper fetched more water. Pouring it with the flair of a magician the scientist said, "There. You will notice that the water flows down clockwise in the southern hemisphere. This is the same effect that causes hurricanes and tornadoes to twist." He went into a long scientific explanation that no one understood.

Interrupting his discussion, Amanda yelled, "Yes! I got it. Look. The egg is balanced on the nail." The entire group went over to look at the egg but before we could see it the assistant bumped the pillar and the egg tumbled, splattering around the nail.

Amanda said, "That egg was lopsided."

The scientist took it in stride and continued, "What do you suppose happens when the basin is held directly above the equator?"

The group was no longer enthusiastic about the show and no one offered an answer until the assistant raised his hand. The scientist ignored him and said, "Well, let's see."

As the assistant filled the bucket the scientist moved the basin over the line. He poured the water into the sink and we all watched. The Israeli woman said, "Hum, it looks like it's going counterclockwise."

One of her students insisted, "No, it's going clockwise."

The scientist was frustrated and looked around the group then pointed to me, "You. What's that you've got in your mouth?"

"Ah, coca leaves. I was having trouble with the altitu…"

"Good," he interrupted. "Come here." He pointed to a spot directly in front of the sink. Then he turned to his assistant, "Fill the bucket again."

When the assistant returned with the bucket the scientist picked it up and quickly dumped it into the sink. As the water pooled in the sink he poked me from behind, "Now, spit those leaves into the sink."

As I turned to look at him he poked harder and demanded, "Now, spit, hurry before the water is gone."

I spit the fermenting wad of coca leaves into the sink and the group watched in amazement. The assistant stuck his finger in and swished them around. The leaves billowed in the sink for a moment and flowed straight down the hole.

The scientist fanned out his hands from the wrist and said with great flair, "The mysteries of nature revealed."

CHAPTER 23

Cleopatra's Place

Baños Ecuador
12,042 miles

Down we drove toward the town of Baños on the other side of the Andes to a lush, humid, subtropical valley, past an invisible line where the jungle exploded in profusion and the long pants stuck to my legs. The road gradually narrowed until it was a road no more, just a slushy mud-black soup where the streams poured over the cliff-side, taking the pavement with them into the green-black abyss. Twisting, snakelike vines strangled and choked the limbs and trunks of trees, covering everything in green, from the decay of black-emerald to the lightness of nearly yellow-lime, dense, thick, stinking, clinging, green. But at lower altitude the van perked up and I perked up.

We parked in the front yard of a hotel near the *baños* (public baths) that gave the town its name. A few entrepreneurial folks had funneled the natural hot springs, creating a tiered set of swimming holes that were full to overflowing with children, like a boiling pot of bobbing, churning guppies.

The robust, middle-aged hotel owner with a short, curly mop of corn-colored hair fanned her moistened face and neck with a fashion magazine, as the fat on the back of her arm flapped wildly. She stopped for a moment to confide behind her fan as if someone might overhear, "I would not go near those pools. You should see what those children do in there. No chlorine and they never change the water, ugh." She shivered then straightened up with a weird little shake as her flowered housecoat stuck to her skin. "But if you want to go, let me know. I have a friend who rents bathing suits, real cheap."

With the roof popped up, the van barely squeezed beneath a massive birdcage hanging from the mango tree in the yard of the hotel. From the corner of her eye Amanda noticed the movement of a dark furry thing inside the cage. Curious, she went over to take a closer look. When the monkey saw her it began running round and round in the cage, faster and faster, eeeeekk, eeeeeekk, eeeeeeeekk, screeching an evil hiss, possessed by some unknown force. Then it stopped and wrapped its thin, brown claws around the bars and poked its miniature protruding mouth through the grate to bare its tiny white needle-like fangs with a screech and a hiss, eek, eek, eek, ssssk, ssssk, sssk. Amanda backed away toward the hotel and asked the distracted owner, "What's wrong with the monkey?"

She was lounging on a bamboo armchair, close to an ancient television, mesmerized by the latest *novela*, and looked at Amanda with a puzzled expression, "Monkey?"

"Yes, the monkey in the cage, in the tree out there." She frantically pointed outside, "Near the van, in the tree out there, in the cage."

A light bulb went on, "Oh, you mean Cleopatra?"

"Cleopatra? Ahhh, yeah, what's wrong with her? She went crazy when I got near her."

Staring at the television, the woman gave a crooked look, and keeping one eye on the screen she waved her hand and said, "Oh, don't worry, dear. She just doesn't like women."

Two plump, burley Irish girls cut across the overgrown garden, wrapped in towels, unsuccessfully concealing their ill-fitting bathing suits and exposing their unshaven legs. They stood poking at the cage, feeding the monkey handfuls of small tangerine wedges. They spoke in unison, one starting a sentence, the other finishing, and asked if I had driven past a friend of theirs, a German cyclist on the road down to Baños.

The taller of the two girls said, "He's traveling around on a budget of one dollar a day. Free-camping along the road…"

The other girl interrupted, "...as he rides south. He's carrying these massive bags of rice and beans, and a box of salt."

Resembling a couple of parrots, they continued the story. The German had flown into New York with his bicycle and a few supplies nearly three years before and had spent only $1,000 slowly pedaling down through the U.S., Mexico and Central America before telling his tale to an Australian sailboat crew who took him aboard and dropped him in Northern Ecuador for one dollar.

Amanda came out of the hotel and passed the cage, consciously ignoring Cleo. The monkey began to hiss and screech. In retaliation for being ignored Cleo threw one of the tangerine wedges and, bonk, hit Amanda right on the head.

The Irish girls and I roared with laughter, but Amanda did not find it funny. Cleo pressed her tiny, furry face through the bars with a cynical smile that made Amanda fear for her life.

Asleep in the pop-top bed that night, Amanda heard whispering just outside the van and elbowed me awake. We peeked out through the screened opening and saw the shape of a woman. It was the owner, leaning her fleshy face against the cage. Cleopatra poked her mouth through the bars and screeched at the owner with an angry monkey hiss. The woman bowed her head in submission and nodded as if she had done something wrong as she said, "*Yo se, yo se. Lo siento mucho. Te prometo, nunca mas.*" (I know, I know. I'm sorry. I promise you, never again.)

Amanda and I looked at each other in the dim moonlight and it dawned on us simultaneously. It was the monkey, Cleopatra, from her perch in the mango tree, who actually ran the strange hotel.

CHAPTER 24

Lunch in the Highlands

Alausi, Ecuador
12,228 miles

We sat down in the restaurant of our $6-a-night hotel in Alausi, Ecuador. Ideally, our nights were spent in a campground, or sleeping in the parking lot of a hotel if necessary, but this hotel only had one secure parking spot several blocks away, and the owner would not allow us to camp in the van.

Word among low-budget travelers was that this was the place to catch the hair-raising roof-top train passage down the Andes to *La Nariz del Diablo*, (The Devil's Nose) a disorienting cliff-edged journey that commonly derailed and left riders stranded for hours.

The streets of Alausi overflowed with the colors of the highland region. Quechua women, dressed in bright wool skirts and embroidered blouses, carried bundles of goods bound for the market, and men strapped machetes to their hip and covered themselves with handmade llama hair ponchos. These interesting outfits, with not-so-subtle differences in color, indicated the village from which the wearer hailed, and made our worn-out travel clothes seem downright dull. The Indians spoke Quechua and Spanish interchangeably and were cordial, but shy with strangers.

Arriving in town hungry and tired, we did not expect much in the way of food as we waited in the restaurant to be served. Two rosy-cheeked, teenaged indigenous girls watched us through the glass divider from the kitchen but did not come out to take our order. Every so often we would turn to indicate our readiness but they would only giggle and look away.

I waited a while before approaching the glass and spoke through the small, semicircular opening. *"Buenas tardes. ¿Tiene menu?"* (Good afternoon. Do you have a menu?)

Their cheeks grew rosier and they gave me blank stares. Silent moments passed before the chubbier girl got up the nerve to ask, *"¿Quiere almuerzo?"* (Would you like lunch?)

If I had had a better mastery of the language I would have reworded my question but I was stuck with the Spanish I knew so I plunged ahead, *"Sí. ¿Pero tiene menu?"* (Yes. But do you have a menu?)

The bolder of the two reached for a bowl and began to serve the first course. I waved my hands back and forth in the universal sign, *"No, no. Quiero un menu."* (No. I want a menu.) Then I opened my hands like a book in front of my face and repeated, "Menu."

They both seemed to freeze in mid-motion, regaining their blank stare. I managed to interpret from their complete lack of communication that there was only a set meal and no menu.

I stammered, *"¿El almuerzo, de que consiste?"* (The lunch, what does it consist of?)

The bolder of the two came back to life and thought for a moment, then answered, *"Sopa."* (Soup.)

"¿Que tipo de sopa?" (What type of soup?)

She looked confused and answered with a question, *"¿Sopa?"* (Soup?)

Not one to give up easily I persisted, *"¿Sopa con que?"* (Soup with what?)

She looked at me as if she finally understood what I wanted to know and nodded her head when she answered, *"Sopa."* (Soup.)

I scratched my head, *"Regreso en un momentito."* (I'll be back in a moment.) The chubby girl nodded and her friend giggled.

Back at the table Amanda asked me, "What's for lunch?"

I smiled and answered, *"Almuerzo."* (Lunch.)

"So what is it?" She insisted.

"Why don't you go ask yourself?" I suggested.

Amanda went over and started from the beginning, *"Buenas tardes. ¿Tiene menu?"* (Good afternoon. Do you have a menu?)

As if on cue the girl answered, *"¿Quiere almuerzo?"* (Would you like lunch?)

Amanda has even less patience for evasive answers than I do and asked, *"Si. ¿Pero que es el almuerzo?"* (Yes. But what is the lunch?)

The girl paused and began her descent into a blank stare and looked away. The chubby girl answered, *"Almuerzo."* (Lunch.)

Amanda was hungry and her tolerance was thinning. *"Si. ¿Pero que es el almuerzo?"* (Yes, but what is the lunch?)

The girl's mouth fell open in the last stage of the blankness. She answered, *"Almuerzo."* (Lunch.)

Trying a different tact, Amanda asked, *"¿Viene con sopa?"* (Does it come with soup?)

The girl replied, *"¿Quiere sopa?"* (Do you want soup?)

"¿Que viene en la sopa?" (What does the soup have in it?) Amanda asked.

The girl walked over and looked in the pot and mumbled, "Blahblahblahblah."

Amanda gave her a confused look, *"Humm. ¿Tiene papas?"* (Humm. Does it have potatoes?)

The girl gave the most assured answer of the conversation, *"No. Tiene maiz."* (No. It has corn.)

From across the room I figured she was getting further than I had so I said, "Ask her what's in it."

Through gritted teeth Amanda hissed back, "I'm trying!" Then, turning to the girls, *"¿Y el plato fuerte, que es?"* (And the main meal, what is it?)

The chubby girl replied, *"Carne con arroz."* (Meat with rice.)

Not satisfied with that, Amanda foolishly pressed on, *"¿Que tipo de carne?"* (What type of meat?)

The girls became instantly frozen with blank stares.

I yelled across the restaurant, "Ask her what kind of meat it is."

Amanda took a deep breath and turned toward me, "I'm trying," then turned back to the girls and smiled, *"¿Puerco?"* (Pork?)

Still frozen.

"¿Carne de res?" (Beef?)

Still frozen. *"¿Es carne de cochi o vaca?"* (Is it meat of a pig or a cow?) "Oink, oink o mooooooo?"

The chubby girl unfroze and looked in the pot, *"No se."* (I don't know.)

With a persistence that makes her who she is Amanda said, *"Enséñeme un pedazo, por favor."* (Show me a piece, please.)

I got up to have a look while the giggling girl used a small pitchfork to pick up a piece of meat that looked somewhat like beef. But it could have been pork as well, or llama for that matter.

I asked, *"¿Y cuanto cuesta el almuerzo?"* (How much is the lunch?)

The girls answered in unison, *"No se."* (I don't know.)

As we were settling in at our table the girls placed two hearty bowls of soup in front of us with huge chunks of potatoes. The meat and rice were both good and filling, though we had no idea what kind it was. Halfway through the meal they brought out two tall glasses of delicious, fresh-squeezed papaya juice. When the check arrived the total was $2.40.

Up in these mountains there are indigenous people who do not have the luxury of seeing their neighbors more than once or twice a month. The isolation of the Andes holds time still and protects the culture from outside influences. When most travelers come in contact with these people they chalk up the resulting misunderstanding to their own lack of communication skills. In fact, it is a combination of a language barrier (Spanish to Quechua) and a cultural one. Their social systems are different from those we know and understand.

We've learned that the most productive language is the universal one, "Oink-oink, moooooo."

CHAPTER 25

The Peruvian Two-Step

Northern Peru
13,063 miles

Fourteen times in one week was a bit much. No exaggeration, fourteen times in seven days.

Each time we went through the same song and dance.
A Peruvian police officer would be leaning against his shiny new Toyota Land Cruiser, concealing his face behind aviator sunglasses. He would lazily stroll to the center of the two-lane highway and signal us to move off to the side of the road.

The conversations would always begin cordially, *"Buenas tardes."* Then the officer would create some absurd infraction. *"Señor,* you were driving at 110 kilometers per hour. The speed limit here is 50."

Politely I would deny it. *"No Oficial, no es posible.* The van can only go as fast as 80. It has never gone up to 110."

Amanda would smile and say, "Oh no. We respect your laws. We would never disobey them."

One officer said, "You obviously do not respect our laws because your license plate is in the wrong place." Another demanded, "You were going over the white line." A third averted his eyes and alleged, "You did not use your turn signal." We hadn't turned for a hundred miles. With each accusation the officers became just a bit ruder and more abrasive, and we in turn became more polite and friendly.

Amanda would use flattery and say, "It's always a pleasure meeting the honest police officers of Peru."

They would grumble and we would smile.

After a while they would conclude that we were not as fearful as they had hoped and would deduce that we would probably not be making a contribution to their lunch fund. They would try a different tactic by becoming instantly amiable and request some unrelated item.

"We can settle this problem right here. Why don't you just give me a can of soda?"

We'd laugh and say, "No."

Another asked, "There is a charity sporting event in the village this afternoon. Maybe you could give me a donation?"

"Ha ha, no."

The most interesting was the officer who told us, "We can help each other. The government has rationed gasoline for our police vehicles. You could give me some of the fuel from your spare canisters and I will let you go."

"Oh, isn't that interesting. No!"

The act was difficult to keep up. Each time we saw the police my heart would race. I was so terrorized that I would drive far out of the way to avoid anyone in uniform. Off-road vehicles parked on the side of the road caused my flight response to kick in with a surge of adrenalin racing through my system. My breathing involuntarily quickened, my blood pressure surged, and I lost all semblance of reasonable thought.

Amanda had had more experience dealing with corrupt officials and understood how to play the game better than I did. Also, our dealings were in Spanish, her first language. While I understood most of the words, I found that the subtleties in a conversation, the slight inflection on a certain remark or the choice of a particular word over another, made all the difference. In Latin America, the way things were said was far more important that what was said, and while I could translate many of the words, I was far from understanding how to interpret what they meant.

The encounters had me so rattled that I searched for a very American solution to the problem. I paged through a local phonebook and jotted down the phone number of the Peruvian Transit Police in Lima. I wrote it on a sticky-note with the words "Police Corruption Unit" written across the top in Spanish and stuck it to the back of my driver's license.

We continued to be pulled over. By the time we reached Nazca we had lost count at fifty. I still got the same jolt each time it happened but we became quite skilled at repeating the script. In the end my confidence grew and I felt satisfaction in knowing that we had never resorted to giving a bribe.

CHAPTER 26

Spacemen and Germans

Nazca, Peru
14,144 miles

The Cessna tumbled about like a Volkswagen Beetle in a washing machine. Jorge, the pilot, fought for control and grumbled through the headset microphone, "Sorry. It's awfully windy this afternoon." As we banked over the giant hummingbird etched into the desert floor below he reached back and handed Amanda an airsickness bag as he asked, *"¿Esta bien?"* (Are you OK?)

She was getting greener by the second.

From above we could see that the Pan American highway sliced directly across one of the figures, dissecting one of the world's archeological mysteries, the Nazca lines and geoglyphs. Carving into the dark top layer of the earth's crust, the ancient Nazcan people dug down to reveal the lighter colored soil, creating an odd assortment of geometric shapes and figures, the meaning of which has confounded experts for nearly a century. At ground level the lines were difficult to see and the geoglyphs were virtually indistinguishable until we viewed them from above. The highway engineers had no idea they were cutting through the lizard when they ran it over with the road.

As we looked out over the flat desert floor that ended abruptly at the edge of the Andes on one side and the Pacific Ocean on the other, Jorge said, "Some people believe this is a massive map to guide the shamans in flight." He pointed out the window and said, "This desert is full of the *San Pedro* (Saint Peter) cactus. As the name implies, the Nazcan people believe it holds the keys to the gates of heaven. There is a shaman in town who says he flies above the desert when he takes a piece of the *San Pedro*."

I thought back to the interesting Argentinean girl a world away in Northern Mexico telling us about how she soared over the desert while using peyote.

"Have you seen the film *Chariots of the Gods?*" Jorge asked.

"Yes, I have, but Rich hasn't," Amanda said enthusiastically. "That's how I learned about the lines."

Jorge banked the plane to the right and circled around what looked like a human figure with a halo around its head. "Then you will recognize the astronaut. In the movie they said this place was a landing site for flying saucers and that the early Nascan people were taught art by ancient astronauts."

"What do you think?" I asked.

"I believe the movie made a lot of money," he answered and turned the plane away.

As we bounced around in the small airplane above the desert floor Jorge told us the unique story of Maria Reiche, the nearsighted German mathematician who came to the Peruvian desert in the 1930s and dedicated her life to the lines. She lived simply in the barren landscape, broom in hand, sweeping away the pebbles that blew into the shallow furrows that made up the lines and figures. She spent her days studying their meaning and protecting them from invasion by clueless drivers. It was the solstice markers, the lines that indicated the sweep of the sun or moon through the sky, that first captured her imagination. Ms. Reiche came to believe that the images of the animals represented the different constellations of the stars and the zigzags symbolized water. Before her death, close to sixty years after her arrival, a massive snake-like figure was discovered. The lines that made up the neat curves of the body were more than a hundred feet across.

As we flew over the spider Jorge said, "Represents Orion," and when we were above the monkey, "Thought to be an appeal to the gods for rain." He explained how different cultures have used a wide variety of symbols to represent what they saw in the night sky as he banked the plane to the right in a steep arc so we could see the full image from the small windows.

The plane jolted and I readjusted my headset to ask, "Now that the German woman has passed away, how are they keeping the lines clean?"

"A group of volunteers, but they are not as committed as she was. It has not been the same since she died."

"She must have lived an interesting life," Amanda said.

"Yes, she was a fascinating woman. Imagine, she came here to live alone, a young German woman isolated in the desert. She really must have loved the place. You know what I think? I think it was her destiny to be here."

As Jorge steered us away from the baby condor and headed toward the whale I heard gurgling in my headset and looked back at Amanda. She was barely keeping her lunch down but made a brave attempt at conversation, "Not many people find the thing they want to do in life. Ms. Reiche was lucky to have found hers."

Jorge was silent for a moment, then banked the plane to the right and circled the whale. "You may be right, but I believe most people know what they want to do. They just do not have the courage to do it." We spun in a large arc around the whale, then pulled up to level and pointed into the sun. "Ms. Reiche believed that the lines were used by the Nazca people to preserve knowledge, like a book. She spent her entire life piecing together her theories, little by little over fifty years. Like putting together a puzzle. She did exactly what she wanted to do and lived to be ninety-five years old. Here in the desert that is a miracle. I believe it was because she had a reason to live."

Jorge fought with the wind as we approached the runway, struggling to keep the small plane in line. "Don't worry," he said as he shifted the stick, "This is my thing. The thing I always wanted to do. We will land just fine."

CHAPTER 27

Lost Souls

Cuzco, Peru
14,622 miles

In the past it was possible to strap on a backpack and follow in the footsteps of the ancient Incas on their stone pathway to the lost city, Machu Picchu. The rules changed just a month before we arrived, making it impossible to hike the trail without a permit from the Peruvian government. The permits were in short supply and we negotiated with three shops in Cuzco to get the best price on last minute spaces available from international tour companies. We decided to go with a company that was a little more expensive than the others, but included the tents, equipment, meals, and an English-speaking guide. Our fellow group members were package tourists who had paid for their trip overseas.

On the road for almost a year, it was the first time we had come across this type of traveler. We often met young backpackers, mostly British and Australian, on "gap year" between high school and university. Once in a while adventurous retirees would cross our path, living out of a suitcase and making their own arrangements. Our new traveling companions were all clean-cut, mid-thirties, respectable-looking professionals, who probably had proud parents at home bragging about them. They worked hard, followed the rules and were clawing their way to the top.

Our peculiar Peruvian guide was chosen not for his profound knowledge of the sites - his explanations often bordered on the ridiculous - but for his skill at managing the long line of porters, two for each client. The porters were paid runners, jogging ahead with massive packs to set up the camp, dig pit toilets, assemble a dining tent, cook three meals a day, clean up, disassemble it all, and run ahead to have it ready when we arrived at the next stop. A miserable job, that of a porter.

Our first day's hike was a relatively easy six-hour stroll up through the valley. Amanda walked with Laura, a talkative software salesperson who announced proudly, "In the past two years I've eaten all my childhood pets. I ate dog in Cambodia, cat in Vietnam, and guinea pig in Peru, and I never got sick."

Looming just over the campsite that night was our challenge for the following morning, the highest point of the trail at 13,780 feet above sea level, the Dead Woman's Pass. After dinner, a short, cheerful British doctor named Roger began showing signs of altitude sickness. Laura promptly offered him a few cubes of Diamox, a medication that increases oxygen metabolism. When he refused she placed a tub of Advil in front of him and insisted, "Take as many as you need."

The next morning four locals waited at the base of the pass, offering for a small fee, to carry our packs over the most grueling section. Knowing my penchant for altitude sickness, I plunked down my heavy pack among those in the large pile and took Amanda's lighter one on my back. Our guide began distributing the packs but there weren't enough porters and some of the men offered to strap a second around their chests. My pack remained on the ground with two others and I resigned myself to carrying it, but one of the porters assured us that he would find someone to haul it up the mountain, so we set off leaving it behind.

The first hours of climbing were utter agony. The higher we went the thinner the air became and I felt a dizzy headache coming on. Amanda walked ahead and I lost sight of her as I slowed down. I began to count my steps in Spanish. At the lower elevation I counted from 1 to 50 and rested for a minute. As I trudged higher I began to lose count so I switched to English, resting at 40, then 30, then 20. Finally I was losing count in English.

Turning a corner, I miraculously made it to the summit where Amanda was sitting on a boulder with Laura and a young local girl. In my oxygen-starved state I thought I was beginning to hallucinate. My backpack was leaning against a rock and I looked at Amanda, confused, "How'd my pack get here?"

She smiled broadly, "Ask our little friend?"

"No, there is no way she carried that thing. It weighs a ton."

"Ask her."

I shook my head in disbelief and sheepishly asked, "*¿Cuantos años tienes?*" (How old are you?)

She answered coyly, "*Doce.*" She was twelve years old.

I slunk off, plopped myself down and guzzled water.

Laura followed. "Feeling OK?"

"No, actually I feel horrible."

"I've got Tylenol with codeine if you need some."

After crossing the pass we hiked for five more hours, descending to 11,800 feet and a grassy field where the porters had set up camp for the night. The tents were erected in a neat line and the smell of dinner filled the air but I had virtually no appetite. The masochistic guide encouraged us to play drinking games with a bottle of rot-gut the porters had carried up the mountain. In my handicapped state I continually lost and had to repeatedly drink the deadly Peruvian concoction. When I finally came to my senses I dizzily staggered toward our tent.

As I unzipped the flap I noticed that the porters were scooping a large pot full of water from the icy mountain stream. They placed it on the primus stove to boil, leaving it overnight to cool so we could fill our water bottles in the morning.

The alcohol kept me warm through the frigid night but Amanda fidgeted, putting on layer upon layer of clothing, complaining about frozen feet. She wore four pairs of socks, then pulled on her boots, all inside her down sleeping bag, but the sub-zero night froze her toes. In desperation she piled every available piece of clothing on top of her feet. When that failed and her squirming woke me, I packed her, sleeping bag and all, into her backpack up to her waist. She fitted nicely and slept like a baby for the rest of the night.

Determined to squeeze as much as possible from the short trip, most of the group stayed up until three in the morning, downing a second, then a third bottle of the rot-gut. They were in a sorry-looking state the next day at the 5:00 am wakeup call. On our hike that day the guide paused at some ruins along the trail and waited for everyone to catch up. Once the stragglers arrived he began his explanation of how the Inca used the area as a security checkpoint. The late night group collapsed and the guide had to shake them awake when we pushed on.

Naomi and Shira, two schoolteachers from Long Island, walked beside Amanda and peppered her with questions as I followed and Laura brought up the rear.

"How did you get away from real life for so long?" Shira asked.

"Well," Amanda said, "We had a dream and, I don't know... we planned."

Naomi said, "But what about debt? Right after graduation I got a student loan coupon booklet from the state. My payments are $288.00 a month. I'm trapped now for who knows how many years before I finish paying them back."

"I had a loan too," I said. "But we really made an effort to pay it off quickly."

"What about a mortgage and car payments?"

Amanda answered, "We didn't want to make that kind of commitment."

"Our only big possession is our old Volkswagen bus," I added.

Laura's voice boomed from the back of the line, "What about this trip, it's got to cost you a fortune?"

I misunderstood her question. "No, we bought it last minute, direct from the agent in Cuzco."

"She means the whole trip," Amanda corrected. "We're just very frugal. We cook our own meals and sleep almost every night in the van. Our biggest expense is gasoline."

Laura persisted and asked directly, "So how much have you spent?"

When Amanda told them our monthly average Laura's voice echoed along the trail, "That means you've spent as much in..." she paused to calculate in her head, "...in three and a half months as I've spent for this two-week trip."

She went on, "My boyfriend paid more for his television than you've spent in six months. It's a nice TV, but hell it's only a TV."

The teachers walked in silence. They seemed as perplexed with us as we were with them.

Our final night was spent at the one permanent campsite on the Inca Trail, a filthy place that stunk of urine and worse. The porters had run ahead to secure the flattest spots for our tents. As it rained, the steep dirt paths turned to slick, mud-covered sliding boards and just about everyone at the camp had a streak of orange mud down their backside. After dinner at the restaurant the late night group perked up and began buying rounds of drinks from the bar. Before heading to his tent the guide announced, "Remember, 4:00 am wakeup call tomorrow." Following him out the door we skidded down the hill to our tent to massage our aching muscles and bandage our blistered feet.

Before dawn the next morning a porter squatted outside our tent opening, *"Buenos dias. Les traigo café."* (Good morning. I have brought you coffee.)

Barely coherent, we hiked into the darkness with our flashlights illuminating the path. We had wanted to arrive at the overlook early enough to watch the sunrise over Machu Picchu, but the valley was covered in a blanket of heavy fog, obscuring our view. As we waited at the sun gate the mist slowly evaporated, revealing a window-like opening to the lush green hills and tiered dwellings of the lost city below.

By the time we weaved down to Machu Picchu, the morning train had disgorged its load of passengers and we found ourselves participating in theme park frenzy. Tour groups meandered in and out of the stone structures as their guides blurted out explanations in six languages.

Our late night group sprawled out on a grassy perch, hung over, staring up at the sky. Amanda and I wandered together, content to be on our own until Laura found us. "I'm not feeling too good," she said, holding her stomach. "I think they didn't boil the drinking water last night." We left her leaning against a wall and went to the gift shop to purchase a few bottles of clean water.

Twenty minutes later we returned and she had attracted a small group of French tourists. "What took you so long?" she demanded. The group stared at us accusingly. "I've been trying to take this anti-nausea medicine but every time I swallow the pill it makes me throw up." We gave her a water bottle and left her in the caring hands of the French.

Boarding the overbooked train back to Cuzco, we reunited with our group. They all looked miserable as we stared out the windows, isolated in our own thoughts. Their faces showed depression. Reality had set in. The British doctor mumbled, "I can't believe it's over."

Another added, "Yeah, I'm not looking forward to going back at all. You have no idea what I had to do to get this time off. I practically bribed my boss."

A Canadian woman said, "I'm dreading it. I don't even want to think of the problems that have piled on my desk and the millions of email waiting for me."

Laura staggered into our car, pale and deflated. "Room for me?" she asked as she slid in to the edge of Amanda's seat, listening to the group complain. With her trumpet-like voice she said, "Yeah, we might as well just plunge off the edge of the cliff right now. Or we could take the easy way out. I've got enough drugs to kill us all."

Stepping off the train at the Cuzco station, we said our goodbyes to the group, relieved to get away from the insulated atmosphere of the tour. In nearly a year on the road we had gone through such gradual changes that we hardly noticed how different we had become. Traveling with the group was like looking at ourselves in a mirror and barely recognizing the people staring back. Our daily concerns had shifted to more basic elements of life; security, food, clean water, and a place to sleep.

As we walked alone down the cobble-path we were excited once again, to fend for ourselves.

CHAPTER 28

Unnecessary Necessity

San Pedro de Atacama, Chile
15,441 miles

Crossing from Peru to Chile was like driving into a different world. Once through the border formalities, we drove along the desert coast and parked on the sand at an empty stretch of beach just north of Arica. I popped up the top, then opened the icebox to pull out the Alpaca steaks we had smuggled into the country and began slicing them into small strips. Amanda watched carefully to make sure I followed the recipe given to us by an old woman at the market who helped us select the pieces.

Within minutes a shiny new four-wheel drive vehicle parked about twenty feet from the van, close enough to seem suspicious with open space for miles on either side. Immediately we were on guard.

Amanda peeked through the jalousie window as two young guys got out and began digging with shovels in the sand. Something didn't feel right. Just as we were about to pack up and leave, we heard the yelling. It sounded like a woman and then a man, struggling. I grabbed a metal bar from behind the seat, slid open the door and jumped out, prepared for a confrontation.

But the two guys were smiling, looking up into the sky.

I followed their gaze to a group of parachutists circling above. A woman maneuvered her chute and swooped by, letting out a stifled yell of exhilaration. She coasted in for a landing, missing the giant X the guys had dug in the sand by several yards. Gathering up her gear, she hurried out of the way for the next jumper. Looking closer at their vehicle, I noticed that it had the logo and address of a local parachute shop.

Amanda pulled out our small table and chairs, and we sat enjoying our lunch as eight more jumpers landed, folded up their gear, and scurried out of the way. It had been a long time since we had encountered people able to pursue such an expensive hobby. In Peru and Ecuador they would have been foreigners out for adventure, but here in Chile they were all locals, using gear bought from a shop in town. We had entered a country with discretionary income, frivolous pursuits, and the time and energy to engage in them.

Driving south on the Pan American highway, further into the string-bean shaped country of Chile, we turned toward the port city of Iquique. I pulled in front of a house and Amanda asked the owner if there was a grocery store near by. The well-dressed woman rocked herself on the porch swing as she answered, "Yes, there is a Lee Der at the waterfront."

"Lee Der?" Amanda asked.

"Yes, Lee Der."

When we got to the waterfront there was no supermarket in sight. We stopped again to ask directions and were given the same vague answer, "Yes, Lee Der. It is one kilometer ahead."

We followed the road as it traced along the sea and there, shining in the afternoon sun, was "Lee Der". We drove up the ramp into the multi-level parking structure shared by a home center and the hypermarket Lider.

Amanda could barely push the boat-sized shopping cart past the ninety checkout lanes, through the consumer electronics, around the big screen televisions and the digital cameras, to get to the grocery section. Like two famine victims we filled the cart to the rim, expecting it to be the first and last time we would encounter such a wide assortment of products. I paid with a credit card, oblivious to the exchange rate and the prices we were charged.

As I rolled the cart back to the van, reality set in. Amanda asked, "Where are we going to store all this stuff?" Up to that moment we had lived by a simple rule. When we bought something it had to replace something else. The massive cart was full of stuff that did not replace anything. It all had to fit.

Later in the day we arrived in the dusty desert town of San Pedro de Atacama. The 970 residents lived in homes made from the same mud bricks that their ancestors had used nearly 11000 years ago. Some survived without television, electricity, telephone, and high speed Internet. Atacameños lived this way by choice. Many were transplanted from the bustling metropolis of Santiago. The artists and wood-fire bakers, the writers and readers, loafers and scientists enjoyed the unique perspective of being away from the modern, living in the middle of the desert, in another time.

Setting up camp in the cactus garden of a guesthouse where the generator was switched off three hours after sunset, Amanda began the task of organizing our hypermarket purchases. The two-kilo wheel of cheese took up most of the spare room in the icebox but somehow she squeezed in the garlic and chive-flavored cream cheese and the strawberry yogurt. The glass packages required unbreakable storage. The bottles of Chilean wine, pasta sauces, balsamic vinegar, olives, and jalapeños were all wrapped in our extra clothing. In an uncontrolled frenzy, Amanda stocked a three-month's supply of pasta, cans of tuna fish, and boxes of chicken bouillon, piling them in a mesh bag. The giant sacks of rice and oatmeal we would use as pillows.

But it was the little things that appeared most ridiculous beyond the fluorescent-induced haze. The boxes of crackers, the sticks of pepperoni and bags of sun-dried tomatoes, the croutons and salad dressings, and the cheese-flavored popcorn topping. There was no place to fit it and we did not need it.

Amanda repeated the same thing over and over, "What were we thinking?"

Hours after sunset we switched off the van's battery-powered light while the other guests sat in lantern-lit cabañas, and we enjoyed the seclusion of almost complete darkness. Looking out at the stars of the Southern Cross, I thought of the abrupt change we had experienced when we drove through the distinct border between Peru and Chile. Suddenly we had returned to what was familiar. The hypermarkets, parachute clubs, four-wheel drives, and popcorn seasoning were all things that we'd never missed, but given the temptation, we desired.

Content in the enveloping darkness, we wondered how many things in our lives were like this. If it hadn't been for the fact that we lived in such a small space, we probably would have never noticed.

CHAPTER 29

Our Own Ignorance

Easter Island, Chile
Flight from Santiago to Hanga Roa
2,300 miles

It was on the coast at Viña del Mar where we saw just how much wealth Chile possessed. As the weekend retreat for the well-to-do residents of Santiago, Viña del Mar is a haven for stretched women in chic jogging suits carrying silly little dogs with bows.

There were no campsites in town and the sky-high hotel prices were out of the question, so we slinked back up the coast to Reñaca, a beach town just slightly less elegant, again too expensive. Further away was Con Con, the town that housed the doormen and maids, but still the accommodations were out of our range. Outside of Con Con, at a beach that captured an unimaginable collection of flotsam, we found the only campsite in the area. It was outrageously expensive, but after spending the day searching for a place to stay, we were hungry and ready to settle for the night. To justify the cost we alternated one night in the campsite and one night free camping in a public parking structure for the week.

In Viña del Mar, we visited a man with a mystifying smile who stood in the garden in front of the Museum of Archeology and History. He was one of only two carved stone figures from

Easter Island that had been removed from the island. He faced the main avenue and seemed out of place as we stood next to him wondering what his purpose had been and how he had traveled so from home. It was this meeting that inspired us to go and visit the island.

Just after takeoff I read from a guidebook that combined two seemingly unrelated places, Chile in South America with Easter Island in the South Pacific. The flight was going to be a long one. More than 2500 miles from the Chilean coast, Easter Island is considered the most remotely inhabited place on earth. The island was first stumbled upon by Europeans on Easter Sunday in 1722 and christened Easter Island. The thousands of miles separating it from the nearest neighbor had allowed the inhabitants to remain in virtual seclusion for almost a thousand years, and with only two flights a week visiting the remote dot, they remained that way.

When the Europeans arrived on the island they found the inhabitants barely surviving in desperate squalor, yet there was evidence of a highly-developed society. Most outsiders who met the Rapa people believed they were incapable of creating the carved stone moai and the detailed writing on rongorongo tablets. The islanders had created legends around the items in their midst but they were unable to read the hieroglyphic scripts and could not explain how the massive moai were moved to their resting places. This was the mystery of the island. If not the pitiable inhabitants, then who created such an advanced culture?

We set up our tent in the damp back yard of a home in Hanga Roa, the only village on Easter Island, in pitch darkness at 1:30 in the morning. Minutes after we'd gotten comfortable in our little cocoon, the rain began. Not a normal rain, but a torrential downpour that hovered over our tent. It was just a sample of what we were in for in the days to come.

The next morning the sun beat down hard and the trapped humidity from the storm turned our tent into a glowing yellow sauna. Making toast and coffee in the kitchen of our *residencial* was Monica, a lean stockbroker in her early forties from Santiago, visiting the island for the first time with her mother, Lula, a plump, smiley woman. Neither Monica nor her mother could drive and they asked if we would share the cost of renting a jeep to explore the island. I was the chauffer, and Amanda, reading from our guidebook, became the navigator for our group.

At our first stop Lula stayed behind in the little four-wheel drive while we hiked around the quarry of Rano Raraku, the spot were the black stone moai were carved. The hundreds of statues held religious significance for the Rapa people and each was unique in a subtle way. As we turned a corner we came upon a half-finished sculpture carved into the black rock. Amanda and Monica rested in the shade, paging through the guidebook, while I climbed over the coarse volcanic boulders to look for more unfinished moai. When I returned Amanda said, "There were different clans on the island competing to carve the biggest and most beautiful moai."

"I wonder how they moved them," I said.

Monica said in Spanish, "I bought a DVD about the island. It said that they used logs to roll the statues."

I looked around and saw only black volcanic soil and patches of low green grasses. The hot wind blew hard across the low hills. "I don't see any trees," I said.

"Yes, exactly," Monica said. "They cut them all down. That's why they had to stop carving the moai. They had no way to transport them."

Amanda said, "And without trees they couldn't make the dug-out canoes they used for fishing, and they couldn't weave their nets."

As we walked back down the hill toward Lula, Monica said, "They didn't realize how dependent they were on the trees until they were all gone. They couldn't build their houses so they began living in the caves."

Bouncing around the island in the back of the Jeep, Monica explained to her mother what we had seen as we headed back to town.

That night the gale-force winds blew the rain up under the tarp of our tent. It dripped mercilessly, seeping into our sleeping bags, drenching everything, and we spent the night in a squishy puddle. Early the next morning we asked about a room at our *residencial*, which was full, so I went searching for an inexpensive hotel while Amanda wrung out our sopping wet sleeping bags. I found a room in a small guesthouse at a reasonable price and I met the owners, a Rapa couple, as they were enjoying a hearty breakfast on their patio. After a warm welcome they handed me the key to the room and didn't even mention payment.

In the tiny municipal market we purchased fruits and vegetables from a Rapa man who had his hair in a long, spiky top-knot, similar to those on the heads of the moai. One massive Rapa woman wearing a colorful tent-like sarong and exotic flowers in her hair was selling wooden rongorongo tablets etched with hieroglyphic writing. We were interested in the detailed work but she asked a price that was more than we wanted to spend. As we were leaving she offered, "You are about the size of my granddaughter. Would you like to trade for your jacket?" She pointed to the windbreaker Amanda wore around her waist.

Amanda had recently purchased it in Chile for a few thousand pesos, a couple of dollars, and asked the woman, "What would you consider a fair trade?"

The woman checked the zipper, then held up the jacket and could barely contain her excitement, "Well, the rongorongo and …" She looked around her stall. "I could give you this carved box and…"

I laughed and Amanda stopped her, "Oh no, thank you. The rongorongo is enough."

She smiled brightly and held the jacket up for the woman in the next stall. "But I must give you more. This is very valuable." She insisted on adding a little box, a shell necklace and a barrette to the bag to ease her conscience.

The next day, bumping around another remote corner of the island, we showed Monica and Lula the rongorongo tablet and told them the story of the trade. As we hiked up to a group of moai a few hundred yards away Lula remained behind. When we returned she stood leaning against the jeep looking at the wooden tablet. "You know, I don't think there have been many trees on the island since Chile took over in 1888." She scanned the horizon and peered toward a few low shrubs that had the same grainy curves as the rongorongo. "Where do you suppose they got the wood to make this?"

She was right, of course. By trading for the tablet we encouraged someone to chop down one of the last remaining bushes on the island to create another knick-knack. Worse yet, we exchanged a piece of clothing, further pecking away their already diminished traditional attire.

The example of this tiny island showed the ugly character of unchecked human nature. The competition to build moai caused some long-dead islander to remove the last tree from his world. Somehow he failed to look past his present desire, ignored the consequence of his actions, and chopped down any hope for his future.

We left Rapa Nui disappointed at our own inability to learn a lesson, and worse, our ability to ignore one when convenient.

CHAPTER 30

A Dollar a Day

Con Con, Chile to Mendoza, Argentina
16,911 miles

Waiting for us in a gated area at the campsite outside Con Con was the van. It had been safely stored while we visited Easter Island. Not that we were concerned. Chile has one of the lowest crime rates in Latin America. Moreover, the country has enviable corruption statistics and is rated less crooked than Ireland. The police patrol the towns with large, intimidating German Shepherds, wearing heavy olive-green uniforms with brown leather cross-chest bandoliers and upward tilting hats.

Resembling Nazi SS commanders, they discouraged crime with their appearance alone.

We thanked the campground owner on our way out and he asked, "Which way are you going?"

"Up and over the mountains to Argentina," Amanda answered.

"Aah, be careful over there. It is very dangerous right now. They are having problems with their economy and there is lots of corruption. I had a customer here the other day who was stopped at a police checkpoint. When he walked over to the officer to show his papers a thief reached into his car and stole all his things."

In virtually every place we visited, the locals told us elaborate stories about the dangers of their neighboring country. It started in the U.S. with tales of *bandidos* in Mexico and continued in an unbroken string of catastrophic legends throughout the continents. Someone they knew would be doing something utterly innocuous "over there" and ended up tied to a lamppost naked or jailed for life, or both. Funny thing was, we never met the actual victim. It was always a distant relative, for some reason deadbeat uncles and estranged mothers-in-law were popular, and they were unquestionably innocent in this case despite the fact that they led otherwise dastardly lives. One of us would always ask the storyteller, "When was the last time you were there yourself?"

"Never, and I will never go," was the inevitable answer.

Leaving the coast, we sputtered up to Chile's central valley, remarkably similar to the central valley of California. Vineyards lined the road and the buds were sprouting on the vines. Most of the fields bloomed in neat rows of bright green while others remained a dormant dull brown, awaiting the nourishment of the summer sun to produce those plump, juicy grapes for the winter shelves of North American supermarkets.

Up further into the Andes, the road narrowed and we began seeing patches of late winter snow. As we ascended the Uspallata Pass the snow cover became deeper, at first a few inches, then a foot, until finally we were driving along in a narrow groove of white walls eight feet deep, carved out by snowplows. Ski lifts glided above as we drove through mountain tunnels and under a series of cement roofs. One famous section of the pass had a series of thirty-two hairpin switchbacks slowly stepping up the steep cliff. Ahead of us a truck had gone over the edge and had tumbled down to the next cut below, slamming into the road, leaving a furrow where it had somersaulted to a stop.

Amidst the heavy snow at the top of the Andes, the border post was one of the busiest crossings in Latin America. The Chilean officials were organized and moved us along through the paperwork process swiftly. As the immigration officer handed back our passports she said, "Be careful on the other side. The economic crisis has made people desperate."

"Did anything happen to you recently?" Amanda asked.

She scrunched up her face as if smelling something rotten, "No. I haven't been across in years. It's what I've heard."

Passing through a tunnel into Argentina, we drove to the border checkpoint inside a massive warehouse. The gloomy darkness made it feel even colder than outside but the Argentinean official, a jolly, hefty Nordic-looking woman made us feel welcome. Bundled up, she stood in a heated booth next to a pile of confiscated vegetables on a counter. We hoped our contraband would avoid a similar fate.

Learning the hard way, we discovered that border officials conveniently enforced laws and confiscated food items based on whims. Some neighboring countries had rivalries and seized provisions tit-for-tat, a game that left the unwitting traveler hungry. Hiding fruits and vegetables in the bottom of the clothing closet, wine and meat in the closed pop-top roof, and yogurt in the back of the tool cabinet, we prepared for the inspection. Having run out of hiding places, Amanda stood watching the guard thoroughly inspect the van, as she carried her backpack stuffed full of smuggled goods, cheese, apples, bell peppers and broccoli.

Hunched uncomfortably in the back of the van the woman began her search through our cabinets, then the closet and finally she lifted the lid that covered the stove and sink. Amanda diverted the guard's attention, "Looks like someone didn't know that they couldn't bring across vegetables," as she pointed to the pile of confiscated items.

The inspector supported her lower back as she carefully stepped out of the van. "Yes, a German cyclist. He left very angry a few minutes ago. He said he is a vegetarian and complained, 'Nobody told me I could not bring this across.'" A gleeful smile took over her face as she said, "But I told him it is in writing on the sign right there." A closer inspection revealed the vegetables to be a stack of dirty onions, carrots with the stems still on, a few potatoes, bruised tomatoes, and wilted lettuce. It looked like homegrown produce and the guard picked up the carrots as she chuckled, "He said he spends only one dollar a day, and this is his only food until he arrives in Mendoza. Imagine that! Lucky for him it is downhill."

We wondered if this was the elusive guy the Irish women in Baños had told us about. Could he have pedaled so far, so quickly? As she stamped our exit papers I asked, "If we follow the road will we pass him?"

"There is no other way."

We watched for the lone cyclist pedaling along the narrow road. The entire landscape was covered in snow and everything stood out in the bright arctic white, yet somehow we did not see him.

The road danced down the mountain in slow, winding curves, with a turbulent river leading the way. Half expecting the city of Mendoza to be in chaos with demonstrators blocking the streets protesting the government's economic policies, we were pleasantly surprised when we drove through the city center. The area was alive with activity. Residents enjoyed the sidewalk cafés along the wide avenues, kids skated in the impeccable stately parks, and business people bustled between the elegant office buildings.

The massive municipal park had a campground in lush surroundings with good facilities, and we found it virtually empty. The supervisor, a friendly older man wearing overalls and rubber boots, came out of the restroom to greet us with a mop in one hand and a pail in the other. He told us to pick any spot and followed the van as we parked in a sunny place on the edge of a grassy field. He watched with amazement as we popped up the roof. "Where is this van from?"

I stood outside while Amanda organized within. "It was made in Germany but we purchased it in the United States."

He poked his head into our living space and Amanda gave him the grand tour: the pop-top bed, the kitchen sink and stove, the swiveling passenger seat. With each new discovery he laughed with amusement. "This is amazing. Where are you going with it?"

"To Buenos Aires next, then to Brazil and finally south to Patagonia," I answered.

He tilted his head and raised his brow, "You must be careful in Buenos Aires. They are like animals there. They will kill you for your hat."

"When was the last time you were there?" Amanda asked.

"Well, I've never been there, but I see on television the protestors and the trouble. Our economy is a disaster, you know. The corruption is everywhere. People think only fools pay taxes because the politicians are all thieves. In the capital they are like rats fighting one another for every little scrap. You must be careful there."

Perhaps a little too confidently I said, "We drove through Ecuador and Peru to get here. I'm sure we'll survive the richest city in Latin America."

CHAPTER 31

Half a World Away

Buenos Aires, Argentina
17,807 miles

Splurging in Buenos Aires, we prepared to celebrate our first anniversary on the road, a day that also happened to be our wedding anniversary, by staying at a nice hotel. Amanda found a small stylish place with old-fashioned elegance that was not far from Plaza Dorrego.

Behind the reception desk stood a jolly, rosy-cheeked old man. His well-rounded physique gave him a presence that would otherwise be lacking in someone of his stature. He was tastefully dressed, with a tiny scarf tied neatly around his neck in a tight knot. His wife, a much younger, bulging woman who spoke with a Slavic accent, leaned on the small table in the center of their living room, just behind the reception area, as she lit a cigarette. A worn antique couch positioned in front of the muted television looked as if their entire life's story could be read in the tattered, discolored fabric. The old man jiggled as he led us up the stairs and through a narrow hallway covered in faded, fraying Persian rugs thrown haphazardly on the wooden floor. Our room at the end of the hall was surprisingly ornate, with just enough space for a diverse collection of furniture which included an antique desk squeezed in the corner with a television set on it. Our only window provided much-needed light plus a view overlooking bustling San Telmo. Perfect for the romantic occasion.

Strolling around the neighborhood, browsing through the old, elegant homes transformed into antique shops and trendy art galleries, we checked out some of the quaint little restaurants along the plaza. To celebrate our anniversaries we chose one to enjoy a candlelit dinner and a nice bottle of wine the following evening.

The residents of Buenos Aires are notorious throughout Latin America as the Parisians of the continent. They are considered arrogant and snobbish by their neighbors. I had heard the cliché, "They consider themselves European", so often from other Latin Americans that I assumed they were jealous.

An old man with an elegant jacket, hat and cane off the shelf of a 1950s men's store, first caught my attention. I actually slowed to look at him. His jacket was worn at the fringes but neatly pressed and patched. His hat showed the sweat stains of many years on the same head but he sauntered along as if he was royalty, jauntily swinging his cane and refusing to yield the sidewalk even partially to oncoming walkers. Then a woman in her late forties clicked past us with her nose high in the air. Her massive helmet of hair and worn dress were straight out of the television series, Dynasty.

Early the next morning we were eager to begin celebrating. While sipping coffee on the rooftop patio we watching the neighborhood come to life. After breakfast Amanda fought to get hot water in the shower while I waited, clicking through the channels on the television. I found Paula Zahn and Aaron Brown of CNN standing in an unusual place, the rooftop of their studios in New York City, speaking in the slow, deliberate voice that television newscasters use when they've got a big story but no details. They switched back and forth, Paula looking a little flustered when it was her turn to tell the billions of viewers all over the world that smoke was billowing from one of the towers of the World Trade Center. I yelled for Amanda to forget the shower and come watch. The newscasters said it could have been a small plane but they were not sure. A blur across the sky and then boom, the second plane came crashing in. We watched live on CNN half a world away.

Never in my life had I experienced such a swing of emotion. Distraught sickness filled me. New York airports were shut down, the tunnels closed. Minutes later all U.S. airports closed, never before in history. Then Paula and Aaron held their earpieces and silently listened for a moment. Paula got redder, visibly disturbed. The Pentagon. We sat frozen in front of the television. The President in Air Force One, the crash in Pennsylvania, hundreds of miles from my family in Philadelphia, yet close enough. I wanted to vomit. I didn't believe it could get any worse, but it did. Washington evacuated. The South Tower collapsed, part of the Pentagon caved in, the North Tower peeled apart from the top.

After having watched the footage over and over by late afternoon, I pushed myself to venture downstairs and pay for another night. The old man's TV blared loudly, the images of the tumbling towers, the roar of cement and steel crumbling, people screaming, the sound so unbelievably loud I had to fight back the urge to break into sobs. My hands trembled as I pulled the money from my wallet. The old man looked me dead in the eyes and nodded his head back toward the television as slow-motion footage showed people diving to their death, that squealing gerbil sound deafeningly loud as the local newscast rewound the footage and showed it again. He mumbled, *"Lo siento."* (I'm sorry.) I tried to thank him but couldn't get my throat to open, couldn't get the words out.

By night-time my sadness had changed. The shock was fading, overtaken by a dark fury. Outrageous scenarios of revenge played out in my head. Nothing was too extreme. My frustration mounted, furious to be so far away, and disheartened by the realization the even back in the U.S. there was not much we could do. But still there was the desire to burn off the rage.

Groggy from a horrible night's sleep of tossing and turning, I immediately clicked on the television as soon as I opened my eyes the next morning. Switching between CNN and the local news, I caught an announcement from the Buenos Aires station about a hastily arranged interfaith prayer service at the obelisk to be attended by the President, Fernando de la Rua, and the head of every religious organization in the country. Feeling the desire to do something, we decided to attend the ceremony and left our hotel room hours before it was scheduled to begin. The downtown pedestrian mall, Calle Florida, was crowded with working people out for their daily lunch break. Most stores and restaurants had television sets tuned to the news and clusters of locals were gathered at each TV, curiously mesmerized. It was difficult for us not to stop and watch for fear that something new might have happened.

Awareness of our surroundings faded in and out as we walked the downtown streets, and our minds wandered. My thoughts were scrambled and confused. As we passed people on the street, I stared into their faces and sensed they were unconcerned about what had happened. It had no effect on their lives. Pounding the pavement, down the wide avenues, plunging into streets bounded by high-rise buildings, looping around traffic circles one street at a time, we walked in a daze toward the obelisk. Deep in discussion, we asked each other the same questions over and over, trying to make sense of it all. "How could this have happened?" "Who was involved?" "Will there be other disasters?"

We walked along the edge of a park with massive statues, a man on bucking horseback, another hunched, contemplating a book. Then I felt something on my back. Two local women came up from behind and one said, "Oh look, you've gotten bird droppings all over you." But Amanda had some on her back, too. It looked and smelled like mustard. It didn't make sense. The women brought out tissues and offered to help us wipe it off, but instinctively I knew something was wrong. "They're thieves!" I said to Amanda in English.

She stared at me in disbelief, "They're just trying to help."

The women insisted on wiping Amanda's back and their fidgeting fingers pulled at the zippers of her backpack. It was then she realized that I was right.

I yelled, "Get away! Get out of here!" and pushed them aside.

A taxi skidded up on to the sidewalk and the back door flew open. The women bolted, jumping head first into the seat as the driver screeched away.

Amanda searched for the police but realized it was pointless. We got napkins from a vendor and cleaned the mustard from our clothing as we sat on a park bench. This was the first time on the entire trip anyone had tried to rob us.

That night Amanda's family back in Tijuana saw us on television on the international Spanish language network Univision. The camera panned in and showed a close up of my intense face listening to the speeches of the assembled clergy. The story focused on how Argentineans were sharing in the pain of the American people. They played a sound bite from the President of Argentina saying, "We, the people of Argentina, share the pain of the people of the United States." They showed a priest and a Muslim cleric saying much the same thing in different words. The report did not broadcast what I saw. They didn't show the groups holding massive peace signs that read, "We are here to support peace, NOT the United States of America." They didn't show what I heard from the crowd, "The United States has meddled too much and now they are seeing the results." They didn't show the chanting, "Peace yes, U.S. no". They didn't play the full sound bites that ended with, "...but now we encourage America to turn the other cheek." I didn't think it possible, but I was even more furious.

On the way back to the hotel I remembered an article I had read a few weeks before about the decaying Argentinean economy, the peso poised to devalue, and the U.S. leading a movement in the IMF to offer a loan package bailing them out. I didn't remember the details but the thought made me even angrier.

The people we passed walking along the street suddenly seemed to be caught in their own personal time warps, wearing the attitude and feigning the appearance of their country's former glory. Normally I would not have cared, but now I wanted to laugh out loud. I wanted to rub their faded, gaudy elegance in their faces. A woman about my age tried to pass us and gave us a condescending look that said, "You know, these pants are Sergio Valenti." Their corrupt economy was in the sewer once again. I took pleasure in observing the outward symbols, the crumbling streets, vacant buildings, expensive cars from another time belching smoke, pawn shops, and overly made-up women selling cigarettes on the street corners.

That night we switched off the television early. The day before the attack I had been thoroughly engrossed in a new novel. But that evening I could not concentrate. I read the same paragraph over and over. When I got to the end of a page, about to turn to the next, I realized I was just moving my eyes. I couldn't focus.

I turned to Amanda, who was half asleep, and said, "What are we doing half-way around the world with all this going on?"

She was quiet for a moment then said, "Do you think we should go home?"

"I don't know," I said. "If we don't go home, will it be safe for us to continue?"

She sat up in bed, propped the pillow behind her back and said, "We could put the van on a ship here and send it back to the East Coast or we could put it in storage and fly home."

I was ready to do something rash, anything, just so I had the feeling I was doing something. Amanda sat quietly and listened, then suggested, "Tomorrow we can go to the American Embassy. Why don't we give ourselves a day to think about what we'll do next." We had seen footage on television of U.S. Embassies around the world inundated with flowers, cards and gifts.

The next morning we walked along Avenida Alcorta toward the U.S. Embassy. The walk did us good. It felt good to finally be doing something, no matter how small and inconsequential. Our hearts beat faster with anticipation as we approached the embassy. From a distance we could clearly see the American flag flying at half-mast, proudly waving against the gray, gloomy sky. We were looking forward to being surrounded by others like us, people who could understand what we were feeling. Then the building came into full view. There was no one around. No flowers. No cards. Not one token of support anywhere on the sidewalk or along the gate. The only evidence of a change was the grim metal barrier positioned around the building. We stood there staring up at the curtained windows.

Dispirited, we wandered in circles and ended up on Avenida Brown walking toward La Boca, an old neighborhood of brightly colored tin houses. At the corner of Brown and Paseo Colon we paused to check the map. A middle-aged woman walked quickly past and squirted mustard on our backs. Another much younger woman approached pretending to help wipe it off while a guy stood nearby and watched. They had no way of knowing the accumulated frustration and fury that had built up within us over the previous days and, unfortunately, placed themselves in a position to experience the brunt of it.

I immediately grabbed the young woman in a bear hug and Amanda ripped her purse from her hand. The young woman screamed and a group of locals at a bus stop were shocked but they all stared and did absolutely nothing. Her accomplice inched his way forward so I raised a fist, holding the woman with one arm and he backed away. Amanda went through her purse and pockets, looking for identification, while I held her tight. She had nothing. We both yelled "*POLICIA*" over and over as loud as we could. A taxi screeched up to the curb and I turned the woman away from it. Another young man came at me from behind so I let go of the woman and she darted toward the cab. She jumped in and the driver, who was obviously involved, began to speed away. I barely got hold of her arm as the door was closing. The driver jammed on his brakes to keep her from being torn from the car. I turned to deal with the young guy. Amanda jumped into the cab, holding the woman by the arm. The young guy backed away again and I turned toward the cab. The woman kicked at Amanda and hit her hard on the shoulder, then again on the chest. Amanda held one hand on the doorframe and reached in, knotting the woman's hair in a fist and holding it firmly. The woman continued to fight. I watched in amazement as all one hundred pounds of Amanda repeatedly bashed the woman's face into her knee. She screamed and I yelled, "Amanda, STOP!" I rushed over and together we held her, partially in and partially out of the cab.

The first cop bolted across the busy street and came straight for the cab, reaching for his gun. We both backed away, holding our hands in the air. The driver jumped out and threw his hands on the roof of the car. We stepped further back, pointing toward the woman. She tried to get out the other door and the cop reached in and grabbed her. Police came from all directions and we pointed at the group of accomplices who were trying to get away. The woman screamed hysterically, "They attacked me! They attacked me!" The few people at the bus stop were not sure what had happened and were reluctant to get involved. Her accomplices turned away when they saw the police converging. It was utter confusion. A dozen police circled the scene. The woman held her face in her hands, crying uncontrollably. The young guy and the middle-aged woman pointed at us, "It was them. They did it." The taxi driver agreed.

Things were looking bad. The officer in charge, a lazy-eyed older man pulled Amanda and me away from the group. He gruffly demanded to see identification. We gave him our passports and he walked away, handing them to a junior officer who read our details into his radio. He walked over and questioned the accomplices, then called several of the officers together and conferred for a few minutes. He and another officer came toward us. He returned our passports and said, "You better get out of here, take a taxi." The young woman saw him give back our passports and screamed, "They attacked ME don't let them go!"

The older officer smiled at her and said, "Dear, in all my years as a police officer I've never seen a tourist attack a local." He blocked traffic as we crossed the street, then stopped a cab and negotiated a price. The cabby agreed and we were on our way.

In the tranquility of our hotel room I realized I was no longer furious. I was still angry at what had happened in the U.S., and mad about the stupidity of the Argentineans, but my fury was gone. I no longer felt helpless. Fighting back gave me the feeling that I had finally done something - Something extremely stupid, but something.

I knew the police probably took a bribe from the crooks and let them go. I knew the Argentineans, would go on blaming America for all their problems. I knew it was silly to fight with a group of petty thieves for squirting mustard on my back and trying to rob me, even though I really hate mustard. I knew, but I didn't care. Amanda and I had done something, fought back, hadn't just lain down and taken it. I had satisfied my overwhelming need to take action. It felt good.

CHAPTER 32

White Man's 'Fro

Paratí, Brazil
19,616 miles

Living in the van in tropical showers was no picnic. At night when it rained we were forced to zip closed the opening on the pop-top roof tent to keep out the pounding drops. The sleeping area grew oppressively hot and our only relief came from a portable 12-volt fan that blew the clammy air around in circles, making the stifling bed just a fraction more bearable.

A few days of this and the inside of the pop-top sprouted a gray fuzzy mold. Like a clean freak Michelangelo, Amanda lay on her back with rubber gloves, bleach, and a sponge, scouring the inside of the roof raw.

We hung our wet laundry inside the van but it absolutely refused to dry. The only way we could free ourselves from the constant wetness was to remain in motion. When driving, a current of air streamed in through the jalousie windows, catching everything in a whirlwind, fluttering the moist clothing and swirling gusts into the damp corners.

The moment we crossed the border into Brazil it began to rain non-stop for an entire week. The rainy season was supposed to begin in November but that year it arrived early. As we approached the coast the showers turned to drizzle, which eventually subsided altogether. When the sun broke out, so did the Brazilians, emerging from their homes wearing an unimaginable collection of exotic and revealing clothing.

The historic port of Paratí was at the end of the old mule trail that connected the gold mines in the interior of Brazil with the Portuguese ships that once carted the valuable cargo back to Europe. When the rail line opened between the inland mines and the port at Rio de Janeiro, the town of Paratí shriveled up over night. It remained virtually uninhabited for hundreds of years until recently. We found the colonial town vibrant. The renovated homes along the cobblestone streets were converted into quaint restaurants, artists' studios, and stylish artisans' shops. Steps from our campground was a lush tropical beach with a magnificent ocean view.

While we traveled Amanda would regularly cut my hair and kept my appearance respectable, but in the coastal town of Paratí I decided to treat myself to a real haircut and searched out a *barbearia*.

The young black barber spoke Portuguese so I peppered him with a combination of Spanish, English and charades to explain how I wanted my haircut. He lifted his brow in a cock-eyed expression that said, "I'm not touching your head until I understand what you want." I glanced around the shop at the magazine pages taped to the walls showing black men with various lines and designs etched in very short hair. Reaching for a magazine, then a second and third, I found they featured photos of young trendy black Brazilians, none of whom had anything close to a regular white guy haircut.

With the barber looking over my shoulder I reluctantly settled on a photo of an older black man with a slight afro and tried to use it to explain the length I wanted. I pointed to the afro, then held my thumb and forefinger about an inch apart, moving them around my head to show the length.

The barber took the magazine from me and gave the photo a long look, then held it up to show the group of men lounging in the seats. He said something in rapid-fire Portuguese and they all burst out laughing.

One guy stood and took the magazine from the barber, holding it next to my head, comparing how the hairstyle would look on me. The other men fought back tears of laughter, and one laughed so hard he began laugh-coughing, then coughing uncontrollably, then choking on his coughs.

I gave up and pointed to the barber's hair, saying, *"Corto, como usted."* (Short like yours.) The audience was disappointed that I would not be leaving with an afro but watched the whole process with great intent. The barber chopped away with his electric trimmer and left me with exactly what I had requested, a practically bald dome with just a hint of fuzz to cover my sparkling white scalp. It took some getting used to, but I soon realized the remarkable practicality of the haircut. I could wash it with any soap, there was no need for a comb, and it was easy to explain in any language.

After the haircut I walked to the small municipal market. Opening early each morning the market closed once the fishermen had sold their catch of the day. I was attracted to the mounds of shrimp the size of lobsters and bought more than a kilo for a dollar. When I arrived back at the campsite Amanda was a bit shocked by my new appearance and said, "You should have told me. I could have easily done that for free."

That night we had one of the finest and simplest meals of the trip, a heaping mound of mouthwatering grilled shrimp. As the sun was setting we were lured by the sound of a strumming guitar to one of the beach bar huts. After a few caipirinhas, a Brazilian drink made from fresh lime-juice and pinga, a fermented sugar cane, we relaxed into the comfortable wicker chairs while listening to the young amateur and his friends belt out Brazilian love songs, lamenting the end of another perfect day.

CHAPTER 33

Grandma's Thong Bikini

Rio de Janeiro, Brazil
19,945 miles

Approaching Rio de Janeiro from the south along the coastal road, we stopped at Barra de Tijuca, a long stretch of beach in the suburbs of Rio with a Camping Clube do Brazil campground. The paved footpath along the beach began at the gate of our campsite and wound past Ipanema and Copacabana, practically to the foot of the Sugarloaf Hill.

The beachfront camp was a paradise and enticed us to settle in and stay. Early each morning we ran along the ocean path, joining the throngs of athletes, weightlifters, walkers, skaters, and cyclists. Men stopped at the edge of the path for fifty pushups and I caught Amanda's wandering eyes checking out their scanty shorts. Women power-walked while curling foam-coated weights. Tanned models played volleyball with intense concentration, smashing and spiking the ball with passion. Surfers, parasurfers and boogie boarders fought for space in the waves.

The vibrant energy and colorful personality of Rio is unmistakable, especially in the women. Confident, bold, boisterous, and full of life, the women of Rio stood in jaunty pose, pointing in the faces of their boyfriends and laughing with their heads thrown back. There were no wilting flowers, no middle road. At the supermarket we saw a woman strolling the aisles with her granddaughter, the pair wearing nothing more than thong bikinis. And they both looked good. Big or small, dark or light, shaven or not, the women of Rio let it all hang out with chin-up pride.

With the sun barely peeking over the horizon on Saturday mornings the beaches were already packed full. These sun-worshipers brought with them every necessity for an entire weekend, grills, tents, coolers, boom boxes, and a change of clothing, transforming the beaches into a massive party.

Being in constant motion was draining and when we discovered a place like Rio that made us feel alive, we gladly set up camp and savored the moment. If not for the return of the rain and days of sticky dampness we might never have left the surf and sand of Barra de Tijuca.

CHAPTER 34

The Little Cripple

Ouro Preto, Brazil
20,340 miles

We had run out of drinking water. Normally we would purchase a 22 liter-bottle of filtered water to fill the tank in the van but in Rio we discovered that if we gradually built a resistance to the different minerals and organisms we could drink the local water supply straight from the tap.

In the city of Ouro Preto I asked the gardener at the campsite, "Is this water good for drinking?".

He seemed to understand and replied in Portuguese, *"Sim. Pois nao?"* (Sure. Why not?), and nodded. I made a few trips between the tap and the van, filling our portable container, then using it to fill the tank beneath our sink.

A few days later we woke to a morning mist, and made our way through the winding, steep cobblestone streets and narrow alleys of Ouro Preto. Amanda complained about an upset stomach that had been lingering since the previous morning, so we wandered into the Igreja São Francisco de Assis and sat down to rest for a few moments as we eavesdropped on an English-speaking tour group.

The guide broke into a passionate speech, obviously enjoying the dramatic effect of his voice echoing between the carved stone walls, "He used his hammer and chisel to chop off his own fingers. He was in such agony." The guide spread his arms wide and continued, "Imagine the pain Aleijadinho must have felt to cut off his own fingers. A sculpture! Unable to use his hands, they strapped the tools to his wrists so he could create the wood and sandstone masterpieces. His crippling disease made walking impossible so he had a team of slaves carry him from place to place around his subject."

Ouro Preto is the capital of the mountainous region of Minas Gerais and is saturated with Portuguese colonial architecture. Using the Minero Baroque style, buildings and churches are designed with richly painted interiors, cedar woodcarvings and spectacular soapstone sculptures. The wealth of the city came from its gold, much of which was used to lavishly decorate the churches.

While sitting in a pew I whispered to Amanda, "You know we bought that medicine in Mexico. Do you want to go back to the van and take it?"

She held her stomach, "How do you know what I have?"

"Well," I said sheepishly, "this morning I looked in the medical book and the symptoms seem just like giardia, a parasitic…"

"Oh no you don't. Every time you read that book you think we have some absurd disease."

"No, but…"

"No. Stop," she said abruptly. "I'll deal with this myself.".

I knew what she was thinking but this case was different.

Getting sick at home is a condition we all despise, but it's bearable. While on the road even the most insignificant illness can become an ordeal. Our constant motion only complicated matters more. Moving from one climate to another while eating strange foods, and perhaps some unclean fruits and veggies, we exposed our bodies to unfamiliar germs. By subjecting our systems to all sorts of microbes, enduring the illnesses, then overcoming them, we convinced ourselves that our bodies would build a resistance. Any future exposure, the theory went, would shorten the duration of an illness or enable us to fight it off altogether. Often Amanda would stubbornly take this belief to the extreme.

"It'll never go away unless you take the medication," I blurted before she could interrupt me.

"I don't want to take any drugs!" she said a little too loudly. Her voice bounced off the walls. The guide hesitated in his speech and two blue-haired ladies from the tour turned to look at us suspiciously.

We stopped arguing and the guide continued the story of Aleijadinho (the little cripple), one of the most remarkable stories in the history of art. The son of a slave and a Portuguese architect, he is considered the mulatto Michelangelo and is credited with a massive body of work as both a sculptor and an architect. Stricken with a debilitating disease, perhaps syphilis or arthritis, he is said to have overcome this disability with monumental determination, becoming one of the most celebrated Brazilian artists.

Back when Aleijadinho was at his most prolific, the miners of Ouro Preto were extracting great wealth from the earth. Many illustrious travelers, writers, and artists visited Brazil, curious to see the results of this prosperity first-hand. They chronicled their observations in letters, publications, and the leading journals of the time. Curiously, there was no mention of Aleijadinho. A sculptor and architect unable to use his hands, yet not one visitor of the time referred to him. He was not discussed as a curiosity for his talent. He was not mentioned in passing whisper for his deformities. He was not alluded to as a brilliant mulatto. Nothing.

There are some skeptics who have suggested that the story of Aleijadinho was invented by the Brazilian government to mold and shape a new Brazilian identity. The passionate tour guide, voice echoing in the church with his arms outstretched, wanted to believe the story. International art collectors and national museums chock-full of Aleijadinho's work wanted to believe. The people of Ouro Preto wanted to believe. Brazilians wanted to believe. With so much invested in this inspiring story everyone wanted it to be true.

It is often easy to criticize the flaws in others that you wish to ignore in yourself. I wondered which of the many legends I hold true, stories designed to build a national culture and to guide people, are actually facts sculpted to serve ulterior motives.

A few days after Amanda's symptoms cleared I woke with horrible stomach cramps and diarrhea. Hopeful that it was a one-day thing I waited to see if my body could fight it. When I woke the next morning with the same symptoms I gave in to the temptation of the simple solution, popped a few Metrodiazole pills, and the giardia infection disappeared immediately.

So much for that theory.

CHAPTER 35

Tropical Windshield Wipers

Arraial da Ajuda, Brazil
21,422 miles

The green, shrub-covered peaks disappeared among the morning haze as the road weaved along the valley floor through steep coffee plantations. An old man riding on a cart with his young grandson plodded along at the pace of his slow-moving burro and blocked trucks from passing. For a hundred kilometers the road was perfectly paved, then abruptly disintegrated into an ancient, pot-holed path, only to return to a stream of clear black asphalt. Trucks trudged up hills so slowly that the van bogged down and stalled in first gear. When reaching a peak they accelerated with wild abandon, making it impossible to pass on the few straight stretches. Small new Fiats sped around and caused the vehicles coming in the opposite direction to slow and flash their lights.

A constant rain of large, pounding drops poured down, filling the gully along the roadside with dull red-brown muddy water and giving the air the damp stench of a summer storm. The drops evaporated when they landed on the hot asphalt, creating a hazy steam that misted the windshield. Turbaned, chocolate-brown mothers balanced large bundles on their heads and walked with children along the muddy roadside. Men rode long distances on bicycles, drenched to the bone, to work with machetes and hoes in the never-ending struggle to keep the dense green tropical vegetation from taking over the roadway. Others gathered in small groups out in the open, squatting together, talking and laughing, oblivious to the incessant downpour that soaked them.

Like food and shelter, rain is one of the most basic elements in the life of the Bahian people. Even though little clothing is worn, each family spreads hundreds of freshly washed T-shirts, shorts, and underwear on the barbed wire fence, in a faint hope that the god of rain will mercifully grant, if not today then tomorrow or the next, a full day of sun. The fast-moving, gray-silver sky, the deep dark puddles of mud surrounding the homes, the clouds of mosquitoes, and the never-ending dampness, all seemed to go unnoticed.

The windshield wipers in the van finally gave out after several long days of constant use.

In the tiny beach town of Arraial da Ajuda, we rented a small, colorful cabana overlooking the sea, with a comfortable white cloth hammock strung on the porch and a mosquito net hung over the bed. At night the bats rattled around in the rafters while we struggled to understand the Brazilian TV news of Anthrax and Cipro, bombs and the Congress. Already news junkies, we turned into information zombies, listening to the half-understood Portuguese commentary while watching the images of war and fear. Every so often we tuned into the BBC World Service on our shortwave radio and received the most up-to-date news from a British perspective. The dropping of bombs, spattered with the results of the most recent Indian test cricket matches.

Arraial da Ajuda is one of a few hippie havens of Brazil. The modern day South American reincarnation of the unwashed, glassy-eyed 60s straggler sells handmade jewelry from purple velvet sheets as they twirl dreadlocks and ignore their children. In the evening they gather in gypsy-like troops at the outskirts of town and camp in the blissfulness of paupers. While they like to think of themselves as travelers who sell to perpetuate their lifestyle, they are actually traveling salespeople with a spiel as practiced as the best door-to-door hack of the 1950s. Just a glance in their direction unleashes an unstoppable sales routine.

Running on the beach each morning, we returned to enjoy a large breakfast of tropical fruits and yogurt. The bright orange papayas bruised easily but melted in our mouths like sweet butter. Juicy, messy mangoes and fuzzy green kiwi fruit were practically given away at the market. Ripe coconuts littered the ground as the hardworking caretaker trimmed the palms for the coming season, and we chopped at them, gorging on sweet coco water and the tender white flaky core.

I spent one morning dismantling most of the major components on the dashboard to get access to the windshield wiper motor. After a few hours of struggling I finally removed it and found that the small plastic driving gear was stripped. Amanda glued it with Crazy Glue and let it set overnight. The next morning I put everything back together and gave it a try. The gear worked perfectly without the wiper blades attached, but once I screwed them in place the thing fell apart. I pulled everything out again and Amanda tried epoxy. Again, no luck.

We were determined to solve the problem using the tools and limited ingenuity we possessed. Many hours were spent lying in the hammock discussing creative ways we could repair the gear. Reading, then rereading the Volkswagen manual we devised absurd plans, "What if we drill a hole in the gear and insert the spoke of a fork?"

"We could drive a piece of inner tube into the hole to add friction."

"How about if we used this wire to tie around the outer edge?"

"What if we carved a new gear out of coconut shell?"

We refused to admit to each other what we both knew was true. We were trapped by something as simple as broken windshield wipers. The constant heavy rain and the narrow roads that offered no place to pull off for twenty or thirty kilometers, trapped us in paradise until it was fixed.

A few days later we made a dash for the parts stores about 100 kilometers away. Surviving a brief torrential downpour with near zero visibility, we arrived safely in the small town. The shop owner looked at the motor as if it was a piece from the Mars lander and said he did not have anything like it. Brazil continues to make a VW kombi virtually identical to ours. A lack of proper language skills kept me from asking the simple question, "Show me the mechanism in that van over there. The one that just passed." I pointed and muttered but the clerk looked at me as if I was from another planet.

After asking directions a couple of hundred thousand times, we found the VW dealer, who took one look at the part, consulted his computer screen and said *"Nao"*. If he had had a spittoon he would have spit in it. "Ain't got notin' like it here." It took several employees to explain in very slow and patient Portuguese that they had never seen this particular part. All agreed it was completely different from the one the Brazilian kombis use.

One of the many loungers around the shop perked up and spoke with hurried enthusiasm, making a windshield-wiper motion with his arms, not stopping between statements to see if I understood, which I did not. He went on and on and when he'd finished with his long, enthusiastic explanation, everyone agreed with frowning nods that it could solve my problem. At the end he realized I didn't understand, and started from the beginning, arms flailing like wipers, counting off the steps on his fingers. Finally, he looked up at the audience. Everyone nodded the look that said, "It might just work". Everyone but me. He shook his head, "Stupid foreigner can't understand simple Portuguese," and yelled at the guy behind the counter to throw him a knife. I followed him out the door and watched as he cut two pieces of twine from a packing crate. Tying one rope to each of our windshield wiper arms, he let them lie down in front of the van.

Palms up, I gestured, "What?"

He shook his head and flung his hand in a gesture that said, "Have I got to do it all for you?" Apparently he did. He passed one rope through the driver's window and another through the passenger's to Amanda, then did a little dance that looked like the twist.

It didn't dawn on me until he did the twist. Pull one rope to bring the wipers up, another to bring them down. Ingenious.

But that didn't fix the problem. The next logical step would have been to visit a junkyard and remove the entire mechanism from an old kombi, but mysteriously, junkyards do not exist in Brazil. Perhaps if old cars were left out in the constant rain they would not last long. Second hand parts stores fill in the gap. We visited one in Ilheus with a wide variety of parts from many different makes and models wrapped neatly in plastic, piled on long, dark shelves. I wandered the stockroom with the owner and found a similar wiper motor that looked like it would fit even though it wasn't exactly right. I took apart the broken one and removed the electrical plug, then connected the wires from the new one and screwed it together. Miraculously, it worked. Not so different after all. The owner of the parts shop was so excited he invited us to stay with his family, tour the city with him and spend the weekend fishing on his boat.

Few vehicles have the personality of an old Volkswagen. Look at one of those functional, unstoppable Beetles and you can't help but smile. It just makes you happy. Car companies try so hard to inject personality into their product but Volkswagen did the opposite, making it so utilitarian that the vehicle assumed the personality of the owner. It was a clean slate, open and simplistic, willing to become anything the owner wanted. Flower-power stickers only added to the luster.

That's the beauty of Volkswagens, perhaps the reason a company born from the maniacal brain of Adolf Hitler, the fussy engineering of Ferdinand Porsche, and the anal retentive German worker could spawn the hippie bus and Herbie the Love Bug. A simplistic design with interchangeable parts, a bomb-proof suspension, good gas mileage, and cheap, cheap, cheap. What more could the public want from the Volks Wagen, the German people's' car?

On the drive to Morro de Sao Paulo it didn't rain at all, but I turned on the windshield wipers every so often, just for the fun of it. When the wipers switched off they swept down past the lowest point and flung back up a few inches, settling somewhere near the middle of the windshield. But heck, it's one of those peculiarities that just adds character.

CHAPTER 36

Blood Suckers

Lençois, Brazil
21,984 miles

Massive, dirt-filled potholes concealed what was left of the road leading to the car ferry in Itacarica, across the bay from Bahia da Salvador. Just before arriving at the port we encountered one of the many police checkpoints that wait at most major intersections in Brazil. Generally the officers are polite and friendly, but this time we were not so lucky. In Portuguese the officer said, "Please produce your fire extinguisher." Spanish and Portuguese are similar languages and we found that when people wished to communicate there was little problem.

"We have two," Amanda said as she pointed to them.

"Your driver's license, please."

I handed over my California license and he smiled.

"In Brazil you must have an International Driver's Permit."

Amanda pulled it out of the glove box. His smile faded.

"And the title for the vehicle?"

"Got it."

"Customs entry paperwork?"

"Yes."

"Passport stamps?"

He went on and on, accumulating a pile of documents; passports, vaccination certificates, AAA card, proof of insurance. When he asked for some absurd item Amanda said confidently in Spanish, "Yes, it's right here," and produced a document from Nicaragua covered in official-looking stamps, which he accepted without question. Realizing he was getting nowhere with this game, he took the pile across the road to his car, then motioned for me to follow.

Sitting securely out of view from the other officers, he motioned to my feet and shook his head. I looked at my feet and shrugged questioningly. I was wearing the national footwear of Brazil, a pair of flip-flops. He underlined an infraction in his ticket book and pointed again to my feet, "It is illegal to drive while wearing those shoes. The penalty for the infraction is seven points."

I thought quietly for a moment, then repeated, "Seven points."

He paused and added with dramatic flair, "Of course, there is also a fine of 254 reals." ($85).

I stood quietly as the officer pretended to write out the ticket.

He broke the silence, "254 reals is a lot of money."

"Yes, it is," I agreed.

"A lot of money," he repeated. "Do you know how long it takes for a Brazilian police officer to earn 254 reals?"

"No, I do not," I said. I could see where this was going and tried to head him off. "As a guest in your country I have great respect for the laws and will never again drive while wearing these shoes." I looked down at the flip-flops as if it was their fault.

The officer doodled for a few moments, then smiled and wrote 100 on his notepad, "You can pay this and leave with a warning."

I did not hesitate and said firmly, "No, we do not want any problems, but thank you."

He insisted, "No problem, no problem. Don't worry." Then went on pretending to write up the ticket. After a few moments of silence he crossed out the 100 on his notepad and wrote 50. "All right, pay this and leave with a warning."

"Thank you, but we do not want any problems."

Again he doodled for a while. When he realized I was watching him draw curlicues on the back of his ticket book he tilted it away from my view and kept scribbling. I stood firm, quietly determined to leave without paying a bribe, and he finally sighed and smiled broadly. Passing the paperwork back to me he shook my hand, "Go, have fun."

Following me across the road he said goodbye to Amanda like a long-lost daughter, "Enjoy your stay in Brazil."

A gigantic tree provided shade to a swatch of dirt in the campground behind the church in the mountain village of Lençois. I imagined groups of kids playing soccer with a home-made ball on the well-worn yard but this day several adolescent boys mixed cement in a wheelbarrow, each waiting patiently for his turn to scoop up the wet paste as a man placed a large block of stone in the half-finished wall along the entryway. The boys showed more interest in us, and gave up their work to inspect the unfamiliar vehicle and its unusual occupants. Shyly watching from a few feet away, they picked their teeth with straw as we set up camp. The smallest boy scurried up the great tree with a machete and chopped at one of the many large green fruits the size of ripe watermelons that hung from it in clusters. When the fruit hit the ground it split open, and the boys picked at the innards with twigs, eating the prune-size white globs that made up the core. The outer shell was hard and green like a fresh coconut and had thousands of pointy bumps that made it difficult to handle. They invited us to taste one of the globs and I found it surprisingly sweet and bitter with a gooey, hard seed inside.

Returning to the ground, the boy with the machete looked into the tree with a malicious grin and pointed out some of the massive fruits hanging directly above the van. As they squatted around their strange treat we moved the van away, to the safety of a nearby mango tree.

The mosquitoes discovered us almost immediately. Attacking our ankles, the back of our necks, and any exposed skin, they took their minuscule samples of blood but left behind welts the size of quarters and a mighty, insatiable itch. Swarming the van, they rushed inside to find hiding spots in remote corners.

Brazilian mosquitoes can carry some nasty diseases like malaria, dengue and yellow fever. While we had gotten our yellow fever shots we knew there was no vaccination for malaria and no cure for dengue fever. Slathering on citronella, swallowing B12 tablets and secreting garlic breath for days, we learned that the only effective weapon to keep these nasty visitors at bay with N N diethyl-meta-toluamide, better known as DEET. DEET works extremely well but has a few annoying side-effects. Once spread on the body DEET caused a warm feeling all over, not the most pleasant thing in tropical heat. When I sprayed some on my arm, a misty droplet landed on my watch crystal and instantly ate away the face, leaving it with a permanently distorted haze. According to the package DEET is not harmful to skin, but will remove paint from a car.

Mosquitoes have risen to the challenge and devised creative strategies to circumvent the repellents we humans place in their path. Relentlessly, they search for the most obscure spot, under watchbands, between toes or on the bottoms of feet, where we failed to cover ourselves with the substance. While we slept they circled around inside the roof of the van like hungry buzzards, wise to the fact that with every passing hour the strength of the repellent waned, then they made their attack at three in the morning, when we were defenseless. Swarming in the shower stall, they waited for the DEET to wash off, then moved in for the kill. Even more effectively, they waited just under the rim of the toilet bowl, knowing there were places on our bodies where DEET could not be slathered. They were remorselessly maddening and could easily succeed in driving a sane person completely crazy.

Yet contrary to popular myth, locals are equally menaced by the mosquitoes. The boys, when they got near us, were attacked just as much as we were, and swatted just as much as we did.

Used to the bites, they ignored the itch, retained their sanity, and discreetly laughed at the welt-covered foreign people with their peculiar obsessions.

CHAPTER 37

Three Thankful Things

Bahia Blanca, Argentina
25,692 miles

Some say bad things come in threes. If a believer misplaces their house keys, then misses the bus, they begin to look out for the third thing to prove the theory correct. Amanda is one of these people. She is a little more fatalistic than most and invokes the three bad things rule long before the second one is on the horizon. In contrast, I do not have a superstitious bone in my body and believe that three bad things in a row happen only to those who want them to. When Amanda mentions it I just get angry. One day she was able to connect the dots between some interesting circumstances in an effort to prove me wrong.

While heading south out of the town of Blumenal in southern Brazil the van suddenly lost power and sputtered like a fifty-year-old tractor. I flipped open the engine compartment to find one of the spark plugs, still connected to the wire, flapping wildly. The van had been running poorly for weeks and we had assumed the cause to be the 60 octane Brazilian gasoline. Fearful that over-analysis of the problem might reveal a catastrophic situation, I accepted the simple explanation that the spark plug must have slowly worked loose, and I screwed a new one into place. The van purred like a kitten.

Crossing Uruguay in one day, we arrived in Montevideo just in time to load the van on the Buquebus car ferry over the Rio de la Plata and back into Argentina at the port of Buenos Aires. As we drove off the boat the sky opened with a hard downpour.

Rush-hour traffic bolted back and forth between lanes and we circled the city looking for highway 3 south toward Bahia Blanca. Once on the highway we drove until late at night, determined to put distance between us and Buenos Aires. Exhausted, we pulled into a spiffy new gas station, parked behind the modern convenience store, and fell sound asleep.

The next morning while listening to tango music on the radio we enjoyed a sunny drive across the pampas of Argentina. Amanda lazily turned to me and asked, "What day is today?"

I looked at my watch. "It's Thursday."

"What number?"

"The twenty-second."

She said with surprise, "I think today's Thanksgiving."

A few minutes later a bird the size of a large seagull with a bright red beak swooped down and splattered itself directly into our windshield. Both were shattered beyond recognition. The impact left a large indentation in the window with a web of veins spreading outward. The window had to be replaced.

Amanda didn't bring it up but I knew what she was thinking.

Just as we entered Bahia Blanca the spark plug I'd replaced so efficiently the day before blew out once again. This time when I tried to screw it in, the threads in the cylinder head stripped. The spark plug would not stay in the hole and without it the van made a deafening sputtering sound and had very little power. Dealing with one problem at a time, we parked the van on a side street and walked around the neighborhood searching for a windshield repair shop or a garage.

As we walked, Amanda seemed uncharacteristically guarded and then she began, "You know, that was the second..."

"Don't even think..." I stopped her, a bit too abruptly.

The search around the neighborhood proved fruitless, so we walked to the nearest hotel, asked for the telephone book, and called the windshield repair shops in town. Only one stocked the windshield we needed and they were able to replace it immediately. Putting the search for the mechanic on the back burner, we hurried back to the van.

When we arrived we found the rear tire completely flat. Not just deflated but torn through the outer ply of the sidewall. It was the first flat of the trip.

In Mexico they have a saying, "*Lo unico que nos falta, es que nos mea un perro,*" which roughly translates to, "The only thing lacking is for a dog to pee on us." But that would be one too many, completely disproving the three-bad-things theory. Once the third thing revealed itself Amanda seemed oddly relieved.

As I replaced the tire with a spare it occurred to me that the three bad things did not actually happen to me. I was just along as a reluctant witness.

As the driver I considered the left side of the van mine, and the right Amanda's. The bird smashed her side of the windshield. The giant cracks stopping suspiciously close to the center, without extending to my region at all. The stripped spark plug hole was also on her side, and the flat tire, hers too. I nearly blurted it out, but then caught myself. I knew if I mentioned that she was to blame, then she would pounce. I imagined her voice as clearly as if she were saying it herself, "See, I knew you believed it!"

I kept my mouth shut and continued wrestling with the lug nuts.

Our fortune changed when we sputtered a few blocks to get the new windshield installed. When the workers removed the old one and tried to install the replacement, the glass was too big. Anywhere else in the world they would have apologized and sent us on our way but these Argentineans were real problem solvers. Grinding away with a special pad, they reshaped the edges, replaced the old rubber seal with a thinner one and pounded the glass in place. It was installed in less than an hour.

A couple of old men sitting outside their hardware store next to the windshield shop told us about their mechanic, an honest guy who was inexpensive. We drove the ailing van with its shiny new windshield to the garage. With a cigarette firmly clasped between his lips, the mechanic took the engine apart. Using a mirror and incredible contortions, he installed a heli-coil in the stripped spark plug hole. The van was back together, as good as new, by late afternoon.

With just enough time to drive from *gomeria* to *gomeria* (tire shop), we found a new tire, the same brand, for less than what we paid at home.

We collapsed that night in the parking lot of the local Wal-Mart where we slept in blissful exhaustion. While it was not our best Thanksgiving, we certainly had a lot to be thankful for that day in Bahia Blanca.

Of course, to Amanda's celestially superstitious mind, everything rounded itself out nicely. The three bad things were negated soundly by the three good experiences, and we drove southwest toward Patagonia feeling strangely fulfilled.

CHAPTER 38

Bank Run

San Carlos de Bariloche, Argentina
26,473 miles

Someone in Brazil went on a spending spree using the number from our Visa Card. Three charges totaling close to $900 were made on one day in a small city in Southern Brazil, but the transactions were dated more than a week after we had left the country. Paying for gas with the card one day, the attendant swiped, then re-swiped the card, but it came back declined.

Being without access to cash so far from home was unsettling. With a few travelers' checks and some U.S. dollars as backup, we were not completely destitute, but we relied on withdrawing cash from ATM machines as our primary source of currency.

In Argentina it was possible to use either the Argentinean peso or the U.S. dollar, but the post office would not allow us to pay the small cost of mailing a letter with a fifty-dollar bill. When one of the employees eagerly handed over a fifty peso note in exchange for the bill we knew something was peculiar. He held it up and showed the other employees and they all nodded as if he had made a good deal. Another clerk asked if we would like to change more money.

Heading toward the auto parts store to buy a battery in the town of San Carlos de Bariloche, we noticed hundreds of people forming an orderly line in front of a bank. Posted in the large plate-glass window was an advertisement for certificates of deposit offering accounts in either pesos or dollars, with the peso account paying nearly double the interest rate. Passing the same bank later in the day, we saw that the line had disintegrated into a pushing, shoving, desperate mob. The security guard pleaded with the people at the doorway, reminding me of Jimmy Stewart in *"It's a Wonderful Life"*.

That evening on the local radio station, commentators speculated that the President was about to sign a decree restricting the amount of withdrawals from bank accounts to $1000 per month. The next morning the government confirmed the rumors and unveiled the decree, causing terrified Argentineans to make a second run on the banks, cleaning out ATM machines.

The Argentinean economy was teetering on the verge of collapse, partially due to their adherence to an artificial exchange rate of one peso to one dollar. Over the past four years the dollar had grown increasingly stronger against most world currencies and Argentina decided to defend the peso while Brazil and Chile devalued their currencies.

Along the main street of Bariloche, the elegantly relaxed Argentineans in town for the holiday season gave the impression of being a million miles away from a country in crisis. Enjoying the trendy resort situated on the sparkling blue lake, they partied in their luxurious vacation homes snuggled in evergreen forest and snow-covered Andean peaks. Shopping in the posh alpine-style boutiques they purchased designer truffles, alpaca-knit sweaters and Swiss watches. With their arms full of packages, these Argentineans spent with the confidence that comes from knowing their wealth was protected from the chaos of the local banks. Their money was in dollars or euros, far away in international institutions. Most seemed insulated, aloof, disconnected from the financial troubles. But even in the wealthiest towns there are people of all income levels.

In North America we take many things for granted. Deposit money into a bank account, and we assume it will be there when we want it. The fluctuations of international currencies matter little to the average person. The dollar is the dollar, the mooring to which everyone else is tied. At the banks of Bariloche we witnessed the 1929 American stock market crash all over again. Desperately frantic people, shop clerks and housekeepers, teachers and librarians, pushing, shoving, and fighting to get their money. In the newspapers we read of its disintegration, on the radio we listened to it trickle away, but it was the impact of television that the fear, the hopelessness, the sickness in the pit of the stomach was most clearly seen. Argentineans watched as their dreams were evaporating.

Battling their way to the teller windows, they grasped bank statements like lifelines only to be told that they were slowly being cast adrift. The money was not yet gone but not there either, still in the account but slowly sinking beneath the surface.

Until that moment we had thought of ourselves as disconnected from the ugly side of money, far from the materialistic world, living in intimate self-sufficiency while roaming around in our Volkswagen van. The crisis in Argentina and the disconnection from our resources brought some clarity. We just assumed our money would be there when we popped the card in the machine. But what if it wasn't?

Amanda has experienced times in Mexico when the peso devalued and money evaporated. My parents told stories of my crazy great-uncle George who lived through the depression and buried money in the back yard because he didn't trust banks.

What if we went to the ATM one day and the balance read zero? Being in Argentina, we understood that this could happen anywhere. Those librarians and postal employees, teachers and housekeepers, desperate to get at their funds, made it all crystal clear. This could easily be us.

CHAPTER 39

Cloud Racing

Patagonia, Argentina
27,020 miles

Filling up with the last of our gas from one of the spare canisters attached to the back bumper, we turned on to the first stretch of paved asphalt road we'd seen for hundreds of kilometers. The van, like some ancient spirit, took to flight and began to chug along at seventy miles per hour. It had never gone seventy, not even down a mountain road when the motor was new. I lifted my foot from the accelerator, but the van continued along with little sign of slowing. Something had to be wrong. I gradually applied the brake and pulled to the side of the road, curious as to what could possibly cause the van to run better.

The force of the wind ripped the unlatched door out of my hand, whipping it open so hard that it hung out completely into the road. Gusting from behind, the wind shook our little world, and we worried about tipping over.

We had not seen another vehicle for more than an hour as we drove on the infamous, unpaved Route 40, and now that we had turned on to a paved section the prospects of seeing another person seemed just as unlikely. Route 40 runs along the Argentinean side of the Andes, down much of the length of the country through Patagonia, and is made with what the locals call *ripio* (rubble). This technique of road building is used in desolate parts of the world where the extreme temperatures and harsh environment wreak havoc on traditional forms of roadwork. Highway crews dig up natural deposits of stone and gravel and then pile it in one long flat stretch to create the road. The few passing vehicles flatten and compact the road surface as they drive. We were unlucky enough to cross some sections of newly-dumped road where the gravel, dust, and big rocks had not yet congealed into a solid form.

Over time, the dirt and gravel roads began to form corrugations on the surface, like waves that grew into ruts just a few inches apart. These rutted sections were tortuous. They ate away our tires, burned up our shock absorbers, jangled every nut, bolt, electrical connection, fuel line, and fastener, causing the van's most unexpected parts to wobble loose. It vibrated every fiber of our being, exhausting my arms and hands from gripping the steering wheel, rattling our teeth and numbing our butts. The dust was unbelievable, penetrating keyholes, cabinets, bedding, clothing, food, ears, and nose. At the end of one of these sections we looked like two doughnuts coated with powdered sugar. Each day after driving a *ripio* road I would spend an hour checking the connections, tightening bolts and replugging wires, while Amanda pulled everything out of the inside of the van, and swept, dusted, and shook the dirt off. One afternoon I found a loose shock-absorber. Another day the muffler hung on by a thread. Had a part fallen off, broken or failed in the middle of nowhere, with no traffic and little hope of getting to a town, it would not have been good.

When driving slowly on these corrugated roads we dipped into each of the ruts, then rolled over the high point, down again then up again, certainly easier on the car, but a thousand miles at ten miles an hour was out of the question. At mid-speed the wheels would dip to the low point in the ripple, then bang over the high point, killing the shocks and tires in the process. The only reasonable option was to drive like a madman. At high speed, over forty-five miles an hour, the tires jumped from the top of one mound to the next, skimming over the low points, minimizing the vibration at the expense of control. It felt like driving a boat. I would set a course in a particular direction and unseen factors would conspire against the steering. Suddenly the van would drift to the left or the right, ignoring my frantic wheel turning to the contrary. We drove down the center of the road to allow a margin of error. Every so often a car came in the other direction and we would slow down, moving as far to the right as possible to avoid being hit by flying rocks. The truck drivers didn't care, and operated at full speed, throwing rocks that pinged and dented the van and glanced off the windshield. A few foolish drivers tried to pass us from behind, but our cloud of dust made them invisible. They would honk and flash their lights but the rumble of our tires would often drown out their horns. Roaring past in their company-cars and transport trucks, they waved fists and yelled into the abyss, kicking up rocks.

Patagonia was a place I wanted to love. Sitting in my tiny cluttered office at work reading travel brochures, I had pictured it as a wild, windswept, rugged, no man's land. A site where only the most daring and hardy go to carve a life for themselves.

Driving hundreds of miles through the barren landscape, with rubble roads and hurricane force winds, the romanticism soon faded. I realized that this could only be a place inhabited and loved by those escaping life, without any other option.

I had read that the Welsh, the first European settlers of Patagonia, came here to flee England's imposing pressure to abandon their culture and language. In an effort to preserve their identity, they chose the end of the world as their new settlement. They were duped into believing that their destination was similar to their homeland. These pioneers were sadly disappointed. Lacking food, water, and a means to make shelter, they set out to overcome the obstacles. Their grit paid off, as the descendants of the daring few now thrive in this wilderness area by herding sheep and farming resilient crops.

Once thrown into this unique world I was resolved to drive to the end of the earth, and my displeasure soon changed as I found Patagonia hypnotizing. It had its moments that far exceeded my expectations. It possessed natural wonders that could only be seen here. Despite the pounding wind and lack of vegetation we saw a remarkable variety of wildlife in this seemingly uninhabited wilderness. Massive rhea, ostrich looking birds, blended into the tumble-weed setting, invisible until they flapped their flightless wings and trotted away.   Bright pink flamingos picked through the shallow, milky green lakes that dotted the roadside and awkwardly bumped into one another as they took to the air when we roared past. Armadillos scattered confusedly across the road, then stopped in the middle, curling into a ball that forced us to swerve. The guanaco, similar to a baby giraffe without stripes, lazily turned to watch as we passed, then fled haphazardly when we stopped. Grazing on the open range, seemingly thousands of miles from anywhere, there were sheep, freshly sheared with their lambs beside them, scurrying to get off the road.

One sunny afternoon we drove along at our normal pace of forty-five miles per hour and realized the clouds were moving just a little faster than us in the same direction. We watched in the rear-view mirror as a shadow raced across the flat plain, engulfing us in its momentary darkness, then speeding ahead to leave us in a wake of sunshine and blue skies. We entertained ourselves with this cloud racing for over an hour until the road took a slight bend and the wind no longer blew in our direction.

CHAPTER 40

The Fortune Teller

Ushuaia, Argentina
28,286 miles

Arriving well before the ferry departure in Punta Arenas, we found the small loading dock surprisingly congested. After spending three blissful days in the tranquility of Torres del Paine National Park we were heading south across the Magellan Strait to Tierra del Fuego. We made a reservation on the ferry the afternoon before and the staff had assured us that there was plenty of room, but that night the weather had not co-operated.

The official-looking guy with the clipboard snarled at Amanda and said, "Look, the ferry did not sail last night so anyone on the list from yesterday has first priority, then I will begin loading from today's list."

A group of gypsies pulled up in a rusted pick-up truck with an old camper on the back and parked directly in front of the loading ramp. The leader got out and insisted he had a reservation. Mr. Clipboard asked his name and scanned the two computer printouts. Nothing. The gypsy slipped his hand through Mr. Clipboard's arm and guided him away from the group.

Amanda figured he was up to no good and followed right behind, saying loudly, "No, your name is not there so you can't get on before any of us on the list."

Mr. Clipboard reluctantly told the gypsy to go to the office and make a reservation.

Three gypsy women emerged from the camper wearing thin, flowing, colorful dresses over their ample girth and immediately began causing a commotion. Surrounding a young vendor, they badgered him to get a better price for his sodas and snacks, stuffing their purchases in the hidden folds of their clothing. At the bottom of the boat ramp they removed their slippers and soaked their feet in the frosty cold water like a group of penguins. A truck driver bundled in a thick parka looked at them in wonder, then turned to us with a questioning laugh, condensation blowing from his nostrils in two cloudy streams.

The ferry workers were frazzled as they struggled to load the vehicles. Every inch of the ferry seemed to be taken by the time the last drivers were positioned on the tiny deck. Minutes before departure, with no room left but a mere foot on either side of the loading plank, we decided to retrace our route toward another ferry crossing. As we pulled away Amanda noticed that the gypsy had cornered Mr. Clipboard, out of sight between two trucks.

What would normally have been an easy forty-five minute boat ride across the Strait to the border with Argentina became a long, round-about drive.

At the border a long line of bus passengers waited for passport stamps, so I went right to the customs office to process the van's paperwork while Amanda waited in the immigration line. The tip of South America is divided between Chile and Argentina and we played hop-scotch over the boundaries of the two countries, making our way toward the end of the road. This was the third time we had crossed into Argentina and we knew the paperwork routine as well as any official.

When I returned to the passport line I found Amanda chatting with her new friend, the gypsy, who had managed, with his professed help from God, to find his way on to the ferry we had abandoned. He and his colorfully dressed wife, two gold-toothed sisters-in-laws, and a pimply nephew saved gas by taking the shorter ferry ride. They were returning to Ushuaia with their camper stuffed full of contraband goodies from a shopping trip at the duty-free zone in Chile. He told Amanda she could find God in Ushuaia, just next to the post office, "Tell them Gypsy Trekko sent you."

After finishing with the border paperwork the customs guards watched curiously as Gypsy Trekko made a commotion of saying goodbye to Amanda, as if they were great friends. The gypsy and his troop took their time climbing into their camper, so we pulled the van to the exit gate first. The guards immediately directed us aside and performed the most thorough inspection the van had received on the trip, knocking on tires, feeling the underside of wheel wells, searching through every drawer, closet, and cabinet. For a moment I thought we might be strip-searched. With all the guards engaged, Gypsy Trekko and his rolling menagerie passed unchallenged.

Ushuaia is the southernmost human settlement on earth and has the slapped-together look of a dried-up fishing camp or failed mining town. The steep-roofed clabber wood huts show absolutely no charm, no trim or frill, just basic wooden triangles and squares with doors and windows. Every home has a pile of clutter in the front yard, a car door, broken panes of glass, a small refrigerator, two barber chairs, a crock pot, cement blocks. It seems the residents refuse to discard anything since it is so difficult to get it in the first place. This was how I imagined the Yukon or rural Alaska. There was a main street that survived off the crumbs of the few people who ventured this far south each year and a few hotels that actually thrived in the frigid environment.

We arrived just after 7:00 p.m. with the Austral summer sun high overhead, and found a campsite outside town along a small river. The last flicker of daylight disappeared around midnight and returned once again before 5:00 a.m. A handful of local kids reveled in this abundance of sun and swam in the glacially cold river, splashing one another and fighting over an old rugby ball.

Among the books we carried to this remote tip of land was a tattered copy of *The Voyage of the Beagle* by naturalist Charles Darwin, who had sailed here aboard the vessel as scientific officer 170 years before. During his travels in South America Darwin first encountered the residents of Tierra del Fuego, and wrote, "I could not have believed how wide was the difference between savage and civilized man: it is greater than between a wild and domesticated animal". He was fascinated with the Fuegians' ability to withstand the frigid cold while practically unclothed and wrote, "…a woman, who was suckling a recently-born child, came one day alongside the vessel, and remained there out of mere curiosity, whilst the sleet fell and thawed on her naked bosom, and on the skin of her naked baby!" He later remarked, "We were well clothed, and though sitting close to the fire were far from too warm; yet these naked savages, though further off, were observed, to our great surprise, to be streaming with perspiration at undergoing such a roasting."

While looking at these perspiring Fuegians Darwin recognized the first hints of his idea of transmutation, that a species can adapt its form or structure to the environment over time. Transmutation was the first step backwards toward his theory of evolution.

Early one morning we arrived at the port of Ushuaia, looking as respectable as possible with our backpacks stuffed to overflowing. The port security officer said in slow, deliberate Spanish, "Only passengers with tickets may enter the port."

I said in equally slow and deliberate English, "Yes, we go to that ship," and walked past with calm assurance. The officer began to follow but we had timed our entrance at just the right moment. Other passengers came to the gate behind us and presented their tickets. He let us go.

I had a little more than two thousand dollars in a pouch strapped around my waist. At the gangplank to the ex-Soviet icebreaker, a burley guard stood with his arms crossed. As we walked closer we deliberately spoke loudly in English to one another and began removing our backpacks. Amanda plunked hers down in front of him, then I did the same. She asked, "Would you please watch these for us?" Without waiting for an answer we brushed past him up the gangplank, along the deck and through a door as if we knew where we were going. We wandered down a narrow hall and through several hatches before finding someone who pointed us to the office. There we met Cyril, a young Australian man in charge of the passengers on the ship for the next sailing to Antarctica. He reached for a clipboard with blocks for various berths and greeted us, "Welcome aboard. May I have your names?"

"Oh, well, we're not on your list yet, but we'd like to be. Do you have space?" I asked.

He turned his clipboard around to show us. "We had a lot of cancellations after September 11th." Upside down he counted the few names on the list and said, "We have plenty of spaces available."

"How much are you charging for last-minute bookings?" Amanda asked.

"When the ship's in port I can't handle bookings. You need to speak with the shore agent," he said.

We had already visited the shore agent, an uptight, abrupt woman from Buenos Aires who refused to budge on the outrageous price she listed on her door. She laughed in our faces when we made our offer and said, "Do you know what the other passengers have paid? Five thousand, six hundred dollars per person, and that's for the least expensive cabin."

I explained to Cyril our plight and added, "Look, you've got plenty of space and we're willing to pay a thousand cash each. What do you think?"

He said hopefully, "Give me a moment," and walked down the narrow hallway and into a cabin. He returned a few minutes later and said, "I just talked to the head office. They told me I can't take less than the shore office price. Sorry, mate." I thought of the gypsy and considered how to reword the offer but then I decided against it.

As we picked up our backpacks at the bottom of the gangplank I said to Amanda dejectedly, "Gypsy Trekko would have gotten on."

She looked up at the icebreaker and said, "It's not worth it if we have to resort to that." Then she turned abruptly and headed toward the gate.

Just south of Ushuaia, a dirt road continues through Tierra del Fuego National Park and marks the end of road at the Beagle Channel. We drove the last few kilometers down this dusty track to the sign that read in Spanish, "Here is the end of route number 3, Alaska 17518 km."

Standing in front of the sign waiting for Amanda to prop the camera on a log and set the automatic timer, I thought back to how I imagined this moment would be. Setting out on our journey, we wanted to learn the simple things for ourselves. We wanted to experience how people in other parts of the world live. We wondered if we could pick and choose some of their best characteristics and meld them into our lives.

Reaching the end of the road, we remained mystified by the dense complexity of what makes a life fulfilling. With each new lesson learned we succeeded in revealing how little we really knew. We could not completely grasp what it was in the lives of these *latinos* that brought them joy and happiness, but we realized that prosperity seemed irrelevant.

Hugging Amanda close, smiling toward the camera with a goofy grin, I wondered how it was that we found happiness in the most unlikely place, living in the close quarters of a Volkswagen campervan for nearly a year and a half.

But before going back home we needed a clearer understanding of the route we had taken to get there. Only then could we plot a course to the future. We had to go where it all began. We had to go to Africa.

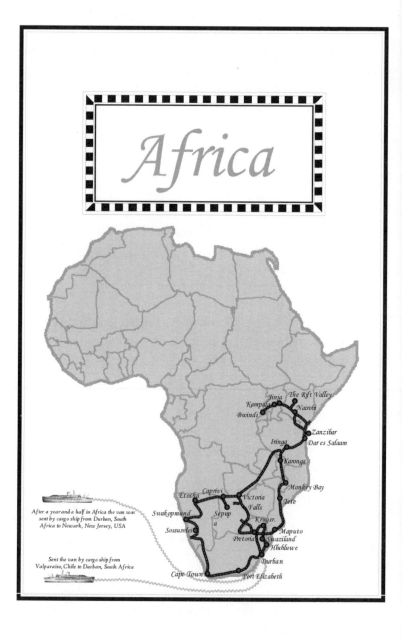

Africa

CHAPTER 41

A Colorful World

Durban, South Africa
31,237 miles

"Africa would be a great place if it wasn't for the blacks," the young man said with the hurried accent peculiar to the Indians of South Africa, as he zoomed through the streets of Durban in his rattling Toyota hatchback. "They turn everything to sh…" He glanced back at Amanda in the rear view mirror. "Excuse me madam, but they ruin everything." He drove like a madman, grinding gears, screeching brakes, cutting off the minivan taxis, then cursing the drivers.

Unconsciously I glanced at my watch, 2:00 a.m. South American time. We were days late. Neither of us had slept more than a few fleeting hours in two, no, almost three days. In a blur I looked at myself in the reflection of the car window, wondering what made the driver think we would not mind his comment, but I was too tired to argue. We were squashed into the back seat and the car was scorching hot. We arrived at the office and he opened the door, flipped the latch on the front seats and said, "Here we are."

Just an hour earlier my unaccustomed eyes had been blinded by the blazing sun as we stepped on to the tarmac at the Durban airport. Sweat trickled from a wet ring on my back made by my heavy backpack. Rushing to the air-conditioned hotel room, I phoned the agent, who sent the maniacal driver.

The agent, a short Indian man, held out our paperwork to show off his fat gold watch and said with a hint of frustration in his voice, "Your van has been at the port for two days. Why did you wait so long to call?"

"We just got in today," I said. "When we bought the airline tickets the shipping company told us it would be here on the 15th."

"Yes, well, the ship arrived early. The port will charge a fine for late clearance. I'll call you at the hotel when the vehicle is ready to be picked up. Tomorrow at the earliest. The driver will take you back."

Back at the hotel, Amanda collapsed and slept instantly. After staring at the ceiling for an hour, I got up and read for a while. Unable to sleep, I strapped on my shoes and went for a run along the waterfront in the blistering afternoon heat.

The Golden Mile is a long swatch of land along the beach in Durban and is one of the finest examples of public planning anywhere in the world. Swirling brick pathways pass through ornamental public gardens, along massive wading pools, into an area of shops and trendy restaurants with names like Joe Kool's, Surf Zone and Debonair's Pizza. The path continues beside Snake Park, and the dolphin shows at the South African version of Sea World, all within a stone's throw of the perfect white sandy beach. I stopped to watch as a lifeguard sat on a red Land Rover with a stopwatch, timing a group of juniors running a relay race.

There was a storm far out in the Indian Ocean, past Madagascar, kicking up massive waves, and the surfers jumped off the end of the pier to get past the violent break. Fishermen tossed their lines from the end of the wharf, covering themselves in broad-brimmed hats and long sleeves as protection from the sweltering sun.

Resting my foot on the sea wall, I stretched while looking out at the sunbathers. This was not what I expected from Africa. In fact, I looked around for any indication that this was Africa at all. Then I saw the rickshaws, elaborately decorated, with the pullers wearing ornate breastplates and massive horned headpieces. Running back toward the hotel, I left the beach and loped along the street side of the public area where curio vendors sold carved wooden bowls, colorful masks, fabric prints, and t-shirts. The traders were African and their curios all had African themes.

I ran past an old Indian man and recalled reading on the plane that Mahatma Gandhi had once boarded a train here in Durban and taken a short ride that would change the world. As the train left the station, one of the other passengers, a white man, complained that he had to share the first class compartment with a "coolie", as the Indians of South Africa were called. In London he had been accustomed to being treated with the respect shown to an English gentleman. Gandhi had spent years in London studying law, had been admitted to the prestigious Inner Temple and had struggled more with maintaining his vegetarian diet than passing the bar exams. A railway official ordered him to move to the third class compartment but Gandhi refused. The official held the train at Pietermaritzburg, a town just outside of Durban, and called the police. The constable promptly deposited Gandhi and his bags on the platform and the train departed. A lesser man might have left the country immediately, but Gandhi used the hardship, resolving himself to help change the country.

During his 21 years in South Africa Gandhi shaped his theories and combined concepts from many religious beliefs to mold together his philosophy of Satyagraha or passive resistance. His tactics of mass marches and civil disobedience were later adopted by Martin Luther King and used during the anti-apartheid movement.

Back at the hotel the next day the phone rang a little before noon and jolted us both awake. It was the agent. He had obtained permission to remove the van from the port. He added with a hint of scolding disappointment, "The customs fine for late removal will be 150 rand." There was a time when the South African rand traded close to par with the dollar. Since the end of apartheid the exchange rate declined and the fine was only $12.50.

As we entered the guarded car lot at the port, we walked by a new, well-equipped Land Rover with European license plates parked inside waiting for its owner. The headlights and front grille had been stolen, and a chain hung limply from the rear bumper. The chain was cut and whatever it had secured was missing. The agent commented offhandedly that vehicles are often stripped on the ship when the sailors have idle time.

Our hearts pounded as we searched for our van. From a few hundred yards it was conspicuous among the new BMWs and Toyotas lined up for export. It looked dirty and out of place. As we got closer we noticed that someone had tried to force open the sliding side door but the extra padlock on the outside had held it in place. Everything else was intact. The spare gas canisters were still on the back bumper and the two spare tires were exactly as we had left them.

As we drove out of the port, jet-lagged from the eleven-hour time difference, it felt disorienting to drive on the left side of the road. Every time we made a turn Amanda chanted, "Stay on the left, stay on the left, stay on the left." Once, out of sheer force of habit, I pulled partially into the right lane, only to find oncoming traffic directly in front. It was a relief to park the van in the hotel lot for the night.

On Sunday morning we went for a run along the Golden Mile and noticed groups of Muslim families power-walking along the waterfront. The men and children wore shorts and t-shirts but the women were sheltered in shapeless black robes with the latest Nike or Adidas running shoes poking out of the bottom. At the north end of the beach, old, rickety buses dropped off black teenagers who walked together in clusters. At first reserved, they gradually grew louder, smiling, pushing one another in embarrassment, enjoying the sunny day. Further along the path a group of veiled women all turned to look toward the public swimming pool. Several husky white men, running in the opposite direction, followed the women's gaze and let out a grumble of discontent as they saw the scene.

In front of the swimming area there was a long line of beach showers where bathers could wash the sand away before entering the pool. About two-dozen black teenagers were using the showers, sharing bottles of shampoo and bars of soap, jostling one another for position under the streams of water. The long, thin boys had stripped down to their briefs and the plump girls were popping out of their see-through bras and panties, chatting happily as they lathered.

Trying to be discreet, I looked out of the corner of my eye while running past and Amanda elbowed me and said, "Hey, watch where you're going."

I turned to look at her with a smile and said, "I think I'm going to like it here."

CHAPTER 42

Safari in Zululand

Hluhluwe, South Africa
31,478 miles

The elderly white woman behind the desk at the Automobile Association of South African warned, "I'll tell you this. If you are in an accident or you hit someone, just keep going. Don't stop to see what happened. Two weeks ago a woman crashed her car in the Transkei. She went to see if anyone was hurt and they beat her to death, then stole her car." She paused and added unconvincingly, "Of course, it's best to go straight to the police."

Just outside of Durban the motorway narrowed from five lanes to three as it cut through the suburban communities and the shanty towns clinging to the sides of hills, then narrowed again to two lanes as we turned north along the coastal road, through sugarcane fields and plantations of eucalyptus trees. Traditional Zulu huts made of cow dung with thatched roofs, sprinkled the hillsides in this region known as KwaZulu-Natal.

In South Africa it is customary for slower drivers to stay on the shoulder, permitting the faster vehicles to pass, and we spent most of the day driving on the left margin, chugging along at our normal pace. A roadblock diverted traffic from the motorway to the top of an overpass, where the police stood waiting. The hefty black officer approached Amanda's window and asked straight out, "Where is your gun?"

"We don't have a gun," she answered surprised.

"You must have a gun. Everyone has a..." then he paused and looked at her strangely, "Incredible, how do you drive without a wheel?" But he quickly realized, "Ah, this is a left hand-drive vehicle! From where does it come?"

"We brought it from the United States." Amanda answered.

"America! You mean to tell me this car came from America?" he said with excitement.

"Yes, all the way from California."

"How did you come? Did you drive it from over there to here?" He made a tracing motion in the air with his finger.

"No, it came by ship and we flew," I said.

He stepped back to look at the van with confusion on his face, obviously wondering why we would send such an old vehicle, but he was too polite to say as much. Ending our brief questioning with a broad smile, he said, "Enjoy your visit in South Africa, but be very careful."

As we were about to leave, a younger officer pulled him toward the front of the van and pointed through the windshield at the plastic toys on our dashboard. Two rubber snakes we'd found washed up on a remote beach in Chile and a plastic spider discovered on our morning run in Brazil, added to the clutter. The young officer looked at the snakes and spider with wide-eyed fearfulness and asked, "Are they real?"

I dangled one of the rubbery snakes, "No, they are just toys."

The young man continued to look at them warily then asked, "Why would anyone want such a toy?"

Passing into Zululand, we went on safari for a few days in the Hluhluwe-Umfolozi Game Reserve. Wildlife was abundant in this reserve and the "Big Five", lion, leopard, rhino, buffalo, and elephant, roamed freely among the rolling hills, streams, and rivers. Once the hunting ground for the Zulu king, Shaka, the reserve was founded in 1895, making it one of the oldest protected areas on the continent.

Tracking game in the early morning hours, our guide Khephu walked stealthily through the tall grass with his high-powered rifle strapped securely around his chest. He motioned for us to remain silent and directed us to walk in a straight line. Khephu, an elderly Zulu tracker, was solemn as he made clear the rules and hand signals. "Be very silent and keep your ears alert. If cheetah or lion approach, stay behind me. Stay close together. Watch where you step, and most important, never make a sudden movement or a loud noise."

Thorny acacia trees surrounded the leafy thickets of the savannah, and the high grassy vegetation made it difficult to spot wildlife. Our guide was one of the most experienced trackers in the region and explained just a few of his methods, handed down through the generations. With a remarkable perception of his surroundings, Khephu searched for footprints, dung droppings, smells, and sounds, to locate wildlife. He possessed a broad knowledge of the plants and animals of the area and explained how the animals use the surroundings as a protection mechanism against predators. A herd of elephant could easily hide in a rocky gorge, among bush willows and woodlands. A rhino could disappear among boulders and a kudu among the trees.

Watching Khephu, we realized we were witnessing a dying tradition. Surely, with so few continuing in his way of life, the ability to merge knowledge with instinct, to interpret smells and sounds, and to read subtle changes in the wind, would soon be lost forever.

We crept through the high brush and passed a burrow. Startled warthogs rushed from their hole with evil grunts, first darting directly toward us, then turning away with their little tails pointing up like antennae. As we were passing through an open field surrounded by low thorn trees, Amanda spotted two white rhinos, a mother and baby. I had lingered a short distance behind, and the mother hesitated, then charged across the opening between us. Khephu yelled, "Move. Move!" and I ran to close the gap, with the rhinos at my heels. Unlike their nearest relative, the black rhino, who would charge toward a moving target, Khephu told us the white rhino is mild-mannered and relatively tame. The mother and child trotted past, leaving some startled humans behind.

In a vast open field of tall grass we encountered a large group of giraffe, wildebeest, zebra, and impala. Khephu explained that the long neck of the giraffe affords a better view of the distant surrounding area. The sharp hearing of the zebra and the acute smell of the wildebeest, combined with the sheer numbers of impala, make the grouping mutually beneficial against the lurking carnivores. Each animal has a strength and each a weakness. They congregate together for the benefit of all.

Khephu climbed into the van and we headed back to the campground on a narrow bumpy trail. He held tightly to his gun and said, "This is a nice vehicle. You must be careful here, they use these for mini-bus taxis and will hijack you for it."

"Is hijacking common?" Amanda asked.

"Yes, it happens every day. You must be very careful. Always keep your doors locked and when you stop at a robot, leave space in front to move. "

"A robot?" I asked.

"Yes…you know…a traffic controller, with a red light and a green light."

A few days later we parked just after sunset in the unfenced campsite of the Mkuze Game Reserve near the border with Mozambique. Beyond the tree line we heard the grunt of a large wildebeest. Khephu had told us that the dominant male wildebeest is constantly challenged by other upstarts and is eventually forced from the group to spend his life in solitude. This lone male was grunting at a threat just beyond the brush. Then the attack began. The grunting of the wildebeest changed to a sad, terrifying scream. The attackers were a group of hyenas and the battle was beyond our view. The laughing howl of the hyenas from all directions was horrifying and the scream of the wildebeest like the haunting wail of a human. We poked our heads out from the window of the pop-top, watching the bushes tremble with violence, listening to the sickening shrieks. There was no barrier between us, nor a fence or cage protecting us from the harsh pitilessness of nature. Then with brutal abruptness the wail was cut off.

Leaving the game park early the next morning, we slowed at a busy intersection. A car coming toward us swerved around at high speed, driving up on to the shoulder where an African woman was walking with a bundle balanced on her head. Jumping off the road, she disappeared as she tumbled down the embankment. The car skidded to a stop and backed up. The driver looked nervously down the steep grade then quickly sped away. Instinctively I wanted to stop and help, but Amanda reminded me of the words of the Auto Club employee. The line of drivers behind gave us restless honks and I reluctantly drove on.

CHAPTER 43

Eye of the Beholder

Malolotja, Swaziland
31,705 miles

The Tony Bennett sing-along festival came to a halt when we stopped along the roadside to take a photo. Children ran toward the van from a grouping of huts made entirely out of straw with the rounded shape of igloos. Other dwellings consisted of mud, held together with a frame of branches, and a roof of corrugated metal. As a precaution against snakes the flat earth was swept clean around the circular kraals, which were surrounded by vast stretches of brown grasses and short, stubby acacia. From a distance the children's colorful clothing, red t-shirts, yellow shorts, blue jacket, stood out against the earthen backdrop.

Amanda smiled and waved to the children as I started the van, slowly letting out the clutch. Nothing happened. The engine spun perfectly but first gear was gone. I shifted to second gear and tried again. Nothing. Third and fourth gears were gone too.

It was Easter Sunday and we were in the mountain Kingdom of Swaziland, a landlocked speck of a nation in Southern Africa ruled by King Mswati III. During his reign, the king's father married over 70 wives, produced hundreds of heirs and somehow found the time to gain independence from the British.

We had read in a South African newspaper some interesting stories about the kingdom of Swaziland, where the young king is not just a figurehead. He maintains an absolute monarchy, holding firm control over the life of the Swazi people. The two official languages, siSwati and English, are used throughout the country and Christian missionaries battle indigenous beliefs for the spiritual life of the people. Struggling with reformers, the monarchy actively promotes traditional Swazi culture in an effort to cling to power.

Participation in the *Umhlanga*, a female coming-of-age ceremony, is encouraged. Thousands of teenage girls wearing little more than jewelry and small, beaded skirts parade before the king who may, on a whim, pick any number as wives. In recent years the king has sparked controversy by choosing several girls against their will and their parents have appealed to the courts, to no avail. As the Swazi Attorney General said, "The truth is, His Majesty is not above the law. His Majesty is the law."

While we were visiting the country the king unveiled a new program to help curb the spread of AIDS. He announced a virginity decree outlawing sex with the country's virgins for five years. Known as Flower of the Nation, the law revives old chastity rites where young virgins must wear a belt with blue and black tassels to indicate their status. When he sheepishly admitted to breaking his own law, the king graciously paid the fine of one cow to himself.

"I can't get into first gear," I said as I struggled with the shifter.

"Can't we just drive in second gear?" Amanda asked.

"That doesn't really solve the problem, and anyway, I already tried. I've got to see what's wrong," I said as I opened the side door and slid under the back end of the van. I heard pounding footsteps approaching. Before I could slither out from underneath, several kids had lain down flat in the dirt next to me while others squatted beside the van. The problem was obvious. Even the children could see that one of the two drive shafts was completely disconnected at one end, hanging down next to the tire. We must have been playing the Tony Bennett tape a little too loud to hear the clatter it had certainly caused. I yelled to Amanda, "Pull out the *Idiot's Guide* and look this up for me."

Lying there in the dirt, I stared at the tangled mess and wondered how we were going to get out of this one. Amanda came to the back of the van, hovering at my feet, "OK. I've got the book. Would I look under gear shifting, gear starter or gear ring and pinion?"

Sucking in a deep breath, I turned my head to look at the children, who watched with smiling eyes. "I don't know," I said. "Let me think."

Amanda started to read from the book, "...the automobile clutch connects the engine to the transmission..."

I tried to interrupt her, "No, wait..."

She continued, "...allowing you to disconnect the engine at will in order to change gears. Does that sound right to you?" She asked.

More kids from further down the road came running up, and the oldest boy explained in siSwati what was happening while a younger boisterous girl loudly disagreed with him.

I didn't know what to do. I said to Amanda, "No. Some of the bolts have fallen off. Only three are left and one is too bent to use."

"Bolts! Your tool kit is full of bolts," she scoffed. "Let me pull it out."

"No, wait! I don't have any of these. They're long things with a funny looking head."

It didn't matter what I said, Amanda was already digging in my tool kit.

The boisterous girl pointed to the other drive shaft and said something that I couldn't understand, then pointed to the disconnected shaft. That's when it occurred to me.

If I unscrewed one bolt from each of the other connections I could secure the loose one. I yelled to Amanda, "Stop with the bolts already. Bring me my ratchet set."

"What's that?" she asked. "Is it the little suitcase with all the circles inside?"

"Suitcase with circles?" I paused to think what she meant, then answered, "Yeah, that's it."

As I began to remove the first bolt the girl broke into a huge smile. I secured the disconnected shaft, leaving each connection one bolt short. Climbing back into the van I said to Amanda, "That's not going to hold for very long on these roads."

"At least it will give us a chance to get somewhere." She anxiously added.

After fidgeting with the clutch, I was somehow able to shift into first gear. The children cheered as we pulled away.

Turning to another bumpy dirt track, we climbed through pine forest over the Saddleback Pass through Piggs Peak to the remote border crossing of Bulembu back into South Africa. After 45 kilometers on a difficult four-wheel-drive track we arrived at the post just a few minutes before closing time. The friendly guards had already begun to celebrate the holiday and seemed a bit tipsy as they stamped our passports.

The campground in Barberton was packed full for the holiday and we squeezed between two caravans, both with *braais* grilling *boerewors*, the drippy brown sausage that is the staple for every South African barbecue. A large man in a tent-like safari shirt, shorts, heavy wool knee socks and hiking boots hunched over a *potjie*, a three-legged cast-iron cauldron bubbling with *bredie*, a pot food of lamb's neck and vegetables.

I scooted under the van to disassemble the makeshift repair. In a matter of minutes we had three offers of assistance from our neighbors.

The following morning the cool breeze energized us on our early morning run through the neighborhoods lined with old Victorian homes. Elaborate buildings left over from the city's gold rush era bordered the side streets. Of all the places we could have ended up with car trouble, Barberton was a pleasant detour.

Walking through the downtown, we picked up the spares I needed to correct the problem and were lured to a small teahouse by the aroma of freshly-baked scones and cups of warm Rooibos tea. At the table next to us, Erin, a young Canadian backpacker with a maple leaf patch stitched to the top of her bag, sat with Margaret, a wrinkled old woman with a contagious laugh. Margaret was from Scotland. Her husband of forty-eight years had passed away two years before and she had decided to take off and see the world. Most remarkably, Margaret was legally blind, suffered terribly from arthritis and was traveling solo. She'd met Erin two days before at a backpacker hostel in Swaziland.

"How are you getting around?" Amanda asked, not quite believing.

"In de minibus taxis mostly. Because I can't read d'signs I usually manage to find a new friend to get me movin' in the proper way. You know, the Africans respect their elders. I b'lieve we might learn a ting or two from'em."

"What did your family think when you decided to leave?" I asked.

"They tink I'm nuts! Me sons tried to stop me but I told 'em I spent most a me life taking care of 'em and der fadher. Cooped up in that house cookin' der meals, washin' and ironin'. Now I'm livin' for me'self. David, me eldest, says to me, 'but ma what if you'er t'die in de middle a' Africa?' Soes you know what I did? I wen'en wrote it up official. I'm t'be buried in de traditional fashion of de place were I 'as t'die." She chuckled, "If I die in Zululand, I'm't'be buried like a Zulu. 'Magine that, me whole family comin' to Africa for me Zulu funeral." She laughed heartily.

Her friend Erin was obviously as fascinated as we and asked, "When you're in a bus with everyone speaking African languages and you can't see what's going on, you must feel very uneasy?"

"Oh my, no. Many times de Africans hev graciously taken me under'der wing. B'lieve me, der's always a helping hand close by. You'd be surprised. And I dink of it like this. I could be home in me comfortable chair, lookin' forward to me favorite program on the telly. I've got friends like dat you know. Dey're wastin' away. Dat's not what ey wanned fer meself."

We could have spent hours listening to Margaret, but she was an active woman on her way to the Kruger National Park, the largest and most famous game reserve in the world. As she stood to say goodbye she strapped on her backpack, then took a telescoping cane from her pocket. She held it in front while her other hand rested on Erin's shoulder, and off they went.

Sitting there stunned by the courageousness of this remarkable woman, Amanda teased, "And you were all freaked out when we broke down in Swaziland. Imagine..."

"I know. It seems ridiculous now, doesn't it?"

CHAPTER 44

A Delicate Balance

Kruger National Game Reserve, South Africa
32,032 miles

The robust Afrikaans woman sat beneath the shade of the awning attached to her caravan in a reclining canvas chair that strained to hold her weight. Next to her on a small folding plastic table her husband placed a perspiring bottle of Castle Lager, then he used the back of a spatula to push around some sort of sausage in an electric skillet. It gave off a noxious smell that instantly zapped my appetite. She leaned forward, bringing the chair to the upright position, and the meaty flesh under her chin jiggled. "Where did you run?" She asked.

I balanced myself against the spare tire to stretch my calves as Amanda wiped the sweat off her face and grabbed our water bottles from the van.

"Just in circles around the camp. They wouldn't let us beyond the gate," I chuckled. We were in the Satara camp of the Kruger National Park, a self-sufficient small village with a grocery store, service station, lodge and campground.

The woman pointed toward the entrance, "This morning we drove out to see a group of lions eating a zebra about a kilometer down that way. They dragged it under a tree not far from the road. It has been quite a while since I spotted lion around here."

"Do you come here often?" Amanda asked.

"We've been coming every year since 1973. It's not as nice as it used to be. They just don't keep it up any more."

"Really? The facilities are far better than the national parks in the U.S." I said.

Her husband spoke. "Have you been to the ablution block? It's a mess. It was never like this before. You should have seen it ten years ago."

Amanda handed me my water bottle and said, "This morning when I was brushing my teeth there was a mom bathing her children in the bathtub. I couldn't believe a national park has a bathtub in the restrooms, and they seemed spotless to me."

This took me by surprise. Never, since meeting Amanda, had I heard her describe a place as spotless. She could always find something, a few errant hairs or a dirty sink, that made a place fail her standard of cleanliness.

I walked to the water tap and rinsed a few pieces of fruit for breakfast while Amanda set out the oatmeal and yogurt on our table. As I chopped an overripe papaya, two mangoes and a handful of peaches, the woman said, "Real health fanatics, I see."

"Just self-preservation, to avoid doctors," I answered.

Her husband served the sausage on foam plates with huge white buns and a pile of cubed potatoes and said, "Before the change we used to have great doctors here. You know the world's first heart transplant was done in Cape Town in 1967. Now our doctors and nurses have all left for your country and England, just when we need them."

The woman took the plate from her husband and dipped one of the pieces of sausage into a yellow glob of mustard, then popped it into her mouth. I hate mustard. Watching her chew up the sausage made me queasy and I looked away as she said, "I'm the Headmistress of a public school and I've got 46 HIV-positive students. That's just those we know about."

Amanda commented, "That's terrible."

The woman paused, biting into another piece, swilling down a swig from the bottle of beer, then said, "Ag, look, everyone in South Africa knows about AIDS. They know about protection. All they must do is control themselves, but they can't. The most awful thing is our President, and his attitude. He must be mad. He should realize what he says influences people."

"Does your school have…some sort of…program?" I asked.

Struggling to sit further forward, the woman's face flushed. She pointed with the bottle of beer in one hand while the sausages rolled around the foam plate in her other, "My teachers are experts about AIDS and talk about it in the classrooms. The students know exactly how to avoid getting it. And when we know a student tests positive we have a counseling program. The counselor's a sharp African lady, always gets them to open up. Three girls tested positive and she got them to talk about their partners. You wouldn't believe how they got infected." She paused and finished her beer, adding the empty bottle to the plastic Spar supermarket bag hanging from the awning of the caravan. "From the teachers, two of them. Can you believe that? And when I fired them they appealed to the bloody union. They're still in the classrooms."

Her husband appeared annoyed with her as he sat down next to her in an identical chair. "What my wife says is correct, but what you must realize is that under apartheid, black men were separated from their families for long periods. That happened for many years, for generations really. It changed the social structure of the African." He set his beer down hard on the table and said forcefully to his wife, "If we want to fight this disease we must first work out how to fix what we broke." They went on eating in silence.

Kruger Park is massive, larger than many countries, and driving through at a snail's pace we felt as if we were the only people on earth. Dangling half her body from the open window, Amanda peered through the binoculars in every direction, catching glimpses of wildebeest, waterbuck, buffalo and the ever-abundant herds of kudu and impala. She became skilled at spotting wildlife many miles away, camouflaged against the dry, brown earth. Most of the animals we recognized from the old nature television programs we'd watched as kids like *Mutual of Omaha's Wild Kingdom,* but other more obscure animals we looked up in a tiny picture guide and marked them on our map.

On a dirt path along a river we heard the cracking of branches not far away. Drawing closer, a loud trumpeting reverberated through the brush. The force of the sound felt as if it penetrated our bodies. Calmly crossing the path, the enormous elephants dwarfed our tiny van. Sitting motionless, we were stunned by their immensity and our vulnerability. The massive piles of their dung littered the road and permeated the area with a familiar, unmistakable stench. It triggered pleasant memories in the depths of my mind of the Ringling Brothers' Circus and the funny little man with a shovel working quickly in the darkened arena to scoop up the giant droppings.

Nature's pooper-scooper, with a remarkably astute sense of smell, makes altogether different mental connections when it detects the odor of elephant droppings. Within minutes the dung beetle zeros in on the fresh pile and begins work, using its paddle-shaped front legs to scoop together and sculpt the dung into a baseball-sized sphere. When finished, the beetle flips around and shoves the ball with its hind legs away from the competition of the pile, and uses it to attract a mate. Once she has been properly wooed they find a spot to dig a hole, bury themselves with the prize, then spend several days of blissful mating as they devour the feast. When the job is done, the couple return to the pile to create another ball that they roll back to the hole. Alone, the female buries herself with the ball, lays her eggs within, and creates a hard crust on the outside to protect it from drying. After several weeks the eggs hatch, the pupae devour the interior while becoming mature beetles, and the cycle begins again.

Looking down from the van, we found mounds of dung around us teeming with busy beetles and understood the importance of the sign at the park entrance warning visitors to avoid squashing them under tires. It seems the dung beetle, dependent on the decreasing elephant population, has become endangered, and the automobile is rapidly flattening the remaining few into extinction.

Awed by the elephants' insatiable appetite, we realized that these enormous creatures are completely dependent on the tiny beetle to spread the nutrient-rich dung among the trees. Without the rich dung the trees would not grow. Without the trees the elephants would not thrive. Without the elephants the dung beetle would be lost. A fine and delicate balance.

The next morning we were up before sunrise, rushing to break camp to see if we might catch the pride of lion just outside the gates. I am a morning person, always have been, and when I have something to do early in the morning I can be ready to go, like a firefighter, in a matter of minutes. Amanda, on the other hand is physically incapable of rushing in the morning. She wakes up moving like a sloth, then slows down for the first hour while contemplating her day.

I was pacing in circles around the van waiting for her to finish in the shower when I noticed the dirty breakfast dishes on the table. Another twenty minutes of waiting, I thought. In a situation like this, where I could get the job done in $1/100^{th}$ the time it would take her, I was downright giddy to wash them. But I could never, no matter how thoroughly I scrubbed, get the dishes clean enough. I knew I had to wash them or we would never get moving so I stacked them on the cutting board and marched to a nearby sink.

When I returned Amanda was still nowhere in sight. Glad to avoid the time-consuming dish inspection, I hurriedly dried them and began shoving them into the cabinet. That's when it happened. I was reaching to the back of one of the small shelves to put away the coffee cups when my watch caught on the container of oatmeal. Knowing that our food would get jostled around, we bought sealable canisters before leaving home and I wasn't concerned as the plastic oatmeal container fell to the floor. But I should have been. It landed directly on the metal hasp and popped open, spewing flakes of oatmeal all over the carpet in the back of the van.

There was nothing more sacred than that carpet. Amanda would sweep it with a small plastic broom about a thousand times a day. She would mindlessly brush the few grains of undetectable dust and sand that had accumulated since her last sweeping frenzy and would spend half an hour scouring the tiny square of carpet each morning before we could leave. I knew if she saw this, all hope of seeing the lion was lost.

I glanced toward the restroom. There was no sign of her, so I hastily scooped up much of the oatmeal and put it back into the container. The remaining flakes I swiped out of the van using my hands, leaving behind a powdery skid mark in the center of the carpet. I searched around for the broom and began to frantically sweep as I repeated to myself, "Think like Amanda…Think like Amanda…Think like Amanda."

I brushed that carpet like a madman. I double-checked that everything was in perfect order, closed up the sliding door of the van, and jumped into the driver's seat. It occurred to me that if I drove over and waited for her by the restroom I would get away from the scene of the crime, so that's what I did.

A few minutes later she came out carrying her toiletry bag. I had forgotten the toiletry bag. I yelled through my window, "Jump in front. You can put that away in the back after we get out into the park."

To my surprised relief she did just that, climbing into the passenger's seat she set her toiletry bag on the dashboard. I figured I was home free as I drove toward the gate.

But then, out of the corner of my eye, I saw her turn her head and stare at me. Without making eye contact I asked, "What? What's wrong?"

Her nose twitched slightly as she said, "What did you spill?"

That evening while walking around the Visitor's Center, we studied the map with the colored push-pins that showed where others had spotted some of the more elusive animals in the reserve. Coincidentally, we had driven past some of the same areas and had spotted nothing.

Leaving the building, we ran into our neighbors coming from the gift shop. The woman was carrying a paper bag and she came over to offer, "Here, have you ever tried biltong? It's dried strips of meat." She tilted the bag in our direction.

"We haven't been eating much meat lately, but thank you." I said.

"Oh, I know, too much meat isn't good for you but I can't resist these things." She shook the bag.

Her husband said, "At the end of the day it's probably for the best that you don't eat this rubbish. It's good to think healthy."

"Yeah," Amanda said, "we figure it's better to take care of ourselves now than have a problem in the middle of nowhere."

He nodded in agreement, "Responsible for yourselves. We could use more of that in Africa."

CHAPTER 45

Biko

Port Elizabeth, South Africa
34,494 miles

"I guess if I grew up in Soweto or another one of these townships I would probably have been a terrorist too," the man said with a distinct Afrikaans accent. We were standing on the beach looking out over Algoa Bay in Port Elizabeth, and the conversation had taken the turn that many conversations in South Africa eventually take. Race relations. "I know in America you are told we Afrikaners are all evil." He shrugged and turned his palms up. "But I tell you truthfully, we didn't know what was happening. We thought the locations were better than the way the blacks lived in their homelands."

I could see in his face that he felt sorry for the way Africans were treated by his government, and he was gentle in pointing out, "You may not see it, but our histories are not so different. Your segregation and our apartheid were very similar in many ways." He tugged at his mustache, then turned toward me. "Look how far we have come in less than ten years. It has taken your country two generations to do the same."

The campground along the bay was only a small section of a sprawling conference center where he was attending a training seminar. Recently he had lost his job, "Because, what they call it, affirmative action," he said. "I could have packed up my family and gone to Australia like everyone else, but this is my country. I will not give up on South Africa."

"What are you training for?" I asked.

"I bought the franchise for my region from this company here," he said, showing a folder with a logo.

"What type of franchise is it?" I asked.

"Bathtub refinishing. A new process that makes the tub as good as new."

We sat looking out at the sea and the conversation meandered. I told him a little about the young man we had met who would be taking us to visit his home that afternoon. He was impressed and a little concerned.

Until then we had experienced much of the first-world infrastructure of South Africa. We saw spotless streets, well-maintained roads, drinkable tap water, reliable electricity, and the elegant homes with manicured lawns. Lurking beneath it all were the hints of the third world. As a white South African this man had never been to the places where the others live. He called them "locations". Most people knew them as the townships.

As I got up to leave he said, "I'm sure your day will be more interesting than mine."

We had read that the townships were the result of the official policy of the "apartheid" government. The races were separated into ruling whites, semi-skilled Coloreds and Indians, and unskilled blacks, each with a distinct neighborhood. The blacks living in the cities were uprooted from their homes and forcibly relocated to new black townships, where they were given one-room brick dwellings with no running water or electricity. The lucky ones had only immediate family members, grandparents, parents, uncles, aunties and cousins living with them. The houses were laid out in rows with no bushes or obstructions between them, allowing the minority government to oversee and control the majority black population with prison-like ease.

When the apartheid government tumbled in 1994, the townships did not simply disappear, as those with wide-eyed hope believed they would. The townships grew. With the new freedom, people began converging on the cities and they were absorbed into the settlements on the fringes.

It is difficult for a visitor to get a feel for these sprawling areas by simply driving past a township, so we found a man willing to take us to see his home on the outskirts of Port Elizabeth. Nelson, a twenty-two year old Xhosa, grew up in Zwide and lived there with his mother and brothers. Seizing the newly available opportunity to attend university, he earned money on the side by offering to guide visitors into his community.

At the Red Location, the nation's first township, we walked with Nelson among the collection of dwellings made from corrugated iron plates that had turned a bright, vibrant red from a hundred years of exposure to the elements. He told us that early in the struggle against apartheid the residents of the corrugated shacks supported the resistance movement of the African National Congress (ANC), and Red Location was often a hiding place for units of *Umkhonto we Sizwe* (Spear of the Nation), the armed wing of the ANC. Since the peaceful transition to democracy, the ANC now runs the country, yet the Red Location continues to lack a basic infrastructure. The closely-packed residents use buckets for sanitation and carry drinking water from community taps.

Most families continue to live in the one-room homes with many relatives. Nelson helped us understand the bleak picture and said, "There's so much unemployment. I know one granny who supports ten people with her pension. The pension is meant to support only her."

"How does she do it?" Amanda asked.

"They eat very little and do not have luxuries like candles or margarine." He continued, "But some people just don't want to work. I have three brothers. My mother gets a pension and I earn some money, so my older brothers sit at home and do nothing all day. Sometimes I get very frustrated with them. They say there are no jobs but they do not get up and try to find one or make one for themselves like I did."

Pointing to a few small shacks on the edge of a wooded area, he told us how the rural traditions continue in the townships. "When boys are eighteen years old they are initiated into manhood. Their father builds a shack in a field away from others where the boy lives for several weeks. He is visited by an elder who performs a circumcision without anesthesia." Nelson added with a grimace, "The men all come around and watch. If you cry or scream or perform badly they tell everyone. When the girls find out, they will not want to marry you. It stays with you for the rest of your life."

Nelson explained that in much of Africa the son is cherished, but among the Xhosa, a baby girl is considered a blessing. When she reaches the proper age to marry, her prospective husband will offer her family *lobola*, the equivalent of at least six cows. Noticing our surprise, he said proudly, "We are negotiating for my brother to marry soon, but it is very expensive."

Stopping at the township pre-school, we met the volunteers who provide three meals a day and teach eighty pupils. Nelson introduced us to the haggard-looking woman from Scotland who ran the school. While making sandwiches in the kitchen, she told us with sad, tired eyes how the children often come on Sunday, the day the school is closed, "For many this is the only nourishment they receive." When Nelson asked about her success recruiting volunteers, she shrugged with resigned regret. "Some days we have a few, others no one comes." Then she turned partially toward us to explain, "I had hoped to make the program self-sufficient before returning home. But I learned that volunteering means a different thing here than what it does in Britain. I'm afraid the school will not be here long after I leave." Piling the sandwiches high, she sliced through the entire stack, neatly cutting them in two with one swoop, and said, "These children have a life expectancy of thirty-five years. And with AIDS that's dropping fast." As we helped her place the sandwiches on napkins around low wooden tables, she said abruptly, concluding our visit, "In ten years half of these children will have no parents. Just imagine." Then she wiped her hands on her smock and went in to gather the children for lunch.

Driving through the township, we noticed lines of people waiting to enter large steel shipping containers. Nelson said that the coated wire for the telephone system is stolen as fast as it is installed, so the company must use mobile payphones, protected in shipping containers, to provide a link to the outside world. He looked back slyly toward Amanda and asked, "Have you seen those colorful baskets at the tourist markets? They are weaved using the telephone wire."

As we drove along Nelson pointed to a pocket of construction where a Swedish development agency was building new cement block homes. From the outside they appeared similar to the surrounding dwellings built by the apartheid government, but on the inside they had plumbing and electricity. Each home included a small workshop and an extra room for a boarder, providing a means for the owner to earn an income.

Long before apartheid, there were problems with unskilled squatters setting up camps on the outskirts of towns, and we stopped to visit one of these squatter settlements. The previous government would sweep through periodically and bulldoze the camp, loading the residents on buses for relocation to distant homelands. The new government, unable to employ the same methods, simply turned a blind eye, and Nelson said with a hint of frustration, "Every few months the residents march through the streets demanding homes, and eventually the government builds them some for free. This only encourages more squatters and more unemployment."

As we passed a police station Nelson offhandedly pointed to it and said, "That's the place where they tortured Biko," then continued talking about something else. While at college in Philadelphia I'd taken a Political Science course taught by the leading anti-apartheid activist in the Delaware Valley, who spoke with a fervent, almost religious reverence for Steven Biko. He told us the story of the Black Consciousness leader who was undergoing interrogation in the police station of Port Elizabeth nearly twenty-five years earlier, and like many before him, was severely tortured. Naked and nearly brain dead from head injuries, he was loaded into the back of a Land Rover and transported 750 miles to Pretoria, where he later died.

While others fought for physical freedom, Biko recognized that the most important battlefield was in the mind. For generations the white government had instilled in blacks the belief that they were inferior, less intelligent, sexually immoral and prone to violence. Biko argued that apartheid could only be overthrown when blacks stopped feeling inferior. "We must accept that the limits of tyrants are prescribed by the endurance of those whom they oppress. As long as we go to Whitey begging cap-in-hand for our own emancipation, we are giving him further sanction to continue with his racist and oppressive system." Biko's forceful ideas led to his banning and eventual murder at the hands of the police, but his theory that "the most potent weapon in the hands of the oppressor is the mind of the oppressed," continues to influence many the world over.

After leaving Nelson and the township, we returned to the campsite. The next day while running along the shore we came upon the Afrikaner bathtub refinisher taking a morning walk before his last day of training. He spoke enthusiastically about his new business and said he was determined to make it successful. As we were ready to say goodbye, he remembered and asked, "Ah, how was your trip to the location?"

I tried to find the right words and settled on, "Confusing."

He nodded knowingly and turned his shoulder against the chilly ocean breeze. "Yes. I thought it might be so."

"Why is that?" Amanda asked.

"Well..." he thought, "...It is not as simple as we want it to be." He was in a good mood this morning and said with optimism, "But don't worry. All will come right. It will get better for the blacks."

CHAPTER 46

Risk

Cape Town, South Africa
35,717 miles

While much of Africa is chock-full of danger, the southern tip operates within a web of protection not much different from the world we knew. Stretching a few hundred miles to the east of Cape Agulhas lies the ingeniously marketed area known as the Garden Route. This playground of adventure sports is wedged between the Indian Ocean to the south and two mountain ranges, the Tsitsikamma and Outeniqua, to the north. Along the route the exploits vary from the tame steam train ride at Knysna to the Great White Shark cage-diving at Mossel Bay. Mountain climbing, abseiling, quad bike riding, windsurfing and sea kayaking were all available at first-world standards.

Along the Garden Route, life glides smoothly and lulls the soul into a feeling of being nestled in the security of a warm blanket. In each town or small hamlet there were several quaint campsites with excellent grocery stores, hip restaurants and trendy shops nearby. Impeccable roads and stylish homes appeared suspiciously European. An air of wealth and gluttony pervaded the place with a sense of ease.

In this zone of comfort we relaxed and days stretched into weeks. Our calloused skin and cunning minds rapidly became soft by the pampering of first-world Africa. Before we knew it, our three-month entry visa was expiring and we headed toward the crown jewel of the nation, Cape Town, to get an extension.

The different races rarely intermingle in South Africa. Scanning the faces of the children wearing their distinctive school uniforms showed that despite efforts toward diversity, particular schools continue to serve particular racial groups. Glancing at diners in restaurants or families leaving a place of worship revealed that, for the most part, people stay with their own kind. Even in public areas like shopping malls and parks there seemed to be a silent agreement as to who belonged where. On the rare occasion when groups did manage to intermingle, they never did so in the true proportion of the population. At one time this division was by design but after the change in government everyone was free to go wherever they wished. It seemed that just a few short years after gaining that freedom, they rarely chose to blend.

The Ministry of Home Affairs is one of the few places where everyone is forced together in a cluttered, confined space. It is the branch of government that issues identity documents, registers marriages, acknowledges births, and does much of the paperwork of the busy nation. Home Affairs was also the place where we could extend our visas.

The building was packed with people and it became abruptly apparent that this was the first time we'd encountered the true racial makeup of the nation. Huge signs plastered above numbered windows indicated the service provided and the clerks' faces were barely visible through the plexiglass barrier covered with posters and stickers explaining regulations, fees and requirements.

Several black women sat on a blanket with infants strapped to their chests while their other children lay on the floor playing with discarded papers. Turbaned Indian men stood in a huddle, practically in an embrace, their wives in colorful silk saris gossiping as their children played hide and seek around their legs. A black man in a suit fidgeted with his mobile phone in deep concentration while another looked over his shoulder with fascination. Amidst the flurry there was order. The lines were straight and places respected as we slowly but steadily reached the counter.

The ambivalent, pinch-faced, white woman sat beneath a sign that read "VISAS". We asked her what we needed to do and she said with a droning voice, "I need your passport, a credit card and your airline ticket back to your home country."

We handed over our passports and credit card and I said, "We have a vehicle. We'll be leaving South Africa by road."

She frowned and pulled a large binder from under the desk. While scanning down a page, holding our passports in her bony fingers, she looked at us and asked, "What country did you say you are from?" Her scowl at my reply did not give us confidence. She jotted the number 3110 on a piece of paper and pushed it across the worn counter along with our passports.

Looking at it, then up at her, we patiently waited for an explanation. Finally Amanda asked. "What does 3110 mean?"

She sighed and answered succinctly, "You must leave a deposit of 3110 rand per person to extend your visa." When she saw our reaction she added defensively, "Once you get to your home country you can request a refund."

Left with little choice, we used our last days in South Africa to take care of loose ends before hurrying toward the border with Namibia. The van had been running a little sluggishly and I felt it was due for a check-up. Rather than do it myself, I decided to take the easy route and hand over the problem to a VW mechanic outside of Cape Town. He was a tactile, quiet man and I got the impression he was doing his best to imitate the character of a German engineer. He outlined a few minor problems that conspired to cause our trouble and his roly-poly assistant, a burned-out old grease monkey with a gray-blond ponytail and a hand-rolled cigarette clenched between his lips, scooted under the rear end of the van to begin the work. I stood close behind and he seemed uncomfortable being watched, but he soon understood my attachment and gradually relaxed in my presence. He worked quickly and harshly, a man who wanted to get the job done, in marked contrast to my slow, careful treatment of the internal workings of the engine compartment. He removed parts with an abrupt confidence that made me feel useless as a mechanic and defensive of the van. I had to restrain myself from saying, "Be careful, would'ya."

A leaky fuel pump was reset with a new seal and the muffler, having suffered considerable damage from a barrage of battering rocks in Patagonia, was replaced. The squealing alternator belt was changed and he tightened the pulley a little harder than I would have. When he finished the van sounded as if it had been given a course of antibiotics. Gone was the sputtering cough to which we had become accustomed.

At the Cape Town waterfront we found a brand-new international travel clinic specializing in vaccinations and medications for those setting out across Africa. The rosy-cheeked young nurse suggested an inoculation to protect against meningitis, an oral polio booster, and a medication to help protect against malaria. She explained the common side effects of the malaria prophylactic, which included panic attacks, paranoia, psychotic episodes and hallucinatory dreams, and warned that those with a history of psychological problems generally experience these. She abruptly turned to Amanda and asked, "Do you experience any psychological problems?" She seemed genuinely surprised when Amanda answered negatively. We purchased one tablet each to test our reaction and decided to wait a few days before taking it.

Despite the fine-tuning, the van began showing signs of a new illness. On a particularly hairy section of the M3 highway the alternator belt tore and the warning lights on the dashboard lit up. I struggled to the side of the highway, dug out the spare belt, and replaced it. As we continued into town the new belt squealed loudly and promptly twisted around, beginning to fray. The pulley was warped. The mechanic had tightened it too hard.

By giving in to the temptation of the easy solution and handing problems over to a mechanic, I was taught an important lesson. After two days of searching for the proper pulley I realized that in the long run what appears to be the easy road can often be much harder.

On our last night in Cape Town we popped the anti-malarial medication and we went to bed early, anticipating psychedelic hallucinations. Tossing and turning for hours, excited and anxious for the adventures ahead, I finally drifted off to a drug-induced sleep. In the morning neither of us admitted to any vivid dreams or peculiar side effects. That day we purchased several months' supply of the drug, in our last chance before heading out into risk-filled Africa.

CHAPTER 47

Have and Have Not

Sossusvlei, Namibia
37,298 miles

The wind blew violently, slapping the canvas sides of the pop-top in and out like an accordion, making it impossible to sleep. It was well after midnight and the bone-chilling cold of the barren Namibian desert penetrated the layers of clothing, down sleeping bags and extra blankets with little resistance. Earlier, we had wrapped our frozen fingers around mugs of boiling tea to take away the frosty chill but the momentary relief was rapidly absorbed into the frigid darkness.

Our tiny catalytic heater could have kept us toasty through the night but the warm glow gulped precious propane gas and if we ran out, our cooking stove would be useless. In the past we had found that if we just gave ourselves enough time to become accustomed to the cold we could endure it, making the heater unnecessary. But this night it was too cold to suffer through. I assembled the heater, shivering violently as I clicked the pilot light and cranked the knob to the high position. Within moments the chill was gone and we were sound asleep.

In the morning the exterior of the van was covered in frost. There were no other guests and the night guard, a lean Nama man wrapped in nothing more than a woolen shawl, his spindly legs poking from beneath, stood watching us from a few yards away. Our campsite at the edge of the Namib Desert was in the shadow of a very unusual dwelling.

After breakfast we climbed the stone stairs, passed through the enormous wooden doors, and paid the admission fee to enter Bavarian style Duwisib Castle. As we walked though the chambers Amanda read a pamphlet, her voice echoing between the harsh block walls, telling the unusual story of the strange citadel.

Near the turn of the last century a German Baron married a girl from New Jersey and together they circled the globe to live in this strange, distant land. She was the daughter of a diplomat, said to be a millionaire, with an income that dwarfed her husband's. They met while she visited Dresden, married shortly thereafter and sailed to the port of Luderitz in what was then German South West Africa. Elegant furnishings, extravagant paintings, and the finest wines were dragged across hundreds of miles of sand and scrub brush in ox-drawn carts. Purchasing vast tracts of barely inhabitable land, they built an ostentatious, unsuitable home using local laborers directed by stonemasons from Sweden and metalworkers from Italy. The couple lived in a shack adjacent to the project, supervising the construction that reached completion in just two short years. The fairy-tale home had fortified walls, embrasures for windows, and turrets at the corners to repel attacks from the surrounding Khoi herders.

As we walked through the castle we wondered what demons or noble desires drove these two young people, with titles and money to burn, to begin life together in one of the most desolate regions on earth. The pamphlet mentioned that the Baron was renowned in his hometown for enjoying a good celebration. Playing the piano and belting out songs, he was the center of attention, and festivities revolved around him. Desert life did not dampen his spirits and he would often pile a carriage full of wine bottles from his well-stocked cellar and set off for the town of Maltahöhe, armed and loaded for a rampage. Perhaps his lovely bride thought the desolate environment would dehydrate his rambunctious nature.

The Baron was a great horseman and he occupied some of his time by breeding the finest Arabian Shagya horses in Southern Africa. His endeavor showed such good results that the couple set out for England to purchase additional stallions to infuse the blood-line.

Shortly after leaving the Southern African port, World War I began, and their ship was diverted to the neutral harbor of Rio. Finding his way back to Germany, the Baron was killed in battle. His wife eventually returned to the expansive pine forests of New Jersey, never again setting foot in Southern Africa.

With the stables of the castle untended, the exquisite horses were eventually abandoned and forced to survive on their own. While driving across a remote area in the Great Namaland days earlier, we had come upon a small herd of feral horses in the simmering desert. Left to roam wild, the descendants of the Arabians evolved through generations with an adaptation to survive for days without water. This mutation allowed them to flourish in the harsh environment.

After leaving the castle, we headed north on the dirt roads that crisscross Namibia. Getting low on gas we planned to stop at a gas station listed on our map at an intersection in the middle of nowhere. When we arrived we found the attendant leaning against the shady side of an ancient pump. He swatted at the red dust lifted by our tires as he lazily said, "No, no petrol sorry, so sorry."

"We are going to Sossusvlei. Where's the next petrol station in that direction?" I asked.

"Yes, at Sossusvlei." He nodded eagerly.

"Nothing between here and there?"

"Yes, at Sossusvlei there is petrol, sorry, so sorry. Delivery comes tomorrow."

Two five-gallon gas canisters were strapped to the back of the van but one was already empty. I poured the second into the tank and we drove on.

At Sossusvlei the small gas station was deserted and I went searching for the attendant, while Amanda walked to the office to register for a camp spot. The attendant was hiding in the shade around the corner of the building and was not happy to be found. The gas tank in the van holds a little more that 13 gallons and according to the pump we arrived completely empty.

A German couple in a rented 4X4 waited behind me at the pump and the guy asked, "Have you driven out to the dunes?"

"No, we just arrived."

"Do you plan to drive out there in your van", he asked skeptically.

"Yes, this afternoon to see the sunset."

"I've heard that the road is very bad. Impossible without four-wheel drive."

"Well, we'll give it a try. If we get stuck you can pull us out."

He snorted a laugh that said, "Yeah, right."

When I finished I found Amanda standing in the shade of the office, chatting with the lean African woman who registered visitors for the Namib-Naukluft Parks. "So do you like living out here in the middle of the desert?" Amanda asked as she signed the registration book.

The friendly woman wore a colorful headscarf with her khaki uniform and smiled. "Yes, I like it very much here. I come from Windhoek, the capital." She carefully separated the perforated sheet and handed Amanda our receipt as she said, "It is very busy there and shopping at the market is expensive. I like it here very much better."

As Amanda carefully counted three Namibian one hundred dollar bills and handed them to the woman she asked, "Is it less expensive to shop here?"

"Oh no, it is very expensive here but I buy just a few things when I go into town." The woman smiled brightly. "In Windhoek I buy things that are expensive. Here I cannot get those things and I am happy."

"What do you buy in Windhoek?"

The woman looked down at the counter as she handed Amanda her change and embarrassedly giggled, "I have a sweet tooth. When I buy sugar I put it in everything. But when I do not have it, I do not want it any more. I like it here because I cannot get sugar."

At the end of the road I parked right next to the German and his rental 4X4. Hiking up to the top of Dune 45, the largest sand dune in the world, we looked over the magnificent burnt-orange hills, denuded of vegetation, sharply contrasting with the near-black afternoon shadows. As the sun set, the colors deepened and the sweeping, seductive curves of the dunes turned a dark blood red. Sitting at the very top, right on the edge, Amanda quietly watched as the strong wind blew the grains of sand over the lip, slowly shifting the dune, one miniscule grain at a time. Stacked in a curving rippled arch, the windward side sloped gently away, but on the leeward it was steeper, and the sand curved back like the tip of a shark's fin before falling over the edge.

The German couple followed our footsteps up the dune and sat down near us with their feet dangling over the steep end, sending sand cascading down in small waves.

"Ah, such a secluded spot. It is beautiful," said the woman. She had wild, matted hair and her blouse was speckled with stains. The man sat further down the edge and the woman continued, "We have been driving in the Sand Seas for two weeks and have seen nothing but dunes." She took a deep breath, "I love the desert. Have you been out into the Namib?"

We told them briefly about our route and they were eager to tell us about their adventures in the remote regions. On vacation from Germany for one month, they spent most of that time in the deserts. I asked innocently, "What do Germans love about the desert? Namibia is so different from Germany. "

The woman thought for a moment and answered, "In Europe everyone lives so close together and our homes are full of things. We leave no space for ourselves." She spread her arms indicating the expansive view. "We have no room to breathe. That is not good." She went on, "I believe we have many problems because we have many belongings around us and no personal space like this."

Standing to leave them alone at the top of the dune, Amanda wiped the sand from her bottom and I took a gulp of water. As we hobbled away down the sharp edge we understood their attraction.

Empty stretches of road offered us an opportunity rarely enjoyed in the modern world, long periods of time to think, to connect conversations and situations that would have otherwise been lost. Discussing minute aspects of an idea, then quietly contemplating them for a few hours before plunging back into the discussion would be considered frivolous in the fast-paced world, but for us this was one of the most important ingredients of our journey.

In the desert our car stereo was useless. Any variation in the landscape, even a small dune, caused the signal to become fuzzy and eventually fade altogether. Starting the trip, we had a handful of cassettes and frequently rotated the selection but over time the player began to reject them one by one. We would pop in a tape and suddenly out of the blue in the middle of a song it would begin playing the other side of the tape backwards in what sounded like fast-forward. Once this happened the tape would never play correctly again. Maybe we could get half a song out of it but just as we were settling in and singing along it would jump to the other side backward. By the time we reached the Namib Desert the only tape that still played was *Jimmy Buffet's Fruitcakes*. Strangely, it also happened to be one I could happily listen to all day, every day. Amanda felt differently and we often drove along in silence.

One idea that spun between us for days was our ability to enjoy remote places not for what is there, but for what is not there. We wondered if isolation helped to balance indulgence with restraint. At home we had become accustomed to having whatever we wanted, within limits. Have we become unable to trust ourselves to acquire and consume only what is necessary? Is modern temptation too great for our ancient passions? Can we not find satisfaction in simply making do with what we have? These ideas twirled round and round between us as we traveled across the barren landscape.

Stopping for lunch at the side of a long desolate road, the sun blazed above and the wind blew fine dust in our faces. Amanda filled a pot with water to boil pasta while I pulled out the cutting board and began chopping vegetables. The flame on our tiny stove burned bright for a brief moment and then disappeared. In the middle of this isolation, with little hope of filling the tank, we had run out of precious propane.

CHAPTER 48

Opinionated Laundresses

Swakopmund, Namibia
37,803 miles

Mexico lost. Amanda strapped on her heavy backpack full of dirty clothes, disheartened after watching Mexico being defeated by the U.S. soccer team in a World Cup qualifying match on television at the backpackers' hostel. Barely visible behind the full pack, she made her way to the laundromat, prepared to do battle with any itinerant laundress who stood in her way.

Many towns in Southern Africa have a self-service laundry and Amanda found herself lured to these establishments with their promise of effortless, sparklingly clean clothes, but she was regularly thwarted by the resident mama, a plump, turbaned woman who ruled her domain like a small kingdom.

In the past we had been enticed by the eager smile of these ingratiating laundresses and handed over our carefully separated piles of clothing. Each time, upon return, there was something not quite right. Once the clothes smelled as if they had been washed in a vat of boiled fish guts. A second time everything came back with a pinkish-purple hue. On the most recent occasion, on a damp rainy day with nothing else to do, Amanda sat and watched the laundress as she efficiently moved our clothing from washer to dryer. She did everything correctly but like a hygienic Houdini the laundress refused to reveal the secret of how she permeated our whites with a green tinge, and the rest with the odor of a bucket of burnt motor oil.

Deflated after the World Cup loss, Amanda arrived at the laundromat where two African girls, barely in their twenties, wearing tight hip-hugger jeans and bright halter tops, smiled and greeted her, ready to accept the dirty clothes.

Amanda said, "No, thank you. I'll do it myself."

The older of the two girls said, "Here's a machine for you," as she moved her neatly stacked piles of clothes aside.

Keyed for a fight that never materialized, Amanda sputtered over-eager thanks and the girls adopted her into their world. With her new best friends Amanda loaded the machine, then sat and chatted a meandering conversation about Namibia.

Julieth was only moonlighting as a laundress. At her regular job she counseled those stricken with AIDS and she held some strong and controversial opinions on the subject. While pulling dirty laundry from a plastic bag and stuffing it into a washer, she said in an angry tone, "The government should stop paying for the medicine for the people with HIV and give it to programs for the orphaned children." She told the story of a family with six children who lost both parents. "They were left alone to live in the streets," Julieth said. "Now the oldest girl is positive also. The cycle will never end if we don't help the children. They're the future of Namibia."

Her friend Selma went even further describing the hopelessness. "We give these people expensive medicine that does not cure one thing. It just makes them live longer and they give AIDS to more people."

Julieth said, "They get the disease because they won't use protection. They think these other countries want them to use a condom so they stop having babies. And they think using a condom is like murder."

Just months before, the President of Namibia, Sam Nujoma claimed publicly that the United States created AIDS as part of a biological weapons program during the Vietnam War. If the President of the country believed such a thing, we wondered what the average person must think.

As they chatted Amanda noticed that the girls had devised an unusual scheme to pocket a little extra money from their laundry gig. They waited until a load completed half the wash cycle then removed it and placed a new pile of clothes in the dirty water to finish the cycle. When half the spin cycle was complete they rinsed the first pile in a sink nearby and switched them once again.

Julieth asked, "What is it like in Mexico with men?"

Amanda explained how the Catholic Church is prominent in the lives of most Mexicans and premarital sex is still frowned upon. She embarrassedly told them that she had been chaperoned by her younger brother when dating, until she was almost their age.

Selma and Julieth found the differences hilarious.

The laundresses talked about the relationship between men and women in Namibia. They felt the men have all the control and the women are grateful if a man chooses them. Julieth said, "The definition for love is warped in Namibia. Women think love is when a man is with them no matter what else he does."

Selma pulled clothing from a dryer and said, "Many women are beaten and cheated on but still continue to have relations and have children with the man." She added, "A women only feels good about herself if she is having a child every year, regardless of the father. To stop HIV, that must change."

As Amanda folded her laundry, the girls placed their piles in carefully marked plastic bags to be returned to the tourists in the five-star safari lodges. On the radio a commercial began, and Julieth started, then Selma joined her in singing along, "The only way to control AIDS is to practice your ABC's. Abstinence, Be faithful and use a Condom." They both giggled as they hugged Amanda goodbye.

CHAPTER 49

Crazy Gods

The Etosha Pan, Namibian Desert
38,383 miles

"It's not like that at all," the young guy said with glassy-eyed discontent as he pointed to the television set.

We were sitting in the dingy lounge of a backpacker's hostel in Windhoek, Namibia, with a group of Peace Corps workers. They were on a short break from their remote posts and they had spent the entire time consuming Wimpy's hamburgers, Coca-Colas and an endless stream of videos.

Michael, a pudgy Coloradoan, was groaning at the portrayal of the San villagers in the cult classic, *The Gods Must Be Crazy*. In the film a soft drink bottle that is dropped from an airplane causes mayhem in a peaceful San village. At first the villagers believe it is a gift from the gods. It becomes a valuable tool for the tribe and they use it to pound tubers and cure snakeskin. But then the once happy group begins to argue over its use. When one woman hits another over the head with the bottle the tribe decides it is an evil gift that needs to be discarded. The leader of the group, Xixo, is determined to throw the bottle off the end of the earth, and experiences an enlightening series of mishaps in his contact with the outside world.

We told Michael about our plans to head into Bushmanland. In preparation to explore the isolated San territory on the fringes of the Kalahari, we had purchased two extra fuel canisters, allowing us to carry a total of twenty extra gallons of gas.

He pointed at the screen and asked, "Have you heard what happened to this guy, the actor?" Not waiting for an answer he said, "This movie destroyed his life."

"What do you mean, destroyed his life?" Amanda asked.

Michael lowered the volume and began to tell us the story of Cgoa Coma, the San villager who portrayed Xixo. Before meeting the film's director, Coma had encountered only three white people and had never seen a settlement larger than his small village. Receiving his first earnings from the film, he was paid the equivalent of $300 in cash but did not fully grasp the value of the bills and let them blow away. But he quickly learned.

He purchased cattle that were soon eaten by lions and bought a Ford truck that he was unable to drive. He hired a driver. By the time the director was planning the sequel Coma had discovered the power of those small pieces of paper and demanded a larger salary. He went on to star in many more films. In one he portrayed the African incarnation of the martial arts legend, Bruce Lee.

Feeling responsible for the transformation of Coma's life, employees of the film company guided him on managing his finances and organized the construction of a fully furnished, three-bedroom brick house in his village. His new home differed significantly from the traditional San dwelling of a modest hut with no electricity and running water. Over thirty members of his family were lured by his wealth. When he was away they traded his refrigerator, furniture, and cupboards for alcohol. Coma lived in fear and worried that the people in his village would use witchcraft to steal his riches. He acted as if he were poor to deflect their attention. His life became so tainted by his wealth that he eventually sold the house and many of his possessions for a fraction of their value.

Coma's last days were spent hunting, living humbly in a small hut in a remote village. On his last morning he woke early, collected firewood and sipped tea with his father-in-law before heading out into the bush with his bow and arrow, bird traps and a hunting pouch, looking for guinea fowl. When he did not return his father-in-law tracked his spoor and found him collapsed on a path, his bow and arrow still strapped to his shoulder.

Michael told us that there are just a handful of San in the most remote corners of the Kalahari Desert living in the ways handed down to them over millions of years. Their once harmonious interdependency was based on the belief that the welfare of the community was more important than one's own well-being. It was once considered immoral among the San to eat in front of someone with no food. Things have changed.

A week later when we reached the town of Tsumeb I stopped at the dusty crossroads and turned off the van's motor. The spare tanks were topped up and we were ready to turn east towards the Kalahari and the San territory. We sat there talking for a moment about the stories we had heard. The stories of the current state of the San people, of alcoholism, degradation, social breakdown, and forced relocation. This discouraged us from probing deeper into Bushmanland. Our purpose in visiting the San was to experience their culture and to get a glimpse into their traditional way of life but, it seemed, our visit could damage the very thing we wished to see. Silently Amanda took out the map. After studying it for a while she said, "We could turn left toward the border with Angola and the Etosha National Park."

I started the car and put on the turn signal.

The Charitsaub water hole at the Etosha National Park was teeming with game. A tour guide positioned a specially-designed Land Rover game viewing truck next to us. Eavesdropping, we listened as he spoke to his elderly English-speaking tour group. "This hole is one of the few places where the animals can drink. Sometimes when it rains, the water collects in puddles on the floor of the pan but the mineral content is so high that the animals cannot drink it." He pointed to some zebra and said, "Watch the way they march up in a group for safety." The tour sat quietly for a few moments, then the guide said in a dramatically hushed voice, almost to himself, "Imagine, groups of Bushmen lived here for eons taking only the animals necessary to satisfy their immediate need, gathering roots and nuts."

An elegantly dressed woman in full safari suit asked, "Do the Bushmen still live here?"

The guide thought for a moment and said sadly, "No, they were moved in the 1950s when the park was created. There were too few animals by then."

"Where did they go?" the woman asked.

"The government created an area for them to the east," he answered vaguely.

"It's a shame they had to lose their home. Did they do it for tourism or to save the animals?" she asked.

Before she finished the question the guide had realized we were listening and had already begun speaking to us, "We saw four lions just to the left of the Kalkheuwel water hole not long ago."

The woman forgot her question and added, "It was really beautiful," so loudly that a nearby zebra spooked and ran off.

Lions are most active at night and we had never seen the animal at the pinnacle of the food chain. The game parks of Southern Africa did not permit guests to drive after sunset, the darkness combined with the dusty roads creating a deadly setting for the wildlife.

Driving directly to the Kalkheuwel water hole, we parked with three overland vehicles. Everyone was looking toward a small bush and Amanda used the binoculars to scan the area but did not see any lion. Suddenly I spotted what looked like a tail flapping just yards from the van behind a log. Amanda looked closer with the binoculars and found five lions, three males and two females, blending into the shade of several small bushes and the log.

Mesmerized like two idiots with binocular rings around our eyes, we raised the pop-top roof and watched these five beasts through the opening. They had obviously fed recently and lazily slept in the shade while zebra, giraffe, wildebeest, kudu, and eland slowly crept toward the water hole from the far side. In the afternoon a herd of elephant appeared from out of the bush and plodded directly into the water, causing the other animals to scatter. Unnoticed by the elephants, the lions sat absolutely still, hunched forward, watching the scene. The mother of a playful baby elephant sensed a threat and fearlessly approached the lions. She was soon joined by others and they trumpeted and stomped their massive feet. The lions reluctantly retreated to a safe distance, waiting for darkness to fall, when they could have their revenge.

On the other side of the pool the playful baby, having learned the power of his size, bullied away a few wildebeest that tentatively crept toward the water. The wildebeests leaped then ran away. When they realized the elephant was no longer chasing they stopped and stood among low brown shrubs, looking longingly toward the waterhole.

CHAPTER 50

Prey and Predator

The Caprivi Strip, Namibia
38,945 miles

Brigitte Bodoin was at the wheel of the rented camper van as the family sped directly into the setting sun along the trans-Caprivi highway in Northern Namibia. Her husband Claude was riding shotgun. This was the journey of a lifetime for the teachers, celebrating the new year at Victoria Falls in the heart of Africa with their three children. They headed west toward the dry Etosha Pan, crossing the Caprivi Strip. Brigitte had driven all the way from Katima Mulilo, stopping at the Omega military base a few short kilometers from the Angolan border to allow her husband Claude to take the wheel. Their eighteen year-old son Michael sat in the passenger seat and Brigitte climbed into the rear of the camper with their daughters, fifteen year-old Aurelie and ten year-old Cecile.

Just minutes after leaving the military checkpoint, all hell broke loose. The windows shattered. Then the tires exploded and the van skidded to a halt. Claude was unconscious, bleeding from the chest. Ten men sprang from of the bush. Some wore military uniforms. Others did not. They surrounded the van and riddled it with bullets. Automatic gunfire echoed in the twilight. Like a pack of wolves the men rushed the van, slashing at the children with bayonets, stealing food, cameras, luggage, even the shoes off their feet. When Brigitte came around the men were gone. Her husband was severely wounded. Her children were dead.

A vehicle approached. Dazed and in shock, Brigitte managed to move, waving her uninjured arm. They were soldiers, members of the Namibian Defense Force. The soldiers rushed the family to the regional hospital in Rundu where doctors stabilized her husband.

Two years later, sitting on tree stumps with our backs to a bonfire looking toward the Okavango River, we first heard the story of the Bodoin family. The glow of the flames made it difficult to see beyond the ring of light. Loud, guttural grunts of nearby hippos brought to mind the dangers that lurked in the darkness. The bush camp owner, Skip, sat on another stump, rapidly getting drunk while he struggled to keep the conversation going and the guests drinking, since most of the profits from the rustic Ngepi Camp came from the bar. Being the life of the party each night, Skip was beginning to show the strain. But he wasn't drunk yet. He could recognize when the conversation took a bad turn. An overstuffed white Botswanan in a safari shirt and khaki shorts sat hunched forward, poking a stick in the fire as he told the Bodoin story. Skip tried to guide the conversation in another direction.

"Yeah, it happened just down the road," the Botswanan pointed.

"But it's safe now," Skip interrupted, "For more than a year the soldiers led convoys across. Now they've lifted the travel restrictions. They've got so many troops in the area, there won't be any more problems here. It's good because now they're also protecting the animals."

The Botswanan fired back, "The Namibians said it was Unita rebels crossing from Angola but the woman said they weren't talking Portuguese. They had to be Namibian. Probably the same group that tried to take over the airport in Katima Mulilo a few years ago."

Skip was getting mad and blurted, "The woman just watched her children getting killed, how could she know what language they were speaking? And anyhow, they speak their native language even in Angola." He realized we were listening intently and said, "You came through there on your way here. You saw there were no problems."

Nodding in thoughtless agreement, our minds were racing. We had to drive back that way to get to Victoria Falls.

We had driven across part of the Caprivi Strip, a narrow finger of Namibia extending between Angola, Botswana, Zimbabwe, and Zambia. Left over from incomplete negotiations between the British and Germans of colonial times, this sliver of land, criss-crossed by the Kwando River in the west and the Zambezi in the east, is the greenest and most truly African area in Namibia.

Leaving the Ngepi bush camp, we drove on a small dirt path running next to the Okavango River and headed into the Mahango Game Reserve on the border with Botswana. The ranger, a robust African woman in a safari suit, smiled broadly as if she'd just met a long-lost friend. Her intricately beaded head of braids bounced energetically as she went through her well-rehearsed speech, "It's the dry season and there are plenty of animals here, lion, hippo, and crocodile, especially around the rivers." Then she paused. Eyeing the van suspiciously, her face took on a serious demeanor. "But it is best for you to stay away from the river paths where the predators hide. They are for stronger vehicles."

Rutted, sandy dirt paths wound through the reserve and we were enticed by an infrequently used road that looked inviting as it looped around to a spot on the riverbank. It appeared similar to the road we were on but as I turned the van on to the path I felt the traction of the tires slipping. Still confident that we could continue, I pressed on the gas, but we barely moved and I immediately realized we were in trouble. The tires were spinning, the engine revving, yet we were going nowhere. I poked my head out of the window as a family of warthogs sped away. Looking at the track beneath us, it was obvious that this had been a trouble spot for 4x4s with a sandy mound in the center and deep ruts on both sides. Like Humpty Dumpty balancing on the wall, the belly of the van rested high on the summit while the wheels spun in the sand. The ranger's warning echoed in my mind.

I had no choice. It was unlikely that another vehicle would come by, so I shut off the engine and rummaged around for the folding shovel we had bought at the Army Surplus for just such a situation. We had never used the shovel and I could not remember where I'd stored it. After tearing everything out of the storage area under the seat I gave up in frustration. Sweating buckets, my shirt was soaked through and I hadn't even started.

Amanda climbed out the window with the binoculars strapped around her neck and sat perched on the roof as lookout. I quickly hopped out of the van and thought to myself, "Here's that risk you've been looking for." At the back bumper I began unbolting the Hi-Lift jack, another handy tool we hadn't used for more than a year. It was so clogged with gunk that it refused to budge. I sprayed it with lubricant and pounded on it with the vice grips, creating a horrible ruckus that could be heard for miles, surely signaling predators.

After several minutes of grunting and struggling, I had the rear end of the van in the air and slithered underneath to scoop out the fine sand with my arms. From her perch above Amanda made a few distressing sounds while I frantically dug. I stuck my head out and asked anxiously, "What, what? Did you see something?"

She stammered unconvincingly, "Oh, eh, um, …nothing, no, em, no, nothing at all….all's clear up here."

"Are you sure? You don't sound too sure."

"I'm sure. I didn't see a thing. Hurry up, dig!"

Slithering back underneath, I continued scooping out sand until I reached firm ground. I got up and dug flat areas a few feet in front of each of the tires. Finally I piled some branches and brush underneath and let the jack down.

Back in the van, with the grit of sand in my teeth, clogging my nose and plugging my ears, I started the engine as Amanda climbed down from the roof. Mashing the pedal to the floor, the tires held and the little motor pushed with a furious effort. The wheels spun and dug in a bit. With the clutch half out and the engine revving at full throttle, the van moved at a snail's pace but finally reached firm ground.

I hung my arms out the window to wipe some of the sand off and asked, "Okay, what did you see?"

Amanda looked away, fighting back a laugh, "When you were under the van that family of warthogs came out of the bush. They sniffed around but when you poked your head out they ran away. I wonder why?"

"Warthogs! Why…why didn't you warn me?"

"They had two little babies and they were so cute with their little tails pointing in the air. What harm could they possibly do?"

CHAPTER 51

Subtle as a Soap Opera

Sepupa, Botswana
39,104 miles

The Belgian soap opera star sipped her beer straight from the bottle and listened intently with a naive innocence that appeared part of her role. Lean and awkward, like a teenager with mature and adolescent features intermingled, Ingrid was in hiatus from the show where she portrayed a conniving, manipulative young villain. The crusty old boatman slid closer, touching her on the shoulder, and said, "Last week we had four funerals in the village, three from AIDS, one from a lion." Ingrid's boyfriend Manuel, a flamboyant Flemish television director with a large scarf wrapped around his neck like a cravat and a long graying beard, repeated, "A lion!" Obviously enjoying the outrageous conversation.

The boatman answered with enthusiasm, "Ya, young guy shot a lion, bad shot and the lion bit his head off, killed him. They ate the lion at the funeral. Good meal." The boatman enjoyed telling stories that kept the drinks flowing in his direction. In the atmosphere of great fun Manuel knew it and didn't care. Ingrid just hung on.

The Sepupa Swamp Stop camp was thrown together at the edge of the Okavango Delta in northern Botswana with bamboo-walled showers and roofless toilets. In a country where rural chiefs can decide on a whim to reclaim land owned by foreigners, the camp represented the minimalist necessity with which entrepreneurs in the region build. Everything, including the kitchen sink, could be loaded on a trailer and hauled away in a matter of hours. The only structure revealing even a hint of creativity was the bar, erected in the shade of a massive baobab tree with a shaky deck poking out over the river and comfortable chairs to lounge away the day.

In those comfortable chairs we sat waiting. The public boat was due to arrive anytime. Anytime could be today or next week. Or never. The public boat hadn't been reliable lately. The foreigner who ran it for the Okavango Polemans' Trust, a European woman, got smacked around by some of the polemen and quit. Her departure left the group in shambles.

As we waited Manuel drew a crowd at the bar by telling of his exploits directing the Flemish version of The Jerry Springer Show. He and Amanda traded anecdotes of how they learned English from American television. Ingrid purposely aimed the conversation toward the episodes of the soap opera Manuel frequently directed. That's how they met. When another Belgian couple enthusiastically said hello, she cringed.

"She doesn't like to be recognized. That's why we are on holiday here," Manuel explained.

Ingrid turned away innocently.

Well greased with free beer and Ingrid's indulgence, the boatman agreed to ferry the four of us across the delta to the Polemans' camp the next morning for a small fee. Moments later Ingrid feigned a yawn and excused herself for the night. Manuel stayed behind and kept the drinks flowing.

The twisting waterways created by the tall reeds of the Okavango Delta seemed to branch off in every direction and narrowed to the width of the flat-bottomed aluminum boat before spreading as wide and flat as an African river. The curving maze of brown water reflected the green, fuzzy papyrus, their feather-duster heads reaching to the clear blue sky on thin stilts.

Manuel, Amanda and I sat hunched in the bow wearing rain jackets against the spray as Ingrid huddled in the stern, her scarf fluttering wildly in the face of the boatman. Hung-over, the boatman sped full throttle through the narrow alleys, using the reeds as bumpers when he overshot a corner. After more than an hour, in what seemed to be the center of the vast delta, he cut the engine and coasted to the bank at the shores of the village of Seronga.

A Botswana man helped Amanda and Ingrid step off the boat and greeted us with bewilderment as he said in halting English, "We did not know you were coming. I am here to meet another group." But the other group failed to turn up and we followed him along the wide dirt path through the tiny village.

As we arrived at the camp run by the Polemans' Trust, the man arranged two simple but clean huts and pointed across the camp to a bamboo enclosure where we found flushing toilets and hot showers.

Not long after settling in, a couple of polers approached, offering to take us for a ride on the river. Lopes, a tall thin man, wore dark blue dress pants and matching pressed shirt with a shiny belt buckle and a black ski-cap. Sitting in the shade of the hut negotiating the price for the trip, I was drenched in sweat from the sticky humidity but Lopes seemed unaffected. His partner, Life, was younger, in his early twenties, and had more experience navigating the delta, having grown up with the waterways as his playground. Life spoke only Tswana but had a gentle, easy smile that instilled confidence and helped to seal the deal with the wheeler-dealer Lopes. Ingrid wrapped a sarong around her head like the turbaned African Queen and attached herself to Lopes as we followed Life to the water's edge.

Cut from a large mukwa tree and hollowed in the center, the mokoro is the traditional means of transportation for the inhabitants of the delta. The boats rot through within a few seasons and demand for proper trees has caused considerable deforestation, so an aid organization introduced fiberglass boats a few years ago. The delta is rarely deeper than a few feet and the poler pushes the mokoro in much the same way a gondolier propels a gondola.

Sitting at water level, submerged within the mokoro, Life pushed us along through fields of underwater vegetation while Lopes propelled Ingrid and Manuel in another. Only the lily pads and their flowers reach the surface and it felt as if we were floating in a meadow of green with purple buds blooming to a bright, waxy white.

After an hour of poling, Lopes was overheated in his heavy, dark clothing and suggested we stop to track a herd of elephant recently spotted in the area, but Life did not seem too keen on the idea. After a brief disagreement in Tswana the more assertive Lopes won and we pulled the boats up on to the bank.

Silently creeping through the brush, Lopes led and periodically paused to ask Life, the more experienced tracker, questions in Tswana about hoof-prints in the sand, then translated the answers into English. At the edge of a stand of tall trees we heard the loud cracking of branches. Life looked nervous, shook his head and said something to Lopes in Tswana. He didn't translate so Amanda asked what was said. Lopes answered, "Life is not happy because that was an elephant and we are in the wrong place, because of the wind. He says we should be above the wind from the elephant. But do not worry. I have done this before." Lopes marched forward confidently with Amanda close behind. Ingrid followed tentatively. Manuel and I stayed back with Life.

Lopes stopped, peering through a clump of green-brown brush, then waved for us to follow but Manuel and I didn't budge. A large lone bull faced away, tearing a branch from a tree, stripping the green leaves with the tip of his trunk. Ingrid and Amanda stood at Lopes's shoulder and Ingrid clicked off a few camera shots, the automatic winder buzzing loudly. The bull elephant turned abruptly and raised his trunk to smell in our direction, then flared out his ears and charged.

The group didn't move so I whispered loudly, "Amanda, get back here."

She swatted her hand, motioning for me to be quiet.

Life backed away and we followed but Lopes, Amanda and Ingrid stood behind the bush, watching. The elephant stopped about twenty feet from them, trumpeting, pounding the earth, and thrusting his head back and forth. Life looked at me and said, "Bad," then moved further back but the others held their ground.

I inched forward as the elephant rushed closer, kicking at the dust, spreading his ears wide.

Amanda turned, looked at me wide-eyed and said, "Isn't this amazing", as I grabbed her by the wrist and pulled.

"We've got to move back. Now!" I said.

"But I want to see. Wait just a second." Amanda said as I pulled her back. Lopes and Ingrid following close behind.

Rushing to the mokoros we jumped in and pushed off into the river. The elephant followed from a distance, feigning a charge then turning away as he neared the water. As they pushed frantically, Life had a few angry words with Lopes, then said nothing for the rest of the journey back.

As we approached the camp Lopes hiked up his pants legs to pull the mokoros up to the bank and Ingrid noticed a large festering wound on his calf. She asked loudly, "What happened to your leg?"

He looked down without concern, "I was cutting brush with a panga and hit myself."

She squatted beside him to get a closer look. "But it's infected. You need medicine."

"Yes. But medicine is expensive. This will heal."

"Come over to our hut. I think I have something in my pack," she commanded.

Lopes reluctantly followed Ingrid toward their hut while we thanked Life and went to our own. We could hear Ingrid tearing through her pack looking for the medicine. "I must have left it in the car in Sepopa," she said, frustrated. A second later she was at our door asking if we had any with us.

Amanda said, "I left everything in the van except for a few band-aids."

"Well, give me them," Ingrid demanded. She impatiently waited as Amanda dug them from her backpack.

Curious to see what she planned, we trailed behind a moment later. Outside their hut Lopes sat on a chair with his pant leg rolled up and his shoeless foot propped on Ingrid's leg. She dipped the edge of her sarong in water and cleaned the wound. It was a deep cut about two inches long oozing clear pus and surrounded by a dark edge. Manuel was equally curious and watched over Ingrid's shoulder as she began to unwrap a band-aid. Concerned, he blurted out, "But it's infected!"

Ingrid swiftly turned her head and glared at him angrily. Instantly he lost his tongue and she continued in her role. Stretching two band-aids over much of the gaping wound she sat back to admire her work, then added knowingly, "Now you must get antiseptic ointment."

Before Lopes could respond Ingrid was already up, walking toward the restroom, dusting off her pant legs, and seemed not to hear when he replied, "Yes, but it is very expensive."

CHAPTER 52

The Son of Ham

Katima Mulilo, Namibia
39,457 miles

Wobbling like a log-rolling contest, the shaky dock was tricky to cross with water-rotted boards and mangled ropes barely holding it together. Just one unsteady step could send us plummeting into the croc and hippo-infested river below. The dock led to a rickety floating bar where locals and visitors gathered for the evening ritual of the sun setting over the Zambezi River. The bright orange ball slid behind the savannah accompanied by the grunting of hippos, and we turned toward the dock, watching the other evening ritual as one by one the drunks tried to cross the shaky contraption back to dry land.

The Caprivi was living up to its reputation. Not because of the violence or the dangers that we had been warned about, but because of the unspoiled, wild frontier feel that only comes from remoteness. Caprivians seemed unaffected by the volatility of changing governments and the modern world around them. Most live by farming plots along the banks of the Zambezi and Kwando rivers.

The small towns scattered along the road offered few amenities, just the basic necessities, a gas station, a few fruit stands, and a market stocked with sacks of corn meal and flour. That was until we arrived in the town of Katima Mulilo.

While we were at the bar Manuel and Ingrid had arrived and set up their tent just a few feet away from the van, blocking our view of the river. When we got back they hurried off to the restaurant while we began tackling chores. Amanda carried a bucket full of laundry to the water tap and scrubbed the clothing while I chopped onions and peppers for dinner.

The harsh onions were making my eyes water and I stuck my head out the door for some relief. Standing just beyond the boundary of our site was a petite blonde girl, about sixteen years old, waiting to get my attention. She timidly asked, "Are you really from America?" She had an Afrikaans accent and was plump and cheerful.

"Yes, from California." Most kids were familiar with California and found it easier to relate to than Mexico or Philadelphia.

The girl's eyes lit up. "California," she repeated, then turned to a group of women cooking at another campsite and said loud enough for them to hear, "They're from California."

A short woman, about twenty-five with long dark curly hair and a face full of freckles, jumped from her chair and came over while the girl bombarded us with questions about the van and our route. "This is Erica and I'm Alma," she said, "Erica's going to Michigan next month. She's going to be a doctor. Is Michigan close to California?"

Erica laughed and said to Alma, "It's all the way across the country," then turned to us, "Not a doctor, a PhD., microbiology. It is all very complicated and boring."

They were from a farming community north of Johannesburg and were curious about our opinion of South Africa. Alma asked question after question until Amanda interrupted, "Well, we want to know about you too. What are you doing here?"

Twisting her hair shyly, Erica answered, "Every morning we go across on the ferry into Zambia. There are thirty-two of us from our church. And we drive fifty kilometers to a Christian camp where we're teaching people how to farm plots of land on their own."

Alma said proudly, "Today we taught them to plant maize." She added with surprise, "Zambian women do most of the hard work here. They're the farmers. The men just lie around, so we teach the women."

A large man in his late fifties, tall and stout, the picture of graying health, approached from where the church group was preparing for dinner and said, "Haven't these girls driven you crazy yet?"

Erica introduced her father. He held out a thick hand and said, "Piet, pleasure to meet you." He put his arm over Erica's shoulder, obviously proud of his daughter. When he asked a few questions Alma said, "I already asked them all of that," and answered for us in great detail. She said, "They want to know about us."

Piet thought seriously for a moment. "Our church is sponsoring a training program for small plot farmers over in Zambia. We purchased the land and divided it up among a village. We're teaching them the skills they need and we've brought along enough supplies, seed and fertilizer for the first crop."

"Teach a man to fish?" I asked.

"Exactly, it's our responsibility."

Amanda wondered aloud, "Your responsibility?"

Erica excused herself to help with the dinner and Alma followed behind.

Piet watched them go and asked, "Do you know the Bible?"

I thought we were in for a lecture on religion and Amanda asked, "How do you mean?"

He scratched dirty fingernails along the inside of his wrist and said, "Genesis, the first book."

We nodded and he said, "Canaan, Ham's son?" Looking to see if we understood, he went on, "The Bible tells us we are responsible for the offspring of Canaan." Again he looked at both of us then seemed to decide something and said, "I'm sure you don't want a Bible lesson right now. Let me tell you that we Afrikaners believe it is important to help the Africans become self-sufficient. A few generations back it was possible for them to live as hunters but most of the animals are gone. Now they are starving. We must teach them how to fend for themselves." He looked as if he was unsure whether he had said too much and excused himself, saying he must wash up for dinner.

The next morning before leaving the campsite with Manuel and Ingrid, and heading toward Victoria Falls to the east, we said goodbye to Alma and Erica. I made a mental note to learn more about Canaan, to understand what could drive these good people into the heart of Africa. I wanted to understand why they felt responsible.

Later I learned that those who believe the literal interpretation of the Bible hold that all humanity stems from Noah by way of his three sons. They say one of those sons, Ham, showed Noah disrespect and Noah responded by cursing Ham's son Canaan, declaring his offspring, "servant of servants shall he be unto his brothers". Even today some fundamentalists believe that dark skin is evidence of this curse.

Rooted in the Bible, this belief was used to justify not only apartheid in South Africa but slavery and segregation in America. Passed from generation to generation, it became the backbone of these unequal societies, fostering a paternalistic attitude toward the African, one of rule and responsibility.

These interpretations help lead good people on the road to righteousness. But they can be used as a tool to manipulate those same people into actions that betray their innate sense of right and wrong. I wondered if Erica and Alma, suddenly open to a world outside their closed community, represented the end of that line of responsibility.

CHAPTER 53

African Babies Don't Cry

Livingstone, Zambia
39,662 miles

"They never cry," Ingrid said, flipping down the hood of her North Face rain parka, as she smiled at one of the little African boys with pity. A cluster of Zambian school children gathered around us and their teacher asked if we would pose for a photo with them.

"Of course," Amanda said and excitedly wrapped her arm around one of the little girls. Leaning toward Ingrid, she said quietly, "We noticed that too." Turning the little girl to face the camera, Amanda complimented the teacher, "The children are so well behaved."

The teacher smiled and pointed the camera to the group. "Say cheese."

In unison the children sang out, "Cheeeeeeeese."

Victoria Falls was roaring in the background, emitting clouds of mist that evaporated in a dance with the noontime sun. A few steps from the base of the falls the sun was winning, the moisture rapidly vanishing into the air. The natural rock ledge overlooking the deep gorge was empty except for a few older boys who removed their tattered clothing and swam in the swirling pools. We watched with uneasy apprehension as they shimmied close to the edge of the falls.

Perspiring under protective rubbery layers of rain gear, we were soaking wet inside and out. Every so often the wind pushed from the Zimbabwe side of the river and the spray drifted, pelting us with a refreshing splash.

"I wonder how things are over there now?" Manuel asked.

Peering over the river from the less-developed Zambian side of the falls, we gazed toward Zimbabwe with its empty hotel resorts and extensive visitors' center. The flip-flopping politics of the two nations, from stability to chaos, had shifted the privilege of hosting visitors to the falls. Ingrid said, "When my father came to visit Africa on a tour just a few years ago, they stood across in Zimbabwe wondering how life here in Zambia was progressing. Now look how the tables have turned. Zambia has found stability and Zimbabwe is in turmoil."

Manuel went on to tell us what he knew about the rebellious leader of Zimbabwe, Robert Mugabe, who had begun a program of farm invasions that sent the economy of his country into a tailspin. Veterans from the war for independence had begun to seize land forcefully, with the government's encouragement, from white farm families who had been cultivating it for generations. With limited experience in raising crops, the new owners could barely support themselves. The wheat and cornfields, once considered the breadbasket of Southern Africa, became wild and untended.

Wiping the droplets from his beard with his long cravat scarf Manuel looked around and eye caught on a group of children standing against a rail at the falls edge. He said, "I think the children are so well behaved because of the mothers. Do you see how they are always connected? They wrap them right next to their skin with the blanket." He pointed with his chin toward a vendor then ruffled his beard in thought. "They get constant attention."

An African woman sat flat-legged on the asphalt just beyond the mist line, selling carved trinkets. Hung in a sash like a hammock around her chest, her infant suckled as she polished a carved rhino with black paste. The sash supported the baby's head, leaving both her hands free to work.

Later, as we drove back to the hostel, Ingrid held her dripping rain jacket out the window to dry. At a stoplight we watched a young mother adjust her baby strapped to her breast as she balanced a stack of flattened cardboard boxes on her head. Ingrid nodded in the woman's direction and said, "They don't have *sucettes* here. What are they called in English?"

Manuel said, "Dummies."

"In America they're called pacifiers," Amanda said.

"They don't use them here," Ingrid added and laughed. "But they have the best substitute."

Later that day, in the yard of the lively backpackers' hostel, two guys were snooping around the van. One lay in the dirt with his blue and white motorcycle boots sticking out from under our muffler while the other, a young African wearing a dressy shirt and pants, peered through cupped hands into the side window. A battered motorcycle with a Danish flag was parked in the shade of a tree, the dented aluminum side-packs open, with tools neatly arranged on a canvas cloth next to the wheel. The guy under the van heard us approaching and shimmied out, asking in flawless English, "Is this your van?" without a hint of embarrassment.

He introduced himself as Arno from Denmark. Arno was a lanky blond nomad, his weathered skin tanned and wind-burned. He spent eight or nine months of the year zipping around Africa on his motorcycle and the other three or four scooping ice cream and saving kroners in Denmark. An African friend would store his motorcycle and a few belongings, and Arno would fly home with a return ticket in his pocket. The owner of the ice cream shop knew the system and helped Arno with the paperwork to collect generous unemployment benefits from the Danish government. In Africa he would pop his ATM card into a machine in Lilongwe or Nairobi and withdraw the bi-weekly allowance amounting to more than most Africans earn in a year.

Tired of living out of his two packs, Arno was curious to see the inside of the van. Amanda opened the sliding door and showed the guys our living area. Arno was enthralled. "I can't believe you have so many comforts, a sink, a stove and drawers. You even have a bowl with fruit and cushions on your seat."

"I made the pillows myself," Amanda said proudly.

"This is like a small living room in a home," said his friend, William.

"I would gladly give up my motorcycle for one day of this comfort." Arno said longingly.

William, a funny, outgoing Zambian, was another story. Arno had befriended him at a backpackers' hostel in the capital, Lusaka, and William had squeezed himself and his modest duffel bag on to the back of the motorcycle. Together they headed for Pretoria where William studied hydrology at the University of South Africa. The university has the largest distance-learning program in Africa and William was making his annual pilgrimage to restock books and meet with his faculty advisor.

Growing up in the Zambian capital, William studied at a private school under a string of young British volunteers, adopting their direct manner without retaining even a hint of African modesty. Whatever flowed through his brain poured out his mouth unhindered.

"So how much money you got in the bank to take this trip?" he asked, unabashed.

"We saved for many years and we're very frugal with our spending," I said.

"How much did you save?"

"Just enough to get by," I answered evasively.

"You're not going to answer, huh?"

We all smiled.

Sitting with cold drinks on the shady front porch of the hostel, we quickly became good friends and Amanda decided to ask William the question we were wondering about earlier in the day, "Why don't African children ever cry?"

He massaged the back of his neck in thought then said, "The question you ask is not right. You should be asking why children from your country are always crying."

"Okay, why do you think kids from our countries are always crying?"

"Money," he said, straight faced.

"Money?" Amanda asked.

"And Power." He sat up and adjusted his shirt.

"Money and power," I repeated.

"Yesssss," he said slowly.

"What do you mean?" Amanda asked, puzzled.

"Look, you have a child in Europe or America, what' you do?" Answering his own question he continued, "You work harder. You buy your child shoes. You buy your child clothes. You buy your child the best food. You take your child to the best doctor. You work and work and work to get money to buy your child more things. You work and work and work for more power to get your child in the best school. You work and work and work for tomorrow." He looked back and forth between us.

"Uh huh," Amanda said, not understanding.

"Africans just want their children to live for today. We treat them like little jewels because it's possible they will be gone tomorrow."

"But parents in our countries also know that's possible," Amanda said.

"Yes," William said, and asked forcefully, "But how likely is it?"

Skeptically I asked, "So you think African parents value their children more than we do?"

"No, no, no." William shook his head and rubbed his hand over his trimmed hair. "We learned to show it differently. Our way has been passed down from our ancestors. Your way is new."

Amanda asked, "Because it's new, is it wrong?"

"No," William said, exasperated. "When I was in the British school my instructors were always frustrated with the students. One teacher believed Africans never looked to the future. He said all our problems are because we never plan ahead." William raised his shoulders and his eyebrows. "He was right! But you people never look at today. You are always planning, planning, planning for the future but you never see today. Your babies are always crying because they don't know the future. Inside your children only know today."

I heard the motorcycle start just after sunrise the next morning and jumped up to say goodbye. By the time I had climbed down from the bed and slid open the door of the van the guys were ready to get going. I could hear the bustle on the street had already begun. Amanda climbed down from the bed behind me and waved goodbye from the open door as I walked over to the guys. Arno held the bike steady, wearing his full blue and white leather crash suit and scarred blue helmet. William climbed on back, wearing the same dressy outfit as the day before, with no helmet and his small duffle-bag strapped to his back. I shook their hands and they pulled out into a new African morning.

That afternoon, while waiting for the slow Kazungula ferry to cross the Zambezi River, Ingrid and Manuel sat in the shade of the van while Amanda trimmed the mold from the last of our cheese and I put together tuna fish salad in a bowl. Without mayonnaise there wasn't much to mix, a little olive oil and chili powder to spice it up, some crackers on the side and we had the makings of an unappetizing meal on the run.

As the boat arrived Ingrid hurriedly pulled closed the van's sliding door from the inside, being careful not to spill the contents off her cracker. To get a better grasp she stuffed the cracker in her mouth and pulled harder with both hands. The door let out an eerie squeal, then got stuck. The cars in front were rolling on to the ferry and a taxi behind began to honk. With our rear door jammed open I drove down the steep hill toward the ramp. A family of walk-on passengers stood next to the van peering into our little home. Once the ferry had sailed I tried to close the door but something was wrong. In the middle of the crammed ferry deck I yanked and pulled on it. Shifting it and repositioning it, I finally got it to close.

It stayed that way for weeks.

CHAPTER 54

Whatever Fuels You

Martin's Drift, Botswana - South Africa Border Crossing
40,762 miles

Crossing through Zimbabwe was out of the question. Mr. Mugabe's gas stations were high and dry, making a drive through that nation in a private vehicle virtually impossible for the time being. To avoid missing any of the East African coast, we traveled in a giant swooping u-turn around the pariah nation with the first leg through diamond-rich Botswana.

Experiencing a boom fueled in large part by the discovery of the precious gems, Botswana was flush with new money. On a visit to a mine we learned that diamonds are artificially scarce, with vast reserves locked in vaults, released in proper fractions to ensure high prices and astronomical profits. Botswana adapted this scarcity strategy to the nation's other natural resource, tourism. High price, low impact was the official policy. Fewer visitors paid exorbitant fees to witness the natural wonders in virtual isolation. In theory it was a wonderful concept, but not our style.

Sweeping easily around the capital, Gaborone, on the sleek ring road, we followed the helpful highway signs past tinted-glass buildings toward the border with South Africa. The entire city was one massive construction site, with modern equipment and teams of local laborers laying down clean sheets of asphalt over Kalahari sand. Recently assembled railroad lines criss-crossed the industrial section, past gleaming factories where workers unloaded the latest European machinery from state of the art railroad cars. The symbols of conspicuous wealth were everywhere, with BMWs and Mercedes waiting at stoplights next to donkey-drawn carts full of people talking on mobile telephones. The old market stalls made of corrugated tin and plastic sheeting shared freshly-laid sidewalks with KFC, Spar Supermarkets and ABSA Bank.

At the border, a puffy-cheeked South African customs official smiled as he directed us with wild hand gestures to a parking space. The tails of his sweat-stained uniform shirt hung out over his belt that strained to contain his girth. "Welcome, welcome to South Africa. Immigration is that way." He pointed to a building nearby and walked around the van in happy contemplation. Just minutes before, the Botswanan officials, known as the most honest in the region, sped us through to the other side of the border more quickly than we expected and the unusual enthusiasm of this South African official gave us cause for concern.

When we returned from immigration the jovial official pointed to the spare fuel tanks on the back of the van, and whispered, "Can you change me some pula?" Pula is the currency of Botswana and I had about ten dollars worth in my pocket.

"I think I have some. At what rate?" I asked.

"I need only fifty pula to fill my car with petrol," he said, tucking in his stretched shirt that popped out right away. I was getting used to the round-about conversation style of Southern

Africans and tried to change the subject. "Is petrol less expensive in Botswana?"

"Less expensive." he repeated in a pensive way.

I silently waited for him to broach the subject again.

He pointed to the spare petrol canisters and asked, "Did you pay customs tax in the immigration office for your extra petrol?"

I'd thought he might ask this and answered, "No, nobody asked me to." I had purposely left the gas tank half full just for this reason. "If you insist, I'll pour the canisters into the van."

The guard scrunched his flabby, deeply lined brow but said nothing, so I began to unstrap the spare canister from the rear bumper.

As I unlocked the gas cap he asked, "You have 50 pula?"

I said a little too abruptly, "Fifty pula is worth about eighty rand. Have you got eighty rand?"

Again he scrunched his brow but this time with more anger than confusion. "These number plates are not normal. I have to look into this more thoroughly. Where are you from?"

As I emptied the gas canister into the van's tank Amanda poked her head out of the passenger window, hoping to save the situation. "We're from California in the United States."

He walked to her window and said with disbelief, "You from 'merica?"

She smiled and nodded.

"And the car too?"

"The van too," she repeated.

"The preacher at my church's from 'merica. Church of Christ the King." He waved his hands violently around his head and said, "That man makes me see God when he preaches. I can feel God in the room and see Him everywhere in the building when that man preaches. He come from somewhere called Dee-trot."

I was listening, still pouring the gas into the van when he came over and rested his hand on my shoulder, "There is no need for that. You can go."

As he lifted the barrier for us to pass he said, "Amen, brother and sister."

CHAPTER 55

Otto's Roots

Pretoria, South Africa
40,969 miles

Otto was late. It was 8:45 am. He had agreed on the phone to meet us at 8:30.

"We'll wait until nine," I said to Amanda as she paced impatiently in the parking lot. "If he's not here by then we'll drive out to the other place." Just before 9:00 a beat-up yellow Volkswagen Chico pulled into the parking lot belching smoke.

"This is the VW guru?" Amanda asked under her breath.

His three-day beard and long ponytail did not instill confidence but the guy at the tire shop swore Otto knew more about Volkswagens than anyone in Pretoria.

The van was suffering flu-like symptoms and felt sluggish. Anything less than perfect was not good enough for the rugged roads we were headed toward in Central and Eastern Africa. Otto was the only mechanic who had agreed to let me work on the van myself at his shop. After the experience in Cape Town where I tried to turn over the problem to someone else, I had learned it was best to fix it myself. If I ran into trouble he promised to steer me in the right direction.

"Sorry I'm late, I got two others running already this morning," he said as he offered a massive grease-stained hand. He opened the hood of his Volkswagen Chico and switched two spark plug wires, then started the little car. "Forces dirt out of the carburetor when you switch them," he said as it sputtered and coughed up a fur ball of dirt. "That should do it. Follow me out to the farm where I have my shop and we'll get working."

Otto zigged through Pretoria traffic with the ease of one accustomed to his route and we struggled to keep up. As we entered the M4 the little Chico began bucking violently and he pulled to the side of the highway. "It seems you will have to give me a tow," he said, without embarrassment as if he'd expected it all along. Using our tow strap we tied the little car to the bumper of the van and pulled away. The underpowered van could barely drag the Chico along.

At the farm a few miles out of town, a young white guy on an old tractor tilled the rich red clay field while a half-dozen black workers used hoes to break up the larger chunks of earth. Otto waved to the men, then pointed to a sunny spot between two rusting old VWs and said, "You can park your van over there and get to work. I want to have a look at your carburetor. It's running too rich. Take it off and I'll get you set up at the bench." He disappeared behind the hood of the troublesome little Chico.

The workshop was attached to what had once been a small house, surrounded by Volkswagen carcasses. A long work area protected by a corrugated roof sprouted from the side of the house like a strangler vine engulfing a tree, and workmen toiled among the piles of farm equipment and old motors.

By the field just next to the workshop two black women were sprawled on the dark earth, sound asleep in the scorching sun, surrounded by a large pile of what appeared to be grayish-brown carrots. Behind them a long row of mesh tables were covered with chopped bits of root drying in the sun.

I removed the carburetor, carefully marking the wires and tubes so I knew where to reconnect them, and took it to the shop. Otto was already working on the one from the sputtering Chico. "They are almost the same, but it looks like yours has enough Namibian dust on it to clog it up good," Otto said. "Strip it and we'll look at the jets." I had never taken apart a carburetor, so I watched and did exactly what Otto did.

As I unscrewed the plug from the sediment bowl I asked, "What are all these roots you've got drying?"

"It's a Zulu cure for diarrhea. We dry it and sell it to a German pharmaceutical company. Not long ago we sold them fifteen tons, but a few years back they allowed Imodium on the market in Germany, so now we only sell 3 or 4 tons. That's why I'm fixing cars again."

A well-dressed older man strolled into the shop and asked Otto a question in Afrikaans. Otto said, "This is my father, Doctor Pieters."

I waved a greasy hand as Otto answered his question.

When he'd left Otto said, "My father was a professor of physics at the University of Zululand just north of Durban, but he quit. He couldn't stand the senseless destruction. The government gave them beautiful facilities but they just tore it apart." He worked quietly for a while but then stopped and turned to look at me. "You know, I never supported apartheid but now, with the new government, I am becoming racist. My grandfather was a German missionary who came here to help the blacks. My father did too. He taught at their school. I'm a Civil Engineer but I can't get a job in South Africa because of affirmative action, so I fix cars and I farm. All my friends have gone to England or Australia." As he turned back toward the carburetor he said in disgust, "Agh. It's miserable to be forced to leave your own country to find a job."

Following his lead, I removed the jet and asked, "Is affirmative action making a difference?"

He shrugged, "Blacks are now in every kind of job, but the problem is corruption. There wasn't corruption like this before. Now every day there's something new." He bent his head to his work. "They get elected and try to figure out ways to get money from it."

We worked quietly for a while and I cleaned then reassembled the carburetor. Otto looked it over and said, "It's ready to go back in."

Slowly, with Amanda looking over my shoulder as she referred to the VW repair manual, I bolted it back in place, attached the wires and the fuel lines, then gave it a fine-tuning, and the van ran perfectly.

"So what do I owe you?" I asked Otto.

"Nothing, you did all the work," he answered. "Would you like a cup of tea? My chef is here."

"A chef, here?" Amanda asked with surprise.

Otto laughed and said, "Yah, I owned a Moroccan restaurant in town, but we had to close because they raised the rent. My chef and waiter stay here until I figure out what to do next." Then he turned toward the house and called, "Salomon, would you please bring us some tea."

A few moments later a meticulously dressed black man appeared with ornate teacups and saucers arranged on an elegant silver tray. He carefully negotiated the path through the greasy shop, carrying the tray as if he were in a five-star restaurant. Resting it on a rusty motor with a flourish and a smile, Salomon poured us all tea.

In that short time, sitting among the clutter of the workshop on a farm in Southern Africa, sipping the flavorful rooibos tea and discussing life in that strange and wonderful land, with nervous anticipation of what lie ahead, and the feeling of accomplishment from getting my hands dirty while learning something new; all mingled together to make up one of the most memorable moments of our journey.

It was Otto's telephone, ringing in the pocket of his jacket, that broke the spell. The old tractor was acting up again and he would have to go out to the field. We thanked him for his hospitality and let him get back to work.

Driving out of the yard, we glanced toward the black women sprawled on the ground chopping Zulu roots. Their movements were slow but constant as they picked up a root and cut it into small bits, accumulating piles in the skirt between their outstretched legs. Their dazed, bored expressions told of having done this same task for years on end. After passing them Amanda glanced in the side mirror and noticed that one of them had gotten up and was walking across the dirt path to the shade of a small tree. Halfway across she broke into a dance and continued toward the tree, dancing in step with a silent beat that only she could hear.

CHAPTER 56

Everything's Backwards

Pretoria, South Africa
41,114 miles

The nifty little rolling hinge on the sliding door of the van had given out. After twenty-four years of sliding back and forth, the Belgian soap opera star had managed to break it. For two weeks we were forced to enter our rolling home by climbing past the passenger's seat, jumping over a storage box, hiking around our tiny library of books, and finally stepping on to the porta-potty. It was like coming home from work each night through the bathroom window.

The red-faced old man at the parts shop rolled his chair across the tile floor and rested his chin on the counter as he spoke through the half-moon opening in the glass, "I might hav a uzed vone. You are Americans, no?"

I answered, "I am, and my wife is from Mexico."

"Ah, I zought zo. Ze oter day America give eight hundred million to Mugabe en fvood aid, vhy you tink?" He walked to the back of the small shop, shaking his head, and took a car part from the shelf, looked it over, put it down and picked up another. "Clinton he vas good. Ya, ya he had Monica, but zat's OK. Here, see'f 'is vorks." He handed the part to me through the slot.

Out at the parking lot I held it up to the spot on the side of the van where the broken one was connected.

Amanda looked at it and said, "It looks exactly the same, but there's something different."

The red-faced old man had given us a part that was an exact copy of the one on the van, only backwards.

Steering wheels in South African cars are on the right-hand side, so the sliding door of their Volkswagen kombis is on the opposite side to ours. This one minor difference made every part of our van's door backward. The key-hole was backward, the handle was backward and the hinge was backward.

Driving on the other side of the road was hard enough. Just crossing the street was terrifying. Since I was a child the practice of "looking left" was drilled into my brain, making it virtually impossible to step off a curb into the street without doing it.

In South Africa we learned to cross streets like two paranoid school children, holding hands, turning our heads left, then right, expecting cars to speed toward us from every which way.

The old man shuffled out to the parking lot. "Iz backvards. Your door iz on ze vrong zide."

"No…," I began to reply but caught myself.

The man chuckled, "Iz like all ov Africa. Backvards!"

A thin black workman in blue overalls who followed the old man from the building looked over his shoulder and said, "Maybe you need…"

The old man interrupted, "Zis von't vork. You need ze von for ze ozer zide. But you vill not find it here in Zouth Africa."

We stood around the van, staring at the door, perplexed.

Amanda broke the silence. "Have you lived South Africa long?"

"Tertyvive year zago I came'ere vrom Czechoslovakia."

"Were you from the Czech side or Slovakia?" I asked.

"Itiz all vone, zhey zhould never ef split."

We were silent once again, contemplating the door.

The thin black workman tried to speak again, "Baas, it is possible to break the fastener from the plastic piece and take the wheel off. To make it work."

He was right. Two small pieces on the van's hinge had broken, a little wheel that slides along a rail, and a plastic guide to keep the wheel on track. Miraculously, these two pieces were interchangeable.

The old man grabbed the part from my hand to look at it. "You mus buy ze whole pieze. I don't zell juz ze veel."

As we were paying I asked, "How did you get here from Czechoslovakia?"

"It'za long story."

"Well, South Africa is a beautiful country."

The old man eagerly scratched inside his ear with his index finger, then inspected a particle as he pondered what I had said. "It all depenz on how you luk at it."

CHAPTER 57

Latin Africa

Maputo, Mozambique
41,484 miles

The young man wearing dirty rags ran with the van, yelling in English through Amanda's closed window, "I will help things go faster for you."

Another with no shoes and spindly legs sprang from squatting and tried to push in front of his larger companion. "It is very difficult to get all of the papers. You will need my help to go faster."

Locking the sliding door, I was surrounded by would-be assistants and said, *"Obrigado, no necesitamos ayuda,"* my standard Latin American response in these situations, a blend of poor Portuguese with Spanish. The young men trailed behind for a moment, then gave up and returned to their perches.

Briefly blinded as we stepped from the bright afternoon sunshine to the darkness within, Amanda nearly cut in front of a crowd of people who gave her indignant stares as they jostled for position at the counter. The sweet, rank smell of unwashed bodies hung like a cloud in the cramped office and the thundering bang of the officer's stamp forced a synchronized blink from everyone in the room. A little man with a large pile of documents and greasy clothing tried to slip past Amanda, but she edged in front of him. Spreading out her elbows to further block him, she whispered to me, "This is just like being in Mexico."

Leaving Amanda to deal with customs, I shoved through the crowd to purchase the obligatory car insurance. Squeezed between the door and the customs window were two older men and one young woman seated behind three decrepit desks, each with a sign displaying their company name and logo. Their indistinguishable policies were sold at an identical price. I took the safe bet with the young woman who just happened to be wearing a tight, purple spandex top that could barely contain her generous bosom. For a moment it was difficult to determine where her chocolate brown skin ended and the darkness of the room began, but her bright smile shone when the two men grunted to one another because they lost yet another sale. The man closest to her looked at me with resigned disgust, as if his financial and physical suffering depended on what she chose to wear that morning. I thought to myself, "Looks like we're back in a Latin country."

With an efficient confidence that demonstrated her success, the young woman had already completed most of the form before I approached her desk. All she needed were a few minor details. Leaning forward, she elaborately swept her pen like a paintbrush, filling the blanks with neat schoolgirl curlicues. As I paid, she scolded in Portuguese-accented English, "If you have an accident, you must notify my office. Do not drive faster than forty kilometers per hour in the villages, or the police will stop you and make you pay." She carefully folded the papers and abruptly handed them to me, then turned and resumed a conversation with one of the men.

This was our first taste of Mozambique and we looked forward to the vibrant change of culture. We had read that for hundreds of years the Portuguese had ruled the country and used the colony as a supply post along their trade route, saturating the region with their culture, religion and language. After decades of war, first for independence from Portugal, then a long civil struggle propelled by the cold war that had ended just ten years before, Mozambique's people were barely resurfacing. Then devastation hit. Storms and floods did catastrophic damage, wiping out many of the roads and bridges we would be using to cross the country.

Driving into the sweaty, cauldron-like capital, Maputo, we were greeted by the Havana of Africa. In the 1920s the Portuguese had designed buildings using the ornate pillars, porticoes, and shady central courtyards that typify much of Latin American architecture, but after the revolution, the new government first flirted, then jumped into bed with Soviet socialism. The austere, utilitarian structures built during that time were muddled together with the elaborate, lavish, colonial style to create a jambalaya where the Latin warmth and Russian cold battled for the soul of each neighborhood.

Clotheslines criss-crossed balconies and neighbors called across to one another from the wide-open windows of apartment blocks. A small number of cars competed with us on the potholed streets as vendors washed and swept the trash from the sidewalks into the gutter. At the municipal market, girls in bright print sarongs wandered with bowls of cashews perched on their heads, pouring piles into cupped hands. Groups of children greeted us with their few words of English and looked away shyly when we responded with a question in Spanish. Women fruit-sellers laughed and talked and danced with bold confidence, more like their cousins in Brazil than their sisters in South Africa.

Like any capital city in a war zone, Maputo offered the curious visitor little to see or do. Of course, the town was bustling with the helpful souls who converged just after the shooting ceased to profit from the destruction. Just two days in Maputo and we were headed up the coast.

On the road out of town, Amanda was wiggling in her seat and I knew what was coming. It never failed. Whenever we were approaching a vital intersection or a place where I needed directions from the navigator, she would have an uncontrollable urge and would bolt out of her seat, slip into the back of the van and on to the port-a-potty. Problem was, when she wasn't in her seat it appeared to everyone else accustomed to seeing right hand drive vehicles, that no one was driving the van.

As we turned a bend, we came abruptly to a police checkpoint while Amanda was sitting on the throne. The officer looked at the van in confusion and waved us over immediately. He knocked on the passenger's window and I reached across to roll it down as Amanda jumped from the back and plopped into her seat.

She was flustered and said in Spanish, "Hello. Good afternoon."

The officer's features were a mixture of African and European and he wore a bright white cap with an oversized badge in the center. His confused look soon faded as he said in Portuguese, "Ahhh, you were driving without a seat-belt."

Amanda motioned to the glove box, showing him that the steering wheel was on the other side and said, "Oh...but I am not the driver."

He looked at the dashboard of the van with a baffled expression. Suddenly his eyes widened. "You have a scapular." He reached under his uniform shirt, "It is just like mine." Tugging at a satin string around his neck, he pulled out a flat rectangular piece of felt the size of a large postage stamp with the image of the Virgin Mary.

Amanda placed her hand under our scapular dangling from the radio knob and said in Spanish, "This belongs to my grandmother in Mexico. I had never seen her without it. But on the day we left for this trip, she took it off and gave it to me, vowing it would keep us safe during our travels."

He reflected for a moment, replaced his scapular under his shirt next to his heart and said, "My mother gave this to me when I became a police officer," he said. "I never take it off." His face broke into a wide smile as he said to us. "I can see that even without a driver your scapular is keeping you out of harm's way.

May God bless you. Have a safe journey."

CHAPTER 58

Afternoon Shower

Tete, Mozambique
42,564 miles

The showers were next to the bar overlooking the southern bank of the Zambezi, where the biting stench of burning palm fronds and the evaporating river water clouded the air with gray haze. Even in winter the heat and humidity were so great that no one was sitting at the outdoor bar. The other guests staying at the place, mostly staff from the massive U.N. facility that dwarfed the town of Tete, paid dearly to sweat in their rooms under the overworked air-conditioners. The tough-looking Arab woman who ran the place stopped scolding the waiters long enough to show us where to set up camp in the shadeless, dirt parking lot. The blazing sun was scorching and we quickly rolled out the awning to get some relief.

The restroom facilities were by the drained pool on the back terrace overlooking the river and the latch to the women's restroom door did not lock. I stood guard outside while Amanda washed off days of sweat under the trickle of brown river-water that poured out of the pipe jutting from the cement block wall. The flowing shower was a luxury. In the last few places we had camped they had simply handed us buckets of water and pointed to a room with a drain where we could soap up and splash ourselves clean.

As I watched the door one of the cooks stepped out from the back of the kitchen, shirtless with long pants rolled to the calf under an apron cut roughly from an old lime-green maid's smock. Wiping his hands on a rag, he stood on the terrace above the shower stall looking towards the frosted glass window of the women's room. He seemed to stare directly into the shower but I doubted he would risk the wrath of the tough Arab owner. After a moment of uninterrupted staring I walked toward him and asked, *"¿Que paso?"* (What happened?), not knowing if the man would understand my Spanish.

He nodded his head slightly with a concerned face and said in Portuguese, *"O rio"* (The river). He yelled something to the kitchen staff while continuing to gaze in the direction of the shower. Three cooks rushed over to the door, shirtless with stained aprons tied around their waists, and poked their heads out.

I walked up the stairs to the terrace to see if they were trying to peek into Amanda's shower. The heat of the stoves in the tiny kitchen poured out and the stench of old frying fat was overpowering. I turned toward the showers and let out a loud laugh. The four men looked at me with surprise. The frosted window to the shower was certainly see-through and a hazy silhouette of Amanda was visible from the vantage point. But just beyond the shower, beyond the motel wall topped with shards of broken glass and the burning piles of palms, was a long stretch of open field with a view of the riverbank. The setting sun illuminated hundreds of men, women and children, in separate areas, completely naked, bathing in the murky brown Zambezi.

It took me a moment to realize that the kitchen workers were not leering at the bathers. They were quiet and serious. Then I turned back to look at the bathers and noticed they had stopped washing themselves and stood motionless, covered in suds, staring at the flowing river. Everyone was mesmerized by something. *"¿Que paso?"* (What happened?) I asked the first man again.

"Um corpo no rio," (A body in the river) he said without emotion.

"¿Que?" (What?)

He pointed toward a cluster of weeds and debris floating a few meters from the bank, *"Há um corpo no rio."* (There is a body in the river.)

We stood in silence and watched the bulk move with the surge of the current. Down river a man and young boy rowed a dugout canoe toward the face-down body. The boy reached out from the bow and grabbed the shirt of the lifeless figure. He held it tightly as the man struggled against the strong current to row the canoe back to shore with the ungainly weight.

One of the cooks looked at another. *"É um adulto. Um homem."* (It's an adult. A man.)

The oldest cook, a man with little flecks of gray fuzz at the temples, turned his head quickly to the side, looking away in disgust, then returned to the steaming kitchen.

The younger bathers hastily finished their washing, dressed and ran to the spot where the canoe had landed. A few moments later, a shoeless boy ran past and yelled something toward us, holding his hands behind his back imitating a person wearing handcuffs. The man to my left spoke a few words but I only understood *"polices"* and *"matado".* I nearly asked him to repeat it, then realized I didn't want to know, didn't want it to linger in my head.

CHAPTER 59

Sweet Schistosomiasis

Monkey Bay, Malawi
43,200 miles

The minuscule girl was just barely able to form the words and her mother looked on proudly as she gazed up at us with massive eyes and a tiny hand extended in the universal greeting for visitors to Lake Malawi, "Sweets, gimme sweets."

Tiny lake waves broke on the thick-grained sand in rapid succession, like the sound of a heartbeat. We took our first steps beyond the gate and the Malawian man guarding the camp acknowledged us with a nod and a knowing smile. We intended to walk along the sandy waterfront. The children waited and the moment we crossed an imaginary line they pounced, all yelling at once, hands outstretched, each with his own special approach.

"Wats yu name?"

"Where yu come from?"

"Ten kwacha, kwacha, kwacha, kwacha."

"Pen, pen, pen, pen for schoooooooooool."

"Gimme moni."

"Taka pitsure."

"Hello, hello, hello, hhhhheeeeeeeellllllllllllllloooooooo."

"Hey boss."

"Hello Madam."

"Camera, camera, camera."

The guard bent lazily and picked up a handful of sand, pretending he would throw it. The kids scattered like stray dogs. As we got further from the gate they followed, trying to hold our hands and reach into our pockets. Ten, fifteen, twenty, they kept coming. Soon we were inundated. Surrounded. Desperate, excited children blocked the path, using the water as a barrier. They screamed anything, sounds, clicking, clapping, dancing, songs, "hey, hey, hey," "watchawatchawhatchawatcha," a boy pretended to ride a motorcycle around us, a girl with a beautiful voice sang *Frère du Jaques*. The further we walked the crazier it became. Surrounded by the pack of children, we turned back to the camp just a minute after leaving. They screamed in unison, "NOOOOOOOO!"

The manager at the campground had told us that a few years before, the village of Cape Maclear had consisted of a handful of fishing shacks and a campsite. Since then, more than 12,000 wretchedly poor souls have built shelters in the small village. Most live off the tiny sardine-like fish they scoop in thin neoprene nets from the banks of the lake.

Determined to explore around the lake, we rented a canoe from the camp and leisurely paddled along the banks to the far end of the settlement. Naked boys ran on the lakeshore trying to keep up with us. The bathing girls were more modest and covered themselves in long, brightly colored sarongs. The men seemed to be constantly lounging or deep in conversation with one another, while the women were always busy, walking from the hand-pump balancing large plastic containers of water on their heads, or lugging bails of laundry to the shore. The older girls carried large metal basins of dishes to the lake and let the sticky paste of the mashed cornmeal soak in the water before scrubbing with their fingers.

Stick-legged tables, fifty feet long, were covered with tiny fish drying in the blazing sun. Bales of dry reeds tied in tree trunk-sized bundles were stacked in neat piles with their tops bursting like the plumes of roosters, waiting to be used as building materials. A handful of sturdy houses closest to the water had doors, a few broken panes of glass for windows, and three or four sickly eucalyptus trees for shade. The rest were temporary reed-walled structures slapped together with dried mud.

At the far end of the lake we rammed the canoe high up on to the shore and jumped over the water, as a white man came out from under a thatched-roof umbrella buried in the sand and said, "Hello, welcome. Don't worry about the flukes here. I had all the reeds and snails removed from my water."

Avoiding the water at Lake Malawi was not easy but we were determined not to get wet since we'd heard that the lake was infested with schistosomiasis. The larva of minute flukes live in the snails of the lake and are able to penetrate unbroken human skin and clothes. Once infected, they set up shop in various organs, causing serious, sometimes fatal diseases.

Lifting a bottle of frosted beer, he said, "Would you like a drink? I started early this morning." His British accent and salt and pepper buzz-cut gave him the appearance of one of Her Majesty's Special Forces soldiers in very early retirement.

I kicked the sand from my sandals, then looked up at him. He seemed happy to have visitors. "Wow, it's quiet here. Where are all the kids?" Amanda asked.

He chuckled, "Guards keep 'em out. You can relax here at my place." We could tell right away that Steve was starved for conversation and had all the time in the world. Wearing little more than cut-off shorts he led us to bamboo chairs in the shade, handed us cold beers, and pointed to a bunch of flooded palm trees he had planted a few months before. "Look how high the water is. Practically took over my bar."

Amanda rubbed her feet dry as she said, "But we keep hearing about the drought here."

Steve sat forward on the edge of an upturned sailboat and began twitching his left leg on the ball of his foot with excess energy. "The lake is fed from the north. There was plenty of rain there but these bloody buggers can't move the water even a few feet from the lake to the crops." He made a scooping gesture with his hand, "If it doesn't rain directly on the fields, they die."

Did he mean the crops or the people, I thought.

He went on, "What are the elements you need to be a successful farmer?" Counting on outstretched fingers, "Fertile land, labor, seed, and water." Pointing with a yellow fingernail, he seemed to be getting worked up. "There is a massive plot of land with rich soil right here."

I began to regret stopping, wondering if he was completely crazy or just suffering from isolation.

He stood and looked down the beach, stretching his tan arm like a traffic cop, "There's certainly no shortage of labor. And the aid organizations compete with one another to give them seed. But they're starving. There's no need for it. There is no reason why it happens but the bloody bastards are starving. They could get two or three crops a year from this land but they can't get it together."

Amanda laid her towel down and sat on the sand as she asked, "What would it take to help them get it together?"

He took a gulp of beer, "That's just it. It's our fault." He let this sink in a moment. "Why would I go to the trouble of cultivating a field if the U.N., the World Food Program and Oxfam give me bags of food every year? If you talk to aid workers they all know it, too. That's the sad part. I have aid workers here all the time. They stay in Africa for what, eight, ten months, a year? Your Peace Corps workers stay the longest, two years. Just when they begin to understand how it works, they go home." He looked at me hard with the glassy eyes of a street preacher. "And you Americans, with all your money, and only what, twelve, fifteen percent have passports? Not many of you travel outside of your country, so you have to trust people with a vested interest in the problem. You like to say 'trust the person in the trenches'. It's like asking the military if they need another billion for the newest weapon. Of course they are going to answer 'Yes'." I wasn't sure if he was angry with me for being American or if it was the loneliness and isolation talking. These thoughts must have flowed through his head regularly, now he had an American to spout them to. We listened as he reached over the bar for another beer. "You Americans have to realize that African governments use your television as a weapon to get you to give more, then they steal what you give. The last two years you gave out starter packs, do you know what they are?"

Silently we shook our heads, guzzling our beers so we could get going.

"Designed by a guy from your big university. Harvard. A box with seeds and fertilizer. Enough to support a whole family on a small plot of land. They gave out millions of them. Twenty kilos each. I had one of the guys running the program here last year. Just before the rainy season they handed out the boxes and told them to wait for the rain." He smiled with a goofy grin, not wryly but with real pleasure. "You know what they did? When the rains didn't come they ground up the grain and ate it." He laughed. "A guy came around an' bought up all the fertilizer for nothing. He'll probably sell it back to you Americans next year."

He sounded like one of those people who criticize but have no solutions, so I asked impatiently, "What would you do, nothing?"

"Absolutely! It might get them up off their arse to plant a crop."

Somewhat exasperated, I said, "Are you seriously suggesting that the solution is to do nothing?"

He calmed and said, "You Yanks have a saying I love," snapping his finger, then rubbing his forehead, trying to remember. "What do you say when a guy's a drunk and his wife calls his boss to lie for him, making excuses. What do you call her?"

"An enabler?" I asked.

"Yes! An enabler, I love that one. Every time your USAID or VSO volunteers drop off a bag of maize or give them fertilizer, they are enabling them to do nothing themselves. Worse, they are encouraging it."

After hearing enough we hastily thanked Steve for the beer and climbed back into the canoe. As he pushed us from the bank he said, "You're welcome to come back to the bar tonight. We still have a lot to talk about."

Slowly paddling back to the campsite we watched as the children called to us from the shore. When we returned, the guard took the paddles as we dragged the canoe up into the camp. A new four-wheel drive Toyota Hilux was parked on the far side of the van, and a young couple argued in Portuguese as they stood over a flattened tent, trying to figure out how the collapsible poles fitted together. Short and stout, the woman gave directions to the lean man by pointing a plump index finger. He reluctantly listened. Eventually they erected the tent in the sand. Exhausted, they plopped themselves under the meager shade of a small tree just in front of the van as they guzzled from tall, clear, water bottles. "Have you been to Mozambique?" she asked in accented English by way of introduction.

"Yes, we drove north from South Africa that way," Amanda answered.

She pointed back and forth between herself and the man. "We work there, in Beira." She went on to explain that they were trained in public finance and had volunteered with a program through the Brazilian government to help the regional administration in Mozambique adopt internationally recognized accounting practices. They had worked for three months and were taking a week-long break.

I asked, "Are you having any success in your work?"

He snorted and answered, "We work every day teaching them but they do whatever they want."

She interrupted, "The people we work with are appointed by the local governor. Some of them can't read or add numbers. I have one woman who was taught by missionaries. She does most of the work for the department but she will only do things her way. What can I do?"

"Who funds your project?" I asked.

"The Brazilian government and the U.N."

"What would happen if they withheld funding?"

She looked shocked at the idea. "I work at the ministry of health. If the U.N. did not send supplies, the people would die. Many people. There is no choice."

Amanda asked, "Is the corruption worse than we see in Latin America?"

The couple laughed and she said, "In Brazil we have corruption, but not like this. In Mozambique nobody cares and everyone steals. The bookkeeper steals pens. The director of the department collects the wages for people who do not come to work. The minister of health steals the drugs and supplies before they get to the hospitals. They say even the President gets a percentage of what the minister collects. Everyone with power keeps it this way."

"How can they do that, knowing people are dying?" Amanda asked.

The woman stood and wiped the sand from her behind, "In Mozambique you cannot think of the politicians as elected officials. They act like a chief. That's what the people know. A chief can do whatever he wants. Everything belongs to him, including the people. He can take anything he wants. It's not stealing, because it belongs to him."

As the sun was setting the Brazilian couple excused themselves to go for a walk along the shore. I was tempted to tell them of our experience earlier in the day but decided to let them learn for themselves.

A group of ten or twelve boys kicked around a ball on the beach next to the camp. Bunches of reeds poked into the sand were used as goal posts. In the dim light the silhouettes of the boys brought back memories of soccer games I'd played when I was young on the beaches of the Jersey shore.

The moment the Brazilians stepped on to the beach the game was abandoned and the boys ran to them, hands outstretched, surrounding them. The Brazilians joked with the boys and sat down on the beach. Through the fence I could see the woman take a bag of candy from the side pocket of her cargo pants and hand one piece to each boy, scolding one who tried to get a second. The couple seemed to enjoy the frenzy of the moment and the boys immediately popped the candy into their mouths and asked for more, sitting in their laps, hanging from their necks, doing anything they could to get another piece. Once everyone had a candy the woman rolled up the bag and stuffed it in the waistband of her pants. The boys began doing stunts, singing songs, and once finished, pointed to her waist and the bag of candy. When the last rays of the sun set the Brazilians stood to return to the campsite. I could hear the boys yelling to them from the imaginary line they knew they could not cross, "Just one more missus, pleeeeeeeease."

CHAPTER 60

A Long and Engaging Life

Karonga, Malawi
43,699 miles

The rough road turned what we thought would be a four-hour journey into a ten-hour ordeal. As the day waned, it became obvious we would not arrive at the border before it closed. Amanda searched the map for any sign of a place to spend the night. There seemed to be none.

As the sun was setting we passed a weather-beaten, barely legible sign advertising a restaurant on Lake Malawi. I hesitated, but at Amanda's insistence I turned the van around and slowly pulled off the main road on to a powdery path that led us through the rusty metal gate of the compound.

More than half the building was in ruins, with a flat section of cement foundation surrounded by low crumbling blocks, but the fence around the property seemed intact. The neglected restaurant had a partially finished patio that overlooked the lake. Wooden tables and chairs were stacked against the faded blue wall, obstructing a narrow passage to what might have been the kitchen. A lean black man in paint-splattered t-shirt and shorts stepped out of a side entrance and came down the patio steps to greet us. He listened patiently to our predicament and asked us to follow him into the building.

A large glass and wood dining table with eight high-back chairs took up most of the space in the center of the cement floor in the room. We followed the man down a hallway to another room decorated with gold-framed beer posters hung above a bamboo movable bar with a small glass-door refrigerator perched on a barstool. Sleek Scandinavian-style furniture faced open French doors, revealing a view of the lake and scattered trees partially submerged in the high water. "Please have a seat. My uncle will be with you soon," the man said, motioning to the stiff chairs.

After a few moments we heard a metallic tap coming down the hallway. An old heavy-set black man, slightly balding, perhaps sixty years old, appeared at the door. As he walked slowly toward us I noticed his face drooped on one side and he had a modern metal cane with a gray plastic support wrapped around his forearm that clicked each time he planted it on the cement floor. He wore a neatly-pressed oxford shirt under a sleeveless wool vest, and tan trousers hung from his large frame. A smile swallowed his face and his meaty lips were framed with a thin gray-flecked goatee.

We stood as he approached and he waved us to be seated as a king might. "Good afternoon," his voice boomed with a strong British accent and a slight slur, "Welcome. I understand you are in need of a place to stay." He sat heavily in the low burnt-orange chair and leaned against the thick armrest as he held the pivoting metal cane like a scepter.

Listening quietly as we explained our predicament, the old man nodded knowingly when I said we had misjudged the amount of time it would take to arrive at the border. He had anticipated our request before I'd had a chance to ask permission and he graciously said we could set up camp anywhere in his compound. He ensured that his watchman would protect us through the night. We thanked him and began to stand, but he motioned us to sit again.

In the awkward silence Amanda asked, "Have you lived here for many years?"

Leaning his cane against the wooden armrest, he answered, "Yes, I purchased the property after the flood a few years ago. My nephew has run the business while I was living in Geneva. This is my village where I went to school as a young boy." He thought for a moment and added, "Of course, I was away for many years." Removing a handkerchief from his pants pocket, he wiped his chin like someone who had just visited the dentist, unable to feel the drool on a numb cheek.

I asked, "What did you do in Geneva?"

He shifted slightly, stuffed the handkerchief into his pocket, and said in a slow, precise voice, "I worked for the United Nations, in Lilongwe for ten years, then in Switzerland for twelve. I was due to retire next February." Then he sat up straight as if something had occurred to him and asked, "Can I offer you a beverage?" Before we answered he called, "Roland, please bring some beverages," then turning to us he said, "I'm afraid we only have beer and cola. Roland, please bring us three colas." He waited quietly while Roland set the tray on the round table, opened the bottles using a flip-top opener, and poured the beverages into short, clear glasses.

He raised his glass and offered a toast like a man accustomed to doing so, "To a long and engaging life."

"A long and engaging life," we repeated.

After drinking he set down the glass and immediately reached for the handkerchief in his pocket, wiping at his chin. "The United Nations was very good to me for many years," he said, almost to himself. "Mind you, I was just a functionary," he snorted a deep chuckle, "Nothing more."

"How did you enjoy living in Europe?" Amanda asked.

"Twelve years is a long time. I know Europe well, better than I know my own country actually. Paris, Cologne, Brugge, Munich for Octoberfest, great fun, great fun. London, I know London well. And Brugge the medieval city, absolutely fabulous." He sat quietly for a moment, reminiscing, then added, "But it is not perfect, Europe. There are problems there, like everywhere else." He seemed to be trying to convince himself of it, then said abruptly, "I had a stroke, as you can see. Seventeen months ago. In Geneva. At first I was unable to move, completely incapacitated. In hospital for twenty-six days," he nodded and raised his brow. "They sent me to a rehabilitation facility. I learned how to speak again, and walk." He took a sip of his cola and dribbled some on his lap.

While he wiped it, I said, "The human brain is amazing."

"Remarkable, really," he agreed. "A remarkable instrument, the human brain." Smiling a half-smile, he added, "One piece takes over where another has failed." Then the smile turned dry, "But I lost my pension."

"Oh, no," Amanda said, "That's terrible."

He slumped forward slightly and nodded, "All those years in Europe I expected to retire there." He looked out at the lake, "I bought this place to help my brother's son," indicating Roland by pointing a full hand. His slur become thicker, "Never expected to live here myself." Suddenly he deflated. His chin turned down and he grasped tightly on to the plastic and metal cane.

I wanted to ask so many questions but could see the conversation had taken a toll on him so I said nothing. A quiet sadness permeated the room.

He finished his cola and pushed himself upward in the chair. "No matter. What can be done now?" He tapped the armrest just once as if knocking on a door. "It's refreshing to meet people out exploring the world. The breeze should return in an hour or so. Nice sleeping weather. Go, situate your caravan."

I helped him to stand and Roland appeared, attaching the cane to his forearm. As he walked down the hallway he said without looking back, "Sleep well."

After breakfast the next morning we asked Roland if we could thank his uncle, embarrassed that we did not even know his name. "Uncle is not feeling well. He asked me to wish you a safe journey."

I asked about the fee for accommodating us and Roland responded, "No, no. Uncle said no charge. You are welcome to stay with us whenever you visit Malawi."

Turning back on to the main road, the van struggled to get over a mound of dirt piled on the verge. The wheels spun and dug in, causing us momentary apprehension, but then the van got traction and moved forward. Teams of workers were busy paving the route toward the fertile mountains of Southern Tanzania. Not knowing what the journey held, we followed in their wake, hoping to reach the frontier and a safe place to stay on the other side before darkness fell.

CHAPTER 61

Cradle of Mankind

Near Iringa, Tanzania
44,029 miles

Border crossings often gave me a headache, but this time it was the thinner air, not the Middle-Eastern looking officials, that brought on the annoyance. The throbbing pain bursting in my forehead was caused by the rapid rise in elevation from the shores of Lake Malawi to the steamy, lush-green highlands of Tanzania.

Normally when meeting border officials we would take care to look respectable, donning my least worn outfit Amanda would pat down my unruly hair with a wad of spit. At this border Amanda took special care to ensure that her outfit would be considered modest and inoffensive, since we were entering a Muslim country.

One guard, eager to escort me to the next office, took my hand and held it in the Arab gesture of friendship while leading me around the corner to the traffic police post. After paying the high fees for our visas, car insurance and road tax we were free to enter Tanzania.

The road we were traveling followed the ancient caravan route on which slaves carried massive ivory tusks, rhino horns, and gold, to the coastal ports of Bagamoyo and Zanzibar. The ancestors of the helpful Arab officials had cut into the heart of this scorching continent in winding caravans, eager to barter with the warring local chiefs who raided their neighboring tribes and sold the prisoners into slavery. Those who survived the harsh journey were loaded as precious cargo on to dhows and shipped to the Middle East.

. The tropical highland of Tanzania, with its dark, rich soil and soaking rains, is home to some of the most fertile earth in East Africa. A sea of green tea and tobacco plantations covered the rolling hills. Along the edge of the road women spread out thin layers of arabica coffee beans to dry in the blistering afternoon sun while vendors slept in the shade near pyramid-shaped piles of tangerines and papayas. Children strolled contentedly along well-worn, puddle-strewn paths trailing long branches of sugar cane, chewing on the sweetly sour core.

We turned on to the access path to the Isimila Stone Age archeological site and a young caretaker ran up to greet us. He watched as I signed into the guest book and said, "From USA. Not many people from USA come. They go only north to see animals."

He introduced himself as Mohammed and said ominously, "I walk with you because some people not good nearby." He took us for a tour that began at a glass enclosure displaying a few neatly lined, yawn-inspiring replicas of hand-axes. The skeletal remains of an extinct hippo with a periscope poking from its head was the most fascinating find.

Mohammed then led us down a sandy trail toward massive stone pillars jutting into the sky from the floor of the gorge, formed when floodwaters rushed through the dry valley. As he walked he commented about the area, then he said, "A man came here from Asia the month past. He very famous scientist." Mohammed repeated the name three times but we were unable to understand, so he continued, "You know about evolution?" He stopped and turned to look back at us. As we nodded he moved on down the path in front, turning to look as he spoke. "This scientist say that evolution is always trying new things, even today. He say that tall buildings and cars and computers are experiment from evolution."

Having a basic knowledge of Darwin's theory, I understood that nature continually produces slight variations to test which characteristics are best suited for a particular environment. In my wildest dreams, I could not imagine how computers and tall buildings could be considered variations in human evolution, so I responded with what I normally say in such situations, "Hum, that's interesting."

Mohammed went on bounding down the path through the gorge. "The scientist say modern civilization is experiment of evolution that will fail. He say there is much evidence of this." He turned to look at us and I wondered if he meant this as a backhanded insult but I encouraged him to go on.

"The scientist say people who grow small farm, live far from city, who do not have car and television will live. But modern people, like in USA, will not." He paused to watch our reaction.

As we reached a viewpoint overlooking the stone pillars Amanda asked, "And what do you believe?"

Mohammed gazed out over the site, where some of the first signs of modern man were discovered, then he pointed toward his own chest, "I go to university to be archeologist. I look for evidence. In Africa people have many babies for the future. In USA I think you not have many babies." He looked at us and when we didn't respond he said, "I think maybe the scientist is true, yes?"

CHAPTER 62

Muzungu

Dar es Salaam, Tanzania
44,375 miles

Sinking into the sticky, hot asphalt, heavily laden trucks created massive mounds in the center of the road with ruts on either side. These mounds were so high that the bottom of the van dragged against them as we descended to the coastal lowlands. Turning the corner, we came upon a caravan of overloaded trucks resting in the center of the steep road, allowing their brakes to cool. One Bedford ground to a halt in the sweeping bend of a narrow s-curve, blocking our passage for more than an hour.

As we approached Dar es Salaam the city drivers became more aggressive. Maniacal dalla-dalla operators, their shared taxis crammed full to overflowing, swerved wildly, squashing people against windows as the young fare collectors struggled to hang from the open side doors.

The bustling city was just as we expected, a tropical, sweltering, third-world New York with rushing people, far too busy chattering away in Swahili to take a second look. Mosques blasted their call from loudspeakers but most of Dar's residents were too distracted by their fight for survival to spend the afternoon in prayer. Down on the Indian Ocean waterfront the traditional sailing dhows jostled for position with barges and international cargo ships as sweaty, muscle-bound young men wrestled with colossal sacks of grain.

As we were shoving on to the ferry with hundreds of other passengers crossing from Dar to the beaches of Kagamboni, a young guy pushed past a group of women with packages, and squeezed on to the bench right next to me. In his imitation American-style clothing with colorful boxer shorts poking out the backside, he seemed out of place among the men in flowing robes and the women in long wrap-around skirts with veils. Sliding closer, he reached toward my pocket as the ferry sailed from the dock. My pocket was zipped closed, but that did not deter him. With my back turned, his hand slowly crept closer.

Amanda spotted him and elbowed me in caution.

Sliding away, I warned, "Go bother someone else," loud enough for the passengers nearby to hear. I expected one of the local men to speak up and tell him in Swahili to go away. In most countries, especially those with an Arab culture where hospitality is paramount, people take pride in protecting the visitor, but on this ferry everyone collapsed into the blank stare and averted eyes of public transport riders.

He jumped up from the bench and yelled, "Don't you tell me what to do!" Then he yelled louder, "Do you know what you are?" The hundreds of other passengers on the decrepit ferry were all Tanzanian, and they quickly shied away at the first sign of conflict. "You are a muzungu. Do you know what that is?" he spat out. The women nearby averted their eyes when they heard the insulting word. "That's right, MU-ZUN-GU. It means white devil." He got louder as he went on. "You WHITE DEVIL! We don't want you here. Why are you here?" He got very close to my face and said, "Think you can tell me what to do muzungu? I am free to be where I want."

With few other options, we chose to adopt the pose of our neighbors and averted our eyes, ignoring him as if he were a spoiled child experiencing a tantrum. This worked. He spewed out a few more insults, then finally strutted away to a group of friends nearby. The women in the corner and those next to us on the bench looked past their veils with apologetic eyes.

CHAPTER 63

Rhapsody in Zanzibar

Boat from Dar es Salaam to Zanzibar, Tanzania
20 miles

The human-sized, overflowing bags of charcoal had to be unloaded before we could get off the boat at the ancient, energetic port of Zanzibar. Taxi drivers, the ones with connections at the gate, pounced on us, shoving plastic badges of every size and color in our faces as if the faux-official documents would instill confidence in their services. Once past an indistinguishable line, a new pack of touts dressed in little more than rags, stalked like hungry leopards, shouting a mishmash of greetings while trying to lead us in the direction that suited them best. With our packs on our backs, we kept our heads down and closely trailed another passenger, an overstuffed man in a flowing white robe, snowy beard and sandals, to the immigration office.

Sultry, sweltering Zanzibar is technically part of Tanzania but the arranged marriage that brought the two together in the early 1960s has not proved fruitful. Mainlander Tanzanians are not permitted to travel to Zanzibar without the proper documents, that few possess, and the immigration officer inspected the Tanzanian passports more carefully than the foreign ones.

As we trudged through a barrage of touts after receiving our entry stamps, an ominous black cloud appeared, accompanied by thunderbolts and lightning. Instantly a drenching downpour forced us under the cover of a bread-seller's stall where we were easy prey. When the rain stopped abruptly, as if someone had flipped a switch, the string of would-be guides followed us through the old section of Zanzibar and would not let us go. Amongst the winding narrow passageways of Stone Town, we got lost in the disorienting labyrinth of streets that seemed to veer with no rhyme or reason. The guides offered advice on the best route to the hotel that would give them the largest tip. Several tried to misdirect us by saying that our destination was no longer in operation. The dizzying maze of alleys was lined with buildings blending the architectural styles of the Arabic, Indian, and European with native African materials. We had a map of Stone Town that was utterly useless, but Amanda studied it with great intent as I swatted away the hawkers. The Muslim call to prayer blared from unseen loudspeakers, echoing down narrow alleys, enhancing the perplexing effects of a house of mirrors.

Farrokh Bulsara was born amongst this chaos, as the son of the Persian cashier at the High Court. He used the frantic energy and intermingling cultures of Zanzibar to propel himself from the tiny island to the stages of the western world. Shipped off to school in Bombay, where the name Farrokh was changed to Freddy, he had a talent for the arts, and excelled at the piano. After graduating in the early 60s Freddy spent more than a year lounging around the cafes and beaches of Zanzibar, before political unrest forced his family to emigrate to England. There he changed his last name to Mercury, and became notorious for shamelessly blending styles and influences in much the same way as his birthplace.

At the old fish market we paused in the unsuccessful search for our hotel to watch as dhows disgorged slimy silver-wet piles into wooden pushcarts. The stinky catch was sold to veiled women, who carried them in head-top baskets on the journey home. Young boys fought one another, clambing the empty dhows to scrub the hold clean, and were rewarded with handfuls of fresh anchovies.

A thousand years ago Arab traders from Muscat and Oman sailed to the island in the ancient dhows, bringing the tenets of Islam to the shores of East Africa, and hauling away the ivory, skins, gold, and slaves that were ripped from the heart of the continent. Zanzibar emerged as the center for these merchants, allowing convenient control of the entire coast from Somalia to Mozambique.

Another downpour battered the puddles with large angry drops, but the buying and selling continued without anyone noticing. In the shelter of a narrow doorway we waited out the rain and a little silhouette of a man appeared from within the darkened vestibule to greet us. Pointing to a sign on the wall, he showed us, skeptical in all the confusion, that we were in fact standing in the entry to the guesthouse we had reserved.

Buzzing along on a wobbly old Vespa with a sticky throttle, we spent the next day exploring the island. The crystal blue water of the remarkably flat beaches vanished at low tide, revealing a marsh-like shoreline with exquisite shells. The frequent rains forced us to take shelter under the palm-thatched stands of roadside fruit vendors. People crowded under the stalls with overloaded bicycles full of firewood, baskets of tomatoes, crates of live chickens, and nets full of coconuts. Nobody seemed to mind. The locals welcomed us with the Swahili greeting, "Jambo," which literally translates to, "Hello person who I know cannot speak Swahili, and I do not expect you to reply in Swahili."

We offered a smile and a "jambo" in return.

Later we visited a plantation and tasted many of the spices that had been introduced to this tropical region from afar. We bit into the tooth-numbing clove, peeled the bark from cinnamon trees, cut fresh pieces from a ginger root, smelled the different aromas of the cocoa used to produce chocolate, and tasted the coffee beans blended to create our morning drink. Ingredients essential to some of the most deeply-engrained traditions of western life. We marveled at our ability to accept them into our culture without even a basic understanding of how they come to be.

Imitating the locals, we zoomed our Vespa through the narrow cobblestone pathways of Stone Town, and laughed along with a group of old men as we unwittingly passed the same teahouse time and again before discovering a new route. Beeping the horn at each narrow bend, we dodged ghostly black-veiled women blinking to control their wandering eyes; sweaty lean-muscled cart haulers fighting against their ungainly loads; elegant bicycle-bound civil servants making graceful curving turns; and young mothers selling piles of rat poison.

The spice island of Zanzibar, the exotic, fragrant, poverty-rich jewel of East Africa, continues in its centuries-old tradition as the place where cultures and customs mix to produce strange and wonderful combinations. Anyone can see that nothing really matters for most of these bizarre blends. But it is the Freddy Mercurys who can turn the dark clouds into the afternoon sun, and cocoa into chocolate, who push the outer extremes of life, sometimes into misery but often into sparkling success.

CHAPTER 64

For Better or For Worse

Nairobi, Kenya
45,460 miles

I swerved the van to avoid a group of locals spilling on to the road, slowed down and asked, "What was that?" The car behind me honked furiously.

Amanda stuck her head out the window to look back while I concentrated on the road. "It looks like..."

"A dead old man?" I asked.

"Yes, and he was all dressed up." Amanda settled back in the van and secured her seatbelt.

The man was lying in an unnatural position with his left arm turned up under him and the back of his head resting on the elevated asphalt road while the rest of him was strewn out on the edge. He had obviously been hit by one of the trucks while waiting, dressed in his Sunday suit, to go to church. Someone had placed his hat on his chest. A group, all in their church attire, stood around his body but none seemed to be upset. They just stood staring down at him.

A sickness was spreading in the pit of my stomach. I kept my eyes on the road and asked, "Had you ever seen a dead body before coming to Africa?"

"I don't think so, maybe at a funeral. I can't remember. I guess it's one of those things I block out," Amanda said.

Within the first twenty minutes of driving on the road between the costal city of Mombasa and the capital Nairobi we saw four trucks flipped on to their sides, with drivers scratching their heads and staring at the wreckage. The trucks would encounter one another head-on and move as far to the edge of the road as possible, each with the outer two wheels hanging over the brink. A lip of asphalt hung over a two foot drop on either side of the road where the sandy edge had been washed away by heavy rains. It was a treacherous tightrope walk each time we encountered a truck.

For hours we drove toward the Kenyan capital in fearful silence.

The streets of Nairobi were empty on Sunday morning, making the usually crammed traffic circles a pleasure to navigate and the favored crime in the car-jack-capital of the world much less likely to occur. The van chugged up Nairobi Hill to a place that has become notorious among budget travelers, the Upper Hill Campsite. There was only one other vehicle, a Land Rover, camping on the lawn when we settled in, but nearly twenty tents littered the yard of the once elegant home.

From the back of the closet Amanda dug out a bag containing our neatly folded respectable outfits, her only skirt with a matching top and my wrinkle-free shirt and pants. From some mysterious cubbyhole in the back of the van she produced leather sandals and a small handbag. Before leaving home she had packed these items in the faint hope that we could use them if we found ourselves going out somewhere fancy.

Propping her tiny double-sided mirror on the table, it took her nearly forty minutes to apply her make-up. She said, "Every morning I did this before work. I used to hate this chore. It's funny how much I'm enjoying it now."

"That was a long time ago," I said.

"It seems like it was another life."

Strolling down the hill on the sunny day, we looked forward to participating in the ritual of afternoon tea at the historic Stanley Hotel, where generations of travelers have pinned messages to the thorn tree in the center of the patio that gives the café its name. Tradition holds that all visitors to Kenya must sample a few of the Thorn Tree Café's scones, pastries, and confections with a cup of their famous tea, but Amanda had gone for such a long time without satisfying her carnivorous cravings that she made a choice she would come to regret. In her enthusiasm among the elegantly clad safari set, she ordered a juicy steak, then finished the meal with tea and a brick-like scone.

It had been months since we had eaten meat but not for lack of desire. Well, not entirely. The color of the beef we found hanging from the hooks in most East African markets tended toward that of the sky, from a grisly gray to a near purple blue. These trips to the butcher's stall could turn the most ardent meat eater to vegetarianism.

The very next day her digestive system ground to a complete halt. After she'd taken an hour on the toilet I was pacing outside the camp bathroom, eager to get started with the day, calling in every few minutes to make sure she was all right. Finally she gave up and grumbled as we drove to the outskirts of Nairobi and the home of Karen Blixen, the author of *Out of Africa*. When we arrived, Amanda headed straight for the restroom and spent the first half-hour on the famous author's toilet hoping for a success that would not come.

Walking through the stone farmhouse, we admired her original paintings of the Kikuyu tribesmen who lived on her massive coffee plantation. The painting of Farah Aden, her faithful Somali servant, was particularly impressive. Most of her furniture had been auctioned off just before she left Africa, and her few remaining possessions were scattered among the props left behind by the crew who used her house to film the movie about her life. After she left for Europe, her land, surrounded by the Ngong Hills, was divided into separate estates and the area is now called Karen in her honor.

The next morning Amanda woke with a beach ball for a belly, and she turned to the first-aid kit for a remedy. I had packed the kit in much the same way I had bolted spare parts to the bottom of the van, then promptly forgotten where I had put them. As a space-saving measure I had removed all the external packaging from the medications and after two years of rubbing together in the kit, the printing on the blister packs of pills had worn off. With no names or instructions, all the pills looked the same. Amanda was furious and she marched over to the toilet for another useless session.

Later she asked one of the campsite workers the location of a good pharmacy and he put a dot on our city map but added, "It is best to wait until you get to your home country to buy medication. What we have here in Kenya is often old and unreliable."

I suggested that a walk around town might get her system flowing and so we set out to see the museums of Nairobi, figuring if she was unsuccessful throughout the day, we could always stop at the pharmacy in the afternoon. Her beach ball wobbled around town with us but never gave a hint that it wanted to be released. The Nairobi map was hard to read, the size of the streets difficult to judge, and when we finally arrived at the pharmacy later that afternoon it had closed for the day.

That night the cramps began and she barely slept. She woke in a miserable mood and demanded, "I want you to go to the pharmacy and tell the pharmacist that I am suffering from severe constipation. Get whatever they suggest. Do NOT choose something yourself. Ask the pharmacist for help."

I did exactly as she wanted and returned with an enema. Not just any enema. A Kenyan enema. It was a plastic bottle full of solution with a long trailing tube and very precise instructions regarding the position of the patient. That position made it absolutely impossible for the enema to be administered by the patient.

After she read the instructions she yelled, "Did you even take it out of the box to look at it before you bought it?"

"Of course not," I yelled back. "There was a whole group of people waiting for prescriptions, listening as I described your symptoms."

"So you just bought whatever they gave you?"

"That's what you wanted me to do," I said, exasperated.

"Well take it back," she blurted, shoving it into my hands.

"No. No way. It was humiliating enough to buy it. I will not return that thing," I said, shoving it back into her grasp.

"Well then, you're going to have to help me," she said.

"Huh? You can do it yourself. Those instructions, they're just guidelines, you don't really have to follow them."

"Don't look at me as if you're not familiar with the area," she shot back.

"But, but, you can just ignore the instructions…"

"Rich," she cut me short. "I need help and you are going to help me."

"But…"

"No buts."

She slammed the door to the van, leaving me outside as she re-read the instructions, then yelled, "Come in and close the door behind you." As she went through the instructions step by step I let out a series of little gasps. Then she got into the position shown on the diagram and said, "Okay, go ahead."

I closed my eyes and my aim was way off. "Not there," she hissed through gritted teeth.

Following each step as she told me what to do, I finally got the tube in the right place. Within seconds she was sprinting off to the toilet.

She left me in the van with my head spinning from the ordeal. This was too much. This went beyond the call of duty for a husband. I thought, "For better or for worse". This was worse than worse. I didn't think our relationship would survive a repeat performance.

I vowed we'd never eat meat again.

CHAPTER 65

Curious Georgette

Rumuruti, Kenya
45,602 miles

The quaintly disheveled stone house sat on a hilltop in the shadows of Mt. Kenya overlooking one of the troughs of the Rift Valley. A young man, dressed in the red-plaid wrap of the Masai, stood outside the gate and opened it for me to walk through, but did not follow. The front door was open and I called, "Hello," from the yard. A monkey dashed out, leaped toward me and landed on my arm as the face of a gaunt white man appeared at a narrow window and said, "We'll be with you in just a minute."

The monkey twisted its tail around my wrist in a firm grasp. I shook my arm but it had entwined itself so tightly that I couldn't fling it off. Waiting for the owner, I stood there holding the monkey far from my body as it spun around and began fidgeting with my watch. A middle-aged woman with a mop of red hair, wearing a tattered man's dress shirt and oversized pants, stepped from the house and greeted me with a firm handshake as she said, "Hello. Welcome. She likes you. Gi'er here and I'll tie 'er up." The woman strapped what looked like a cat leash around the monkey's neck and placed it on her shoulder. The monkey immediately began picking through her wild red mop, finding a few choice morsels.

"We were hoping to camp with you and go on a camel…"

"Hello," a skinny little pixie of a man interrupted from the doorway. "We're happy to have you with us," he said as he adjusted his pants. Two large dogs followed him into the yard, tails wagging wildly, and one went right for my crotch, burrowing with its nose.

"Thank you," I said as I tried to shove the dog away. "I already parked the van in the campsite. We wanted to stay the night and rent camels tomorrow for a trek into the valley."

"Camping is no problem and a ride t'morrow's fine, jus' fine. I'll organize it with the herders and come over later to let you know," he said with a grin, watching me struggle to the gate with the sniffing, wagging dog glued to my pants.

Amanda had already popped up the roof, set out our table and chairs, and was busy taking out the few meager ingredients for our meal when I got back to our campsite. The dry desert breeze of the Rift Valley was a welcome change from the moist, semi-tropical humidity of the highlands and Amanda washed our dirty sheets and towels as I prepared dinner.

Just before sunset she boiled a kettle of water for tea and brought it to the table among the hanging laundry. She poured herself a cup and was ready to pour some for me when the monkey came bounding along.

With the kettle in one hand, her cup of tea in the other, Amanda tried to scoot the monkey away from the open sliding door of the van. It jumped toward her, landing on her upper arm, reaching for her cup. Amanda spun in a frenzy, yelling, "Get off, get off, get off!"

The monkey dropped to the ground, then hopped from the chair to the table, and picked up my cup.

I reached for a bamboo reed lying on the ground and said to Amanda, "Get inside the van while I chase it away."

Amanda glanced towards our things spread around the campsite and said, "No, I don't want it to take anything." Then she began to kick dirt at the monkey while holding the kettle and her cup of tea. "Go away, go, go, go!"

I swung the stick near the monkey and said more forcefully, "Amanda, get in the van."

She kept on kicking. "No. Monkeys steal things."

"I have a stick. Get in the van."

"No. It might take…" she looked around, "…something from the table." Just as she said it the monkey leaped again and landed on the back of her shoulder, its tail curling around her arm.

"Errrggh. See, I told you to get in the van!" I insisted.

"I can't!" She yelled back, "Ow ow ow…" The hot tea spilled on her hand as she tried to hold the cup still. "Get it off. Get it off. Ow, ow, ow! It's burning." She spun in circles.

"Don't move. I'll scoot it off with the stick," I said, frustrated.

She continued to spin, shaking her arm, trying to balance her cup and the kettle.

"Stop moving so I can get it," I yelled.

Spinning in circles, she was getting frantic. "Get it off, get it off, get it off!"

"Stop moving." I was getting angrier.

She spun, flapping her arm.

"Stop! Stop! STOP MOVING!" I shouted.

I swung the bamboo reed as she spun, hitting her on the back and swatting the arm of the monkey. She spilled the rest of the hot tea on her hand.

The monkey screamed, "Eeeeeeeeeeek!"

Amanda screamed, "Ahhhhhhhhhh!"

The monkey thrust downward, sinking its teeth into her shoulder.

When I saw the monkey bite her I whacked wildly, swinging blindly and hitting hard.

It leaped from her shoulder and hopped under the van. In blind fury I hurled myself to the ground, banging the tires.

The monkey ran toward the house and I chased it at full speed.

I slammed through the gate, through the open front door, right into the living room, panting, dirty, ready to kill, searching for the monkey. Out of the corner of my eye I saw movement through the back door of the house. I rushed out into the courtyard and was stopped dead in my tracks. There, unchained, was the reason for the gate.

I came face to face with a cheetah.

I was breathing heavily from the run and fought back the instinct to bolt. Looking me straight in the eye, it hypnotically wagged its tail.

A dog barked and the cheetah twisted its head with lightning speed. The dog ran at me, burying his nose in my crotch. The cheetah watched the dog, then slowly turned and walked away. I cautiously backed into the house with the dog in my crotch. When I reached the gate the young Masai man waited for me on the other side.

Struggling to breathe, I stammered, "There's, ah, ah, ah cheetah in there," as I opened the gate, heart pounding, mind spinning.

"Yes, he lives here," the young man said calmly.

Then I remembered. "The monkey…" Gasping, "…it bit my wife."

"Ohhhh…" he said slowly. "The screams…I see. It is a bad monkey."

Then the fear turned to anger once again, "You better catch that monkey because if it comes back near us… I'll whack it. You hear me? I'll whack it hard." I shook the bamboo reed.

He backed away and looked at me as if I were crazy.

"Where are the owners?" I demanded.

He gave a vague reply. I could see that I was getting nowhere so I left and rushed back to the van.

From a distance I saw Amanda dashing madly back and forth, moving like a whirlwind, throwing our wet laundry, dishes, teakettle, and books into the van, then I heard her slam the sliding door. When I arrived she said hysterically through the jalousie window, "I rubbed alcohol on it. I didn't know what else to do."

"Let me see it," I said.

She opened the door just a crack and pulled off her t-shirt. She turned and I saw two punctures on the back of her neck.

"How does it look?" she asked, concerned.

"It looks like a vampire bit you," I answered. "But what's this?" I reached down and touched a red streak across her back.

"Ouch. That's where you hit me. Why were you hitting me?"

"I'm sorry. I didn't mean to…"

"The monkey was on my shoulder, way up here."

"I know. You were spinni…"

"But you didn't have to hit me."

"You were spinning in circles, jumping around. I didn't mean to hit you. I'm sorry. But you won't believe what happe…."

"Get in the van. I want to get out of here."

"Wait. Let me tell you what hap…"

"GET IN THE VAN!" she shouted.

"OK. OK. We'll go. Right now." I said, and walked to the driver's door. "Keys. Where are my keys?" I said, patting my pockets.

As Amanda pulled on her t-shirt she reached across and unlocked my door. The keys were already in the ignition.

CHAPTER 66

Close Shave

Jinja, Uganda
46,107 miles

"They're in the cabinet above the back seat. Get them out and I'll do it when I come back," Amanda said just before marching toward the restroom.

In silent defiance to her bossiness I sat watching the foaming rapids of the White Nile. Leaning the chair back I became mesmerized by the rolling water. The van rested on a small mound in an open grassy field overlooking the source of the Nile where the river meets Lake Victoria at Jinja, Uganda.

After she was out of sight I climbed in to the van and flipped open the cabinet, then stared with bewilderment. I could not remember what Amanda needed.

The cabinet was in a place that required uncomfortable contortions to reach, and consequently was stuffed like a jigsaw puzzle with items we rarely used. The small sewing kit was right in front, and I moved it out of the way. Behind it I found the binoculars. I took them out and played with them for a few minutes, looking at the huts further down the river, then set them on the table. I found a small box of votive candles that Amanda periodically produced on quiet evenings. I had often wondered where she kept those. I kept digging, removing items and setting them on the stove and the floor in the hope that my memory would be jolted when I came upon the item she wanted.

Then I found my collapsible fishing rod stuffed way in the back corner. I had to remove a two-year's supply of sunscreen and insect repellant to get it out. When I purchased this nifty piece of equipment at a flea market, I had such high hopes. But I hadn't used it as often as I would have liked, primarily because I couldn't remember where it was kept. Amanda teased that I had never actually caught a fish with it, but it was one of those things I had to bring. I took it out and began spinning the reel. It was rusty. The last time I used it was in salt water, so I set it on a greasy towel and began to take it apart for a good oiling.

The oil was in my tool kit in a separate closet Amanda liked to call Tool World. She called it that because it was the only place in the van that was a mystery to her, a lost world full of tools. Every time I opened it she would cluck and shake her head, hoping one day to get the opportunity to reorganize it so that each item had its own place. I learned from hard experience that if Amanda poked her nose in there, Tool World would be far neater and much more logically arranged and, from that moment on, I would have to ask her where everything was kept. Tool World was a cluttered, disorganized mess and I liked it that way.

When I unscrewed the bolt that held Tool World's door in place everything came tumbling out on the floor of the van, conveniently spread out so that I could find the exact item I needed. With everything scattered, I promptly forgot what it was that I wanted. Then I saw the disassembled fishing rod on the table and began digging for the oil. The can was buried under a heap of junk that I piled on the port-a-potty. Grabbing the oil, I got to work lubricating the fishing rod.

That's when she returned. "What are you doing? Did you find them? Where are they?"

"What?" I asked. "I'm oiling my fishing rod."

"What? What do you mean, what? The scissors," she demanded.

"Oh, yeah. I looked but I couldn't find them."

"I told you…the scissors are in the sewing kit, in the front of the cabinet."

"Oh, the sewing kit. I didn't see that."

I sat with a towel wrapped around my neck, as motionless as humanly possible, while Amanda trimmed my hair. There aren't many situations in life where a man appreciates a gentle touch. In fact, at the time I could think of only two, but that day I added the Barber Shop to the list. It's strange that such a petite woman could have two hands made from such heavy bricks.

Snipping around my ears, she pulled them down and peeled them out of the way so hard that my eyes watered. As she trimmed the back of my head she shoved it so far forward that my chin rested in my belly button. But it was the last part that was humiliating.

A group of Ugandan teenagers had come to sit in the grass overlooking the rapids, and they were all watching as Amanda stood in front of me and said, "Now turn your head so I can see if the sides are even."

I turned first to the right, then to the left.

She said, "Faster so I can see both sides. Real quick."

I turned faster, left then right.

"I can't tell if it's even; keep turning, left, right, left, right," she said.

I looked over at the group who were laughing. "I don't care if it's even. Don't worry about it."

She insisted, "No, I want to get it right. Just turn, back and forth, real quick. C'mon."

"But my barber never makes me do that," I pleaded.

She was already angry from the mess in the van and said, "If you want me to cut your hair, this is what you have to do. Now turn, fast, and keep going until I tell you to stop."

Normally I would have relented right then but I saw the teenagers laughing and said, "But…but it doesn't matter if they're even. Nobody can see both sides of my head at the same time."

Just then a raft floated by with seven helmeted white people paddling in unison as they effortlessly rolled over the foaming rapids. We both silently watched as they passed.

The Ugandan teenagers ran along the banks, following the rafters down the river, and they all disappeared around the bend. Once they were gone I did my head twisting routine and Amanda finished up the haircut by trimming a wedge from my left ear lobe.

A few hours later a young Ugandan man with tightly twirled dreadlocks approached and asked, "Did you see the rafters as they passed here?"

I told him we did.

He squatted a few feet away and said, "Tomorrow we're organizing a trip down the White Nile and we have a group of four. Would you like to join?"

Amanda was skeptical and said, "I don't know. We've never been rafting before. Is this a good place to try it for the first time?"

The young man said with assurance, "Ah, it is not bad at all. Nothing to worry about."

I asked him the price for the trip and a few other minor details then said with confidence, "Sounds great. I'm gonna do it. How about you?" I looked toward Amanda.

She was reluctant and asked, "Ah…well…does this include safety equipment?"

I turned and saw a crowd of locals lining the banks as Ben, our rugged Australian raft leader, steered us to a calm spot above the second rapids. He had stopped the raft to give our group a pep talk and yelled above the roar of the water, "This is the one I was telling you about yesterday."

I wanted to mention, "Ah, what? Yesterday. We weren't there yesterday." But I didn't.

Ben continued, "You can fall out of the raft at any other rapid, but for this one you want to stay in. This is the most technically difficult commercially rafted rapid in the world. There's a four meter waterfall and sharp rocks at the bottom."

"Huh?" I was in the front and turned to look at Amanda, who was behind me, but she was facing Ben who was at the back of the raft spewing instructions.

Ben yelled, "OK! This is it! A class five-plus rapid. Are you ready? OK. Let's go! Right paddles back, left paddle forward, all paddles back. Here we goooOOOOO!"

I was thinking "four meter waterfall....most...difficult...rapid...in the world," and I missed Ben's instructions. My oar got tangled with Amanda's. I messed up the paddling and we hit the rapid all wrong. Everyone else in the boat was in a squatting position, holding tight, but Amanda and I were struggling to unknot our oars as we crested the waterfall. We crashed in. The nose of the raft dug under and bent like an accordion. I was dragged directly underwater at the base of the falls. I knew Amanda was also thrown, but I didn't know where. I immediately lost all sense of direction. I opened my eyes and saw only churning brown and white. Despite the heavy life preservers, the mass of water pulled me under with ease and spun me around and around.

Ben had warned us about this. He told us that if we were to fall out we should not fight current. His advice was to stay still, keep from trying to swim, and let the life preserver do its job. Eventually we would be pulled to the surface, he said. The best course was to stay calm.

Easier said than done. I fought against the rushing avalanche of water and finally remembered his words. Those few seconds underwater, spinning in a tumbling, brown, out of control washing machine seemed to last forever.

I somersaulted in the water at the base of the falls, never moving more than a meter from where the raft landed. I bobbed to the surface right next to the raft and Ben yelled, "Pull him in!"

But Amanda wasn't in the raft so I began to swim away. I couldn't find her and refused to get into the raft until I saw she was safe. As we hurtled down the rapids I gripped the side of the raft, scanning the water, looking for any signs of her bright red life vest.

After what seemed like an eternity, Ben yelled and pointed near the bank. Amanda was floating in a swirling eddy, but I was too low to see if she was injured. One of the rescue paddlers rushed over and pulled her up on to the front of his snub-nosed kayak.

The group pulled me back into the raft, and I discovered that the force of the water had ripped the sole from one of my sandals.

The rescue paddler deposited Amanda back into the raft, soaked and exhausted. She sputtered as a delirious grin spread across her face from ear to ear and said, *"¡Hijole mano! ¡Increíble! ¿En donde estoy?"* (Oh my goodness! Incredible! Where am I?) She babbled away in Spanish before collapsing flat on her back on the floor of the raft.

Glancing toward the bank, my eye caught on the teenagers from the day before. When they saw me looking their way they elbowed one another and burst into laughter.

CHAPTER 67

In God's Hands

Kampala, Uganda
46,184 miles

It took three calls to get through to the health clinic. The receptionist transferred me to the nurse, who sounded like a middle-aged British woman. "Was the animal acting strangely?" she asked.

"Well, I'm not really sure. I don't know how monkeys normally act. It jumped on us without being afraid. Is that normal?"

"Is it a pet or wild?"

"It's a pet."

"Do you have it there?" she asked hopefully.

"No, this happened in Kenya."

A hint of concern crept into her voice. "How long ago did the bite occur?"

"Uh…" I had to think and count, "Five, no six days ago."

"Did your wife get the pre-exposure inoculation as a precaution before leaving home?"

"No," I said, then added lamely, "I wanted to get it, but she didn't."

"Hum. Have you contacted the owner?"

"I've tried, for three days now, but these telephones…every time I call they connect me with a wrong number. I don't even know if I'm getting a line into Kenya."

"Let me suggest that if you are unable to make contact with the owner within the day, then bring your wife in and we'll begin the treatment."

"What does the treatment involve?" I asked, remembering horrific tales from years ago of needles in the stomach.

Sensing my concern, she said, "Rabies is not as frightful as it once was. We'll give her one injection today, then four more on days three, seven, fourteen and twenty-eight."

Walking back to the van at the campsite in Kampala, Uganda, I went over in my mind how I was going to tell Amanda everything. Since leaving the Rift Valley she had assumed a resigned, fatalistic stubbornness that scared me as much as the possibility of rabies. While the chances that she had actually been infected with the virus were slim, I couldn't get the haunting words from our medical book from my mind, "If someone with rabies infection begins showing symptoms, that person usually does not survive."

I got halfway to the van and remembered that I wanted to try to get through to Kenya once again, so I turned around and walked back to the pay telephone.

Earlier in the week I had read aloud to Amanda from a precaution sheet published by the Centers for Disease Control, "After the incubation period which may last for weeks, it is usually within a very short three to five day period that the animal is infectious and begins showing the unmistakable signs of rabies." I told her, "I'll try to call the owner and ask him if the monkey is acting weird. If it's not, then we have nothing to worry about."

Amanda shrugged as if she didn't really care and said, "I am not getting any injections here in Uganda so it doesn't really matter."

"Look," I said. "Rabies is deadly. We shouldn't take any chances. If you start showing symptoms it's too late and there's nothing the doctors can do. You must get treatment before the symptoms appear. Do you hear me? Are you listening?"

"Richard, stop worrying. I'm feeling fine. Anyway, it's in God's hands."

Back at the telephone I put in a pocket full of coins and dialed the number with meticulous precision.

Someone picked up and said, "Hum?" into the receiver.

"Hello, is this the Sobong Camp?"

"Milton...no here."

"Is this SOBONG?"

"Unakaa wapi?"

"Camp? S-O-B-O-N-G?"

"Nisamehe sifahamu."

"Is this 324-484?"

"Nisamehe sifahamu."

"Are you in Kenya?"

Click. The line went dead.

This was the fifth public telephone I had tried. Each time I was connected with a different person, and I began to wonder if the owner was purposely avoiding speaking with me. The monkey would have definitely been dead by now if it were rabid.

When I got back to the van I said to Amanda, "Well, it looks like we have no choice."

"I told you, no needles."

"It could be worse. At least Kampala has a good clinic."

"No, I am not getting any shots here. Absolutely not."

"I called the clinic and they said we can come in anytime."

It took me twenty minutes to entice Amanda into the van. We were ready to leave the campground when she yelled, "Wait. Stop! I want to try to call the camp. What's the number?"

Amanda just wanted to delay the inevitable. I knew she would not get through but I indulged her because she was the one getting the injections.

After a few rings someone answered and she said, "Hello, is this Sobong Camp? It is? Thank goodness!"

I didn't believe that she had gotten through to the right number and said loudly, "Hand me the receiver."

She said, "It's them. It's the right number."

I took the receiver and said, "Hello. Is this Sobong Camp?"

A man with a proper British accent answered, "Yes, this is John at Sobong."

I said, "Ah….John….ah… we were there with you last week."

"Yes, the Americans who left. Why did you leave so abruptly?"

"Didn't your staff tell you about the monkey?"

"My monkey, what about her?"

"She…she attacked my wife, bit her on the shoulder."

"Oh, my."

"John, we're on our way to the clinic here in Kampala for the rabies shots. Is it necessary?"

"Heavens no. That monkey is a pet. We've had it inoculated for rabies along with the cheetah and all the dogs."

"So the monkey is still alive and well."

"Right here on my shoulder as we speak."

I hung up the phone with a great sigh of relief as Amanda shrugged and said, "I told you so."

CHAPTER 68

Gorillas in the Jungle

Bwindi, Uganda
46,718 miles

I knew it was a bad idea from the start, but Amanda insisted. It is more than three hundred miles from Kampala to the remote corner of the country where the world's few remaining mountain gorillas survive. The dense mountainous jungle is the spot where Uganda, Rwanda and the Congo converge. The far-flung patch of Central Africa often makes the news as the birthplace of Ebola and AIDS, and the deathbed of untold millions in the tribal clash between the Hutus and the Tutsis. I wasn't enthusiastic about driving into such a volatile region on our own.

But Amanda argued, "How many times in our life will we have the opportunity to see gorillas in the wild?" She said it in the tone of voice that made it clear she would not accept no for an answer.

I knew she was right. Years earlier when we decided to travel around the globe, we looked forward to being forced to conquer our fears and drive beyond the world we knew, the one that was guaranteed and insured. It's funny how easy it was to contemplate stepping outside our comfort zone while sitting in our comfortable home. When reality hit, on the ground in Uganda, with no back up plan, no safety net, and no idea what was ahead, we felt entirely exposed.

Nearly half the world's 600 mountain gorillas live in the Bwindi Impenetrable Forest, and Amanda was navigating us there using a hand-drawn map she had gotten from a gas station attendant in the small town of Kabale. The dirt roads were completely unmarked, and we stopped at a fork to ask directions from a hunched old man weeding a small plot. He pointed to the right to a trail that headed up a hill.

At the top we came to a swinging gate with a wooden, hand-painted sign dangling from it that announced we were entering the boundary of the Bwindi Forest. Amanda said, "Wow, we arrived faster than I thought we would," as she jumped from the van and opened the gate.

"That's good. I'm getting hungry," I said to myself.

The dirt road narrowed to a rugged trail with two brush-covered tire tracks. It wasn't long before we crested another hill, turned a bend, and began to descend one of the steepest paths we had encountered in three years. I slammed on the brakes. "This isn't gonna work. This is too steep. We've got to go back."

I tried to reverse up the hill but the van did not have enough power. The tangled vines and vegetation grew to the edge of the path, leaving no room to turn around. I realized there was no going back and we continued down the rocky hill. The situation was rapidly disintegrating.

An hour later Amanda scanned the map in frustration and said, "We were supposed to pass two villages by now. I don't understand." All we had seen was the endless tropical forest.

We continued on.

Starving and tired after many hours of excruciatingly slow driving, with the sun beginning to set, we came to a steep uphill section with large rounded boulders poking through the path. Disheartened and disoriented, we had no idea where we were or where the path led. I stopped the van at the bottom of the hill and together we walked up the path to scout out the course. When I saw what was ahead I knew it would be challenging even for a high-clearance four-wheel-drive vehicle. It was much steeper and rockier than any route we had ever driven. I tossed a rock into the vegetation and said to Amanda in laughing desperation, "This isn't even a road. If we were on mountain bikes we would have to walk them up this hill."

"Do you think we'll make it?" she asked, concerned.

"We can't turn back now. All we can do is move forward," I answered without much hope.

I revved the engine and built up some momentum, then unleashed the feeble power of the van. I thought of all the things that could go wrong. Hitting one of the rocks incorrectly could break the suspension or a tie-rod, leaving us stranded. Something simple like a busted shock absorber, and we would spend the night wherever we stopped rolling. As we hit the first bump I thought, "What have I gotten myself into?"

Struggling up the hill, something happened to the van, something strange and unbelievable. With rocks scraping along the bottom and wheels spinning on the damp boulders, the van got a burst of power it had never had before. I said, "I think I can, I think I can, I think I can…" It just kept chugging along, pushing forward. It slowed when it hit an obstacle, but it continued to move. As we crept close to the top Amanda chanted, "I know I can, I know I can, I know I can…"

On top of the hill a small break in the foliage revealed a view of the vast jungle canopy. Through it we could see the main road and the forest headquarters. I never imagined the van could do it. But it did. We were exhausted as if we had run a marathon, but we made it.

Relieved, we parked in the cramped yard of a basic campsite. Too tired to move or eat, we collapsed to sleep, knowing we were in for another ordeal in the morning.

A week before in Kampala we had visited the Bwindi Forest office, but had been unsuccessful in securing permits to be in the area. The friendly Ugandan woman told us, "There are only a few permits issued each day. You must make reservations one year in advance."

We had made the tortuous journey into the remote region without knowing if we would actually be able to see the gorillas. Once in Bwindi we had hoped for a last-minute cancellation. The next morning we walked to the warden's office.

He was a serious, overly-efficient man, and he looked at his watch as he shook his head, "Two people have not arrived as of yet. If they are not here by 8:00 am I may sell you their permit. But mind you, chances are not good."

"What is the price for the permit?" I asked.

"One hundred sixty five American dollars per person," he said. Then he added as if apologizing, "The funds are used to provide security and to protect the habitat of the gorillas."

Resting our daypacks on a bench in a small cement pavilion, we waited with a group of soldiers in full camouflage carrying AK-47s. Anxious that the other visitors would arrive, Amanda paced nervously and I walked over to read a plaque bolted to a post on the outside of the pavilion. It was a memorial to a group of tourists and locals who had lost their lives while trekking in the nearby hills. I remembered hearing something about it in the news but couldn't recall the details. One of the young soldiers watched as I read the plaque and I asked him, "Did this happen here?"

"Yes," he said regretfully. "The rebels came from Rwanda. They were in a camp, there in the Congo." He pointed to a hill to the east. That's when I realized how close we were to the border.

"Is that why you soldiers are here?" Amanda asked.

"Yes, to protect the visitors, and also the gorillas..."

At exactly 8:00 am the warden opened the door to his office, broke into a wide smile and said, "You are in luck. It seems they have not come." He completed the extensive forms and we were paired with a group of soldiers and a guide.

Benson, the ranger who worked for the Ugandan government, was in front, hacking the dense foliage with a curved machete to create a clearing through the jungle as the five soldiers followed behind. "Do not be concerned. This will grow back in a matter of days," he said. Every so often he looked down at the GPS receiver to determine the direction where the gorillas were last seen.

After two hours of tracking, we hiked along the edge of a steep, slippery hillside and my boots skidded on the wet vines. I grabbed at the foliage to keep from sliding down, but my foot sunk further and I grasped for anything firm. My hand landed in something squishy. The brown grassy glob oozed between my fingers. One of the young soldiers pulled me up and was unable to fight back a laugh when he saw that my hand was clutching a pile of fresh gorilla dung. Good sign. We were getting close.

Startled by a noise that seemed foreign to the jungle, we froze to listen. It sounded like a drumming combined with a massive exhalation. Amanda turned to look at me with excitement in her eyes. Benson said something to one of the soldiers, then explained to us, "The troop is very near. That was the silverback. He was warning a young male that has been trying to steal a female from the troop. The young male is not habituated to humans. He is not used to us so we must be careful."

"Are we in danger?" Amanda asked.

"No, no danger," Benson answered. "The entire troop is feeling tension, especially the silverback. We will see a lot of activity."

Ducking to pass under some thorny vines, we noticed a strong, musk-like scent, similar to the smell of human body odor mixed with decaying vegetation. Benson squatted to look under a low arch of green vines, then pointed for us to follow. Through the clearing we could see the silverback, the dominant male of the troop, hunched forward, looking aggressively at the bushes to our right.

Benson said, "You can see he is anxious. The troop has not slept well. They must always watch for the threat."

The bushes shook and a dark figure slid past. The silverback rushed at the figure, hunched on all fours, his massive hump protruding from the back of his neck.

Amanda crawled through the brush for a better view and I followed. We found ourselves just a few feet from a baby gorilla and mother. The female rolled her index finger and adeptly stripped the tender green leaves from long, fat vines before shoving a handful into her mouth. Benson said, "See how fast she is eating and how she is protecting her baby. It is because of the young challenger."

The massive silverback male was on guard and kept careful watch over the three females, two babies, and one juvenile male in his troop. A rustling of bushes behind us caused him to stand at attention and gave us all a fright. The unhabituated male rushed toward us from behind. Before we could move the silverback had cleared a path through the thick brush, pounding the earth with fierce power, and placed himself between the aggressive young male and our group.

The wide-eyed soldiers erupted into frantic chatter. Excitedly Bensons said, "He protected us. Did you see? Did you see?" He pointed as if we had not seen it ourselves, "The silverback came from over there to protected us." As we stood marveling at what had happened, the massive silverback moved back to his nest and sat heavily to rest.

Fighting to guard his domain and defend his territory, the silverback had barely slept and was subjected to extreme stress. Benson said, "This young male will not give up. They have been fighting like this for weeks. One day soon the silverback will lose. If he chases away this one, another will come. He must always be alert."

Once again it was hard to witness the mercilessness of nature. Even in victory the gorilla, always struggling to remain the strongest and to defend his troop, could never let down his guard.

Benson looked at his watch and said, "We have three minutes until we must leave." Amanda hastily loaded another roll of film in her camera and asked one of the young soldiers if he would take a photo of us with the jungle and the troop of mountain gorillas in the background. He swung his AK-47 to his back, pointed the camera and said, "Say cheese."

It had taken fifty thousand miles of driving for us to reach this remote corner of the world, and we had come to the end of the road. At that moment, a new adventure began. This photograph would capture our turning point, where we set out on our journey home. I wrapped my arm around Amanda as we said, "Cheeeeeese," in unison.

Neither of us noticed the camera was switched off.

CHAPTER 69

Homecoming

San Diego, California
59,338 miles

After nearly three years of constant travel we were driving the van toward the roller coaster at Mission Beach in San Diego. The local media had heard about our homecoming and cameras waited to capture the images of our leap into the Pacific Ocean.

Amanda had pulled all of her clothing from the closet and was in the back of the van trying on different outfits as I took the Mission Beach exit from Interstate 8. It seemed unreal to be driving on familiar roads for the first time in years. The traffic was overwhelming. As I stopped at a light not far from Sea World Amanda said, "Quick, look in the mirror. Should I wear the flower top or this red one?" She held up a bright pink tank-top with a huge yellow flower-power flower in the center.

"The flower one. Definitely the flower," I answered.

It was one of those warm, sunny spring afternoons when everyone takes a half-day off from work and heads to the beach. Summer was just around the corner and there was a buzz in the air. Roberto's Taco Shop was teeming with surfers and the open-air bars were packed with sun-worshippers. As we drove up to the boardwalk the smell of sunscreen mingled with a faint scent of the sea. A crowd of skaters, cyclists, and walkers were drawn to the van by the cameras.

Hopping out, we ran toward the water with the camera crew in tow, and plunged into the ocean. I had forgotten how cold the Pacific gets and shivered as we trotted back out of the sea. The reporter moved in. I put my arm around Amanda as the camera zoomed in close. I was glancing around at the crowd, taking in the scene, and barely heard his question. He tilted the microphone toward me and stared in anticipation. I had to replay it in my head, "What did you learn on this journey of a lifetime?" I hadn't prepared. What could I say? A million things flashed through my mind. How could I explain the complexity of what we learned about ourselves and about each other? What could I say about the thousands of people we met and the many places we visited? How could I describe the difficult roads and the way it felt to be almost perpetually lost? I couldn't possibly compress it all into one brief sentence.

I started to mumble, "Well, ahhhh…" but my thoughts were tangled. I wanted to tell him about the nervous anticipation we felt when crossing a border into a new country. I wanted to explain the simple pleasures: of learning a new recipe from an old woman in a market; of hearing the whistling purr of the motor when the van was running perfectly; of living a thousand nights in our tiny pop-top home.

Amanda perked up and he shifted the microphone to her. Without hesitation she said, "We discovered how little we need to be happy." Then after pausing for a second she added, "And also we learned that good things can come from obstacles in the road."

With a chance to think, I began to talk, and the reporter moved the microphone over to me. "We also discovered that we can count on each another, no matter what."

The reporter said, "OK, that's all we need." Then he started wrapping up the microphone and said, "Can I take a look inside your van?"

As we showed him the sink, the stove and the fold-out bed he asked, "So what's next? Where to now?"

We looked at each other and Amanda answered, "We're on our way to Tijuana to visit my grandmother for her 90th birthday. But before we cross the border we're going to our storage garage to dig out our dressy clothes."

The bright orange door on the storage unit was caught on something. Together we forced it up and Amanda crouched under to get inside. I heard her banging around and could see her tiny feet shimmying on the floor. She said, "Aargh, all this stuff. One of the rugs is....caught...there. Now try it."

The door rolled up and suddenly the light flooded in on our possessions for the first time in three years. I couldn't believe how much we had stored. Squeezed in front was my antique reading chair, covered with a sheet. I remembered how I used to look forward to coming home from work and collapsing into the chair with a good book, trying to get my mind off the problems of the day. As I pulled off the sheet Amanda said, "Don't start taking things out. There's too much. We'll never fit it back in."

"I'm not taking anything out. I just wanted to sit in my chair again." I stood there looking at it. "Remember how carefully I refinished the legs?" I asked.

I began to sit down into it, but before my rear end hit the cushion I stopped, supporting myself on the arm rests. Then I pushed myself back up.

"What's wrong?" Amanda asked.

"I don't know. It just doesn't feel right. I don't want to sit in it."

As I tossed the sheet back over the chair Amanda said, "Look, we have two vacuum cleaners. Why did we keep two?"

"I don't know. Does that one still work?"

She wasn't listening and went on, "And all these books. I forgot we had so many books."

"And look at that," I responded, pointing to a box with a picture of an ornate glass punch bowl and ladle. "Why did you keep that?"

She shrugged. "It was a wedding gift."

"When was the last time we served punch in it?" I asked.

She answered glumly, "Never."

We stood back and stared at all the stuff. The furniture, paintings, books, dishes, and clothing packed tightly in boxes and bags, piled from floor to ceiling. The belongings that we'd collected in another lifetime.

Objects once so important to us now seemed foreign.

EPILOGUE

Life of the Lottery Winner

San Diego, California
59,405 miles

Amanda was in back of the van gluing together an antique teacup with Krazy Glue when the woman in the next space, a shrewd grandmotherly type wearing gold-framed reading glasses on a beaded chain, asked with a husky voice, "Is your wife in retail?"

I laughed. "No, why do you ask?"

"She hasn't stopped rearranging things since six o'clock this morning, and the way she deals with the customers. She should work at Nordstroms."

Chuckling, I said, "Yeah, she's a real people person and she loves to reorganize."

The woman held her hand up beside her mouth as if she were telling a secret and said in a hoarse whisper, "I wouldn't tell her about that vase you just sold."

"Why not?" I asked.

"This morning she told me the price was five dollars. You just sold it for a quarter."

It was the third weekend in a row that we had packed up the van and driven to Kobey's Swap Meet, a giant flea market in the parking lot of the San Diego Sports Arena. That morning I unloaded the boxes and Amanda arranged what remained of our belongings on an old oriental rug. When someone came along and showed a genuine interest in an item, we would quietly give it to them or sell it for a token amount. Each time we made a sale we felt just a little bit lighter, as if the weight of the item had been lifted from our shoulders.

At the end of the day we were packing the few remaining items that no one wanted and Amanda paused to pick up two brass candleholders we had once used for special occasions. I watched her stare at them and thought, "Oh no, here we go. She's having second thoughts." We had given up virtually all of our possessions. It was too late to do anything about it. Nearly everything was gone.

She turned to look at me, cradling the candleholders, and said, "Do you have any idea how many times I polished these things? I can't wait to get rid of them."

The Goodwill was a few blocks away on Rosecrans Boulevard and we unloaded the van as one of the employees, an older Mexican lady with dyed bright red hair, helped us drag the boxes to the donation booth. When we were handing her the last of our things she pointed to the few small boxes in the back of the van and asked Amanda in Spanish, "What about those?"

"Oh no, we're keeping those. They're our family photos and our wedding album," Amanda told her.

"Did you give everything else away?" she asked with surprise.

"We did," I told her. "Now everything we own fits in our van."

Her eyes lit up. "Wow. And where are you going?" she asked.

"Wherever the road leads," Amanda said with a laugh.

The little lady grabbed Amanda by the arm and hugged it tight as she said wistfully, "Take me with you."

Driving south on Interstate 5, we passed the running paths along Mission Bay that we once knew so well. Beyond the downtown area we came to the Coronado Bridge and Amanda began telling a story I had heard a thousand times about our wedding on the island. Just past the exit to the bridge I saw a familiar billboard and laughed, interrupting Amanda's story. Pointing up at the sign advertising the next lottery jackpot, I asked, "What would we do with twenty-two million dollars?" As

I asked the question I felt a surge of nervous anticipation pass through me.

Amanda was quiet for a moment. Then she turned to look at me and said in almost a whisper, "You know, I wouldn't change a thing."

A thought passed though my mind like the bright piercing reflection of sunlight from a car window. It happened so quickly, I was afraid I would loose it if I didn't focus and really think about what it meant. In that spit second I pictured the pampas of Patagonia, the jungles of Belize, the deserts of Africa. I thought about how we had explored, searched, looked for the elements that make up a fulfilling, joyful life.

We knew that no matter how much we wanted them to be, these mysterious elements that make us happy were not hidden in the dull everyday routines we created. Nor were they stashed away in our bank accounts, or in the possessions, the stuff, the piles and piles of things we had given up.

But they weren't buried under the snow in the Andes either. They were not obscured by the vegetation in the tropical forests of Uganda. They were not percolating in the ancient blood of the indigenous people of Central America. And when we arrived back home, they weren't covered in the sand on Mission Beach.

That Christmas morning feeling, of being alive, vibrant, thriving, pulsating, came the moment we put ourselves beyond what was comfortable, what was familiar, what was known. Once we were responsible for ourselves in almost every conceivable way, we began to feel as if we were living. In taking chances we made mistakes and learned, and at the same time built rich memories to look back on. It was when we took the greatest risks and relied on our own ingenuity that we felt the most alive.

Pressing on the accelerator to speed up and change lanes I listened to the contented, whistling purr of the van's exhaust. I knew the sound so well, like the beat of my own heart, and I could hear in it the faint difference between simply living and being alive.

The Ligato's have hundreds of photographs on their website that compliment this book perfectly. Visit their site at VWVagabons.com. You may also contact them directly at WideEyed@VWVagabonds.com. They are happy to answer any questions you may have about travel, book publishing, car maintenance, and how to survive while living with your spouse in a confined area for more than 24 hours.